The Child's
Point of View

THE DEVELOPING BODY AND MIND

Series Editor: Professor George Butterworth, *Department of Psychology, University of Stirling.*

Designed for a broad readership in the English-speaking world, this major series represents the best of contemporary research and theory in the cognitive, social, abnormal and biological areas of development.

The Child's Point of View

Second Edition

MAUREEN V. COX

Senior Lecturer in Psychology,
University of York

HARVESTER WHEATSHEAF

New York   London   Toronto   Sydney   Tokyo   Singapore

First published 1986 by
Harvester Wheatsheaf
66 Wood Lane End, Hemel Hempstead
Hertfordshire HP2 4RG
A division of
Simon & Schuster International Group

Second edition, 1991

Typeset in 10/12pt Garamond
by Witwell Ltd, Southport

Printed and bound in Great Britain by
Billing and Sons Ltd, Worcester

British Library Cataloguing in Publication Data

Cox, M. V. (Maureen V)
  The child's point of view – 2nd, rev. ed
  1. Children. cognitive development
  I. Title
  155.413
  ISBN 0–7450–0936–0

---

1 2 3 4 5   95 94 93 92 91

For Amy

Contents

List of Figures

List of Tables

Acknowledgement

I am most grateful to Dr. A. J. Wootton, first of all for encouraging me to write this book, and then for so generously giving his time in critical discussion of the evidence and ideas presented here.

Introduction

'A point of view' can refer to many different sorts of experience. We may, for instance, speak of a person's political affiliation, religious beliefs, or allegiance in a family quarrel. We can also interpret the phrase in a more literal way, that is in terms of a person's *visual* experience – what she actually sees from a particular place. The subject areas, then, in which one can have 'a point of view' are quite diverse, but the *point* about a point of view is that an individual's own experience is only *one* of a number of possible views which could be held by herself or by others.

Someone who does not appreciate that her own view is simply one of a number of possible alternatives may in certain circumstances be at an advantage, but generally we would regard her as narrow-minded, inflexible and insensitive. She may behave as if her own view is the 'natural' one and is shared by everyone, and appears unaware that there are alternatives. We may even call her *egocentric*. However, we would not regard her as *cognitively* incapable of considering alternative views; we would be more likely to think of her as lacking the sensitivity or inclination to do so. When we consider young *children* we may think of their egocentrism also as a lack of awareness of the need to take account of other views; on the other hand some writers, notably Jean Piaget (1896–1980), have regarded childhood egocentrism as a *cognitive* deficit, an intellectual inability to put oneself in another person's shoes.

The development of an awareness and understanding of other points of view, whether it be through greater sensitivity or more advanced cognitive functioning, is important if we are to operate efficiently and effectively in our social and natural environment. In this book I shall focus on this development through childhood. In doing so, I shall question the notion that young children are egocentric and shall present evidence which throws doubt on this claim. However, I do not wish to get bogged down in the debate about egocentrism; my aim is to focus positively on what children can do, rather than to approach them as inferior beings and evaluate them in a negative way.

Although I could have chosen to write about a great many subject areas related to 'a point of view', I have selected just four:

(i)   What do people see? The development of visual perspective-taking.

(ii) The artist's point of view.

(iii) Conversational role-taking.

(iv) What's on your mind?

I have not attempted to give an exhaustive account of the literature in each area; rather, my purpose has been to select some of the most relevant and interesting studies and to discuss these in more detail than would otherwise be possible. Although my background in psychology biases me towards accepting mainly experimental evidence to answer the questions posed, I am also interested in evidence from other traditions and I have drawn on different approaches throughout the book.

I have treated the four main topics separately, but they should not necessarily be regarded as distinct and unrelated. I have begun, in Part I, with the development of visual perspectives. It seemed to me that this is perhaps the most literal interpretation of 'a point of view', and is a good place to start. The ability to understand what people see is not merely of academic interest; it is part of our interaction with others from an extremely early age. We need to know what other people are attending to and referring to; conversely, we need to be able to draw others' attention to objects or people that we are concerned with. These visual abilities are particularly important in the pre-verbal phase of development when young children do not yet possess words to refer to things, but they also continue to be a fundamental part of our face-to-face interaction with others. For more enduring communication, nevertheless, through space and time, we frequently need to represent a particular view by pictorial or linguistic means.

So an understanding of visual perspectives is bound up in the communication process between people. Two important aspects of this communication process are the pictorial and linguistic modes of representation, and these are dealt with in Parts II and III respectively.

Clearly, there are problems when we want to represent objects in the three-dimensional world on a two-dimensional surface. We need to know the conventions for doing this if we are to 'read' correctly the pictorial images around us as well as to maximize our chances of successful communication. A dominant convention, particularly since the Renaissance, is to draw a scene as it looks from one particular viewpoint, the artist's own. This is only one way that we could approach the task, yet we often regard it as the only way and we may even consider other approaches, particularly the efforts of young children, to be quaintly primitive or eccentric. The adoption of one's own particular viewpoint for the purposes of pictorial representation seems to be a rather late development.

This section on drawings links back with that on visual perspectives. When we aspire to draw a picture from a particular point of view we are obviously concerned with what we, as observers, can see from that viewpoint; thus, visual perspective-taking is directly related to the way we think objects should be represented in pictures. And when researchers in the area of perspective-taking have tried to assess the extent of people's understanding of others' views they have very often asked subjects to draw or choose a picture of the view. Each of these two main topics, then, has relevance for the other and, indeed, may have confounded the findings of the other.

Rather than looking at children's use of language in particular cognitive tasks, I decided in Part III to examine language in a more 'natural' setting, that is in conversation. Successful communication involves the adoption and adequate fulfilment of conversational roles by the participants. Typically, we adopt the role either of speaker or of listener and are continually exchanging these roles during the interaction. We may need to modify our speech in a number of ways to take account of the listener, especially if that listener is perceived to be cognitively and linguistically immature. Thus, we must judge appropriately when and how modifications should be made in our speech. Even when we are speaking with other adults we need to understand when our communications have been problematic in some way; we need to appreciate that there is a problem, identify what it is, and then be able to remedy it.

The constantly shifting roles of speaker and listener that each person plays makes the apparently straightforward activity of 'having a conversation' a very complex enterprise. Deictic terms (often called 'shifters'), such as *I* and *you* and *here* and *there*, are a category of words which reflect or even establish these different roles. For instance, the speaker uses *I* to refer to herself and *you* to refer to the listener; when the conversational roles change, each term now refers to a different person. A fluent communicator will have a proficient use and understanding of these terms.

In Part IV I have examined some of the issues in the recent surge of research activity on the child's understanding of people's mental states, a topic not covered in the first edition of this book. Although one might imagine that young children must have considerable difficulty with the more covert and mentalistic phenomena in our lives, it turns out that they exhibit quite remarkable sophistication in their understanding of the beliefs that people hold and the feelings they have. Far from being locked in a world of their own beliefs and desires, children from a very early age treat others on the assumption that they possess these qualities too.

I shall review evidence in these four main areas which shows that infants and young children display considerable awareness of other people's behaviour and of different points of view. But they do have a lot to learn before reaching the level of adult competence, and my purpose is to chart this progress towards a sophisticated understanding of different points of view, including one's own.

PART I What do People see? The Development of Visual Perspective-taking

My main task in this first section of the book is to examine what young children know about other observers. Do they realize that other people see things and do they realize that others' views may be different from their own? Can they work out what these other views are like? In Chapter 1 I shall examine the research evidence on what these very young children do know about other observers and their views. The conclusion I shall draw is that preschool children have considerable understanding of other people's views of the world.

The idea that young children are egocentric and cannot understand other points of view comes mainly from the work of Jean Piaget. Although this idea was first introduced in relation to the young child's use of language in Piaget's first book *The Language and Thought of the Child* (1926), perhaps the best-known body of work with which it has now become associated is his investigation of visual perspective-taking (Piaget and Inhelder, 1956).

In Chapter 2 I shall describe Piaget and Inhelder's method of study and the stages of development in visual perspective-taking which they found. Not only did they regard children up to about the age of 7 years as egocentric, but they thought it pointless to investigate perspective-taking in those below 4 years of age because these children simply did not understand the meaning of their questions. Piaget and Inhelder's conclusions are perhaps rather surprising, particularly in the light of the evidence discussed in Chapter 1, namely that preschool children seem to be rather good at working out what other people see.

I shall re-examine Piaget and Inhelder's meaning of the term *egocentrism* and find that Piaget and Inhelder, and later Flavell, can accommodate the findings outlined in Chapter 1; most of these rely on a *practical* understanding of the spatial environment. Although young children have developed their abilities in this way, a difficulty that they still face is how to *represent* their understanding, particularly in a pictorial form. It was in this representational sense that Piaget and Inhelder used the term *egocentric* to describe the young child's deficiency. I shall go on to outline the developmental steps in the ability to represent perspectives.

1 The very young child's understanding of other observers

William James (1890) described the newborn baby's world as a 'blooming, buzzing confusion' and considered that it might take some time for the senses to become organized. In *The Construction of Reality in the Child* , Piaget (1954) also argues that at first a baby does not appreciate that objects and space have the quality of depth, nor does she understand that objects which go out of sight still continue to exist. Through handling objects the baby gradually discovers their various properties, in particular their three-dimensionality.

Many researchers (such as Bower, 1974, and Butterworth, 1981), however, are opposed to Piaget's constructionist theory of perception. Although they would agree with Piaget that the baby's 'knowledge' is not the same as the adult's and has yet to be developed, nevertheless they would not agree that the newborn baby lives in a chaotic world which can only gradually be structured through the infant's own *activity*. In contrast, they take a 'Gibsonian' view (e.g. J. J. Gibson, 1950, 1966, 1979) that some properties of objects in space (such as three-dimensionality) are *directly* perceptible by the sensory system and not dependent on the experience mediated by motor activity. Although the baby's behavioural repertoire is limited, some capabilities are apparent at birth or shortly afterwards. For instance, within their range of focus (about 7½ to 8 inches) babies are sensitive to light at birth (Pratt, 1954; Kessen, Haith and Salapatek, 1970), and, they can detect figures from ground. They can also discriminate among different stimulus patterns and seem to prefer the characteristics of the human face rather than other complex patterns (Fantz, 1963; Dayton, Jones, Giu, Rawson, Steele and Rose, 1964). The newborn can follow a slow-moving object with her eyes (Greenman, 1963; Dayton *et al.,* 1964; Haith, 1966) and, at 4 weeks, can fixate several points in succession passing rapidly from one to another (Gesell, Thompson and Amatruda, 1934). Some knowledge of three-dimensionality is demonstrated by 2-week-old babies. Bower, Broughton and Moore (1970) found that these very young babies can discriminate between objects (or shadows of objects) travelling towards them on a 'hit' path or a 'miss' path; babies show defensive behaviour towards the former but not to the latter. That objects themselves are three-dimensional is known by 16-week-old babies (Kellman, 1984); they detect information from the many different optical projections presented by an object as it moves or as the babies themselves move.

These research studies show that very young babies are already living in a three-dimensional world 'populated' by three-dimensional objects and are able to deal with three-dimensional information. The reader is referred to Chapter 3 of Bremner's *Infancy* (1988) which gives a fuller review of babies' visual–perceptual abilities.

Are people special?

As Fantz's work shows (e.g. Fantz, 1963), babies prefer to look at complex rather than simple patterns and, in particular, they prefer the human face. At an average age of only 9 minutes they will attend more closely to a moving schematic face than to a blank head or to a head with scrambled features (Goren, Sarty and Wu, 1975). And, at just 2 days' old, babies can discriminate their mother's face from that of a stranger roughly matched for similarity (Bushnell, Sai and Mullin, 1989). Such impressive findings at such a young age certainly suggest that babies must have an *innate* mechanism for attending to facial patterns. And some researchers (e.g. Bower, 1979) argue that babies are born with distinct social predispositions: they are supposed to have a set of behaviours specific to people. To back up his case, Bower cites evidence from studies of smiling (e.g. Dunkeld and Bower, 1979), imitation (e.g. Maratos, 1973; Meltzoff and Moore, 1977), interactional synchrony (Condon and Sander, 1974), and babbling (Wolff, 1963).

Now the evidence on *imitation* is very interesting. By imitation we usually mean that an infant observes an adult's action, identifies the part of the adult's body involved in the action, and then co-ordinates her own body movements in order to match the visual stimulus. This behaviour is called *active intermodal mapping* by Meltzoff and Moore (1983, 1985) and such extraordinarily sophisticated behaviour could

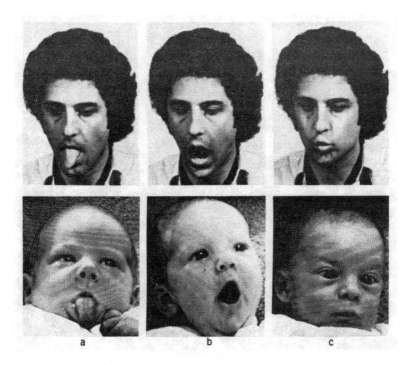

Figure 1.1: Sample photographs from videotape recordings of 2- to 3-week-old infants imitating (a) tongue protrusion (b) mouth opening and (c) lip protrusion demonstrated by an adult experimenter (Meltzoff and Moore, 1977, Figure 1, p. 75). (Reprinted with the permission of the authors.)

not occur, according to Piaget (1951), until the second year of life. All the more surprising, then, that Meltzoff and Moore (1977) claimed that babies as young as 2 to 3 weeks can imitate an adult's tongue protrusions (see Figure 1.1) and the opening and closing of a hand. Despite some initial failures to replicate these findings (e.g. Hayes and Watson, 1981), a number of studies have since shown the same effect in even younger babies – at 3 days' old (Meltzoff and Moore, 1983) and within the first hour after birth (Reissland, 1988).

There is no doubt that babies do exhibit these remarkable behaviours and since they occur so soon after birth they are likely to be innate. But are we really justified in assuming that babies engage actively in such cognitively sophisticated behaviour as the term 'imitation' suggests? Even though Piaget recognized that very young babies do behave in an apparently imitative way, he claimed that it is not true imitation and evidence from a number of studies would seem to support his view (see review by Bjorklund, 1987). Jacobson (1979), for example, reported that moving a small ball or a felt-pen towards the faces of 6-week-old infants resulted in comparable levels of tongue protrusions as did actual tongue protrusions modelled by an adult. Since any object moved towards the baby will elicit tongue pro-trusions, it's not necessarily the case that, when the baby 'imitates' an adult's tongue protrusion, she has engaged in an active process of matching to that particular body part; she may simply have an innate, fixed response for any approaching object.

A further difficulty is that the infant's readiness to imitate actually declines over the first few months of life (Jacobson, 1979; Fontaine, 1984; Vinter, 1986) to re-emerge later in the first year. This pattern supports a view that the early imitative behaviour is based on an innate, 'wired-in' response mechanism which involves no higher-order or intentional cognitive processing and whose function is, or was, primarily the baby's immediate survival. It may be similar to the 'walking' reflex that is present at birth but which declines and then gives way to more autonomous walking later on.

Although it is difficult to know whether or not this early 'reflexive' imitation serves as a basis for the subsequent development of imitation proper, Vinter's work (1986) has sought to describe the changes from the early to the later kind of imitation. She found, as had other researchers, that whereas neonates and 1-month-olds imitated the tongue protrusions and the hand opening–closing move-ment, 3-month-olds did not. She went on to observe in more detail the babies' general behaviour at both these stages. She found that at the earlier age, as well as producing the tongue protrusion or the manual gesture, babies also made gross movements of the head, the arm and the hand. From these observations, it seems that neonates may not be able to decompose action into isolated and specific movements but that they produce a predetermined general response.

Although by the age of 3 months babies no longer imitate either the facial or the manual gestures they do not lose interest in the adult model; indeed, Vinter reports that they display a more focused interest in the relevant body parts – smiling and vocalizing when the adult models a facial gesture and looking at their own hand when a manual gesture is modelled. These activities suggest that the earlier gross imitation has given way to a more detailed analysis of the adult's gesture and to the beginnings of a process of matching up of the baby's own relevant body part. When the baby eventually does produce an imitation of the adult's gesture, it will be a more precise movement and one which we might regard as less contentiously fulfilling a cognitively complex definition of imitation.

As well as imitating adult gestures, another example of the way in which babies may respond in a special way to people is in the turn-taking pattern of their 'conversations' (Brazelton, Koslowski and Main, 1974; Trevarthen, 1977, 1979). During these synchronized interactions, both participants – the baby and the parent – appear to regulate each other's behaviour: one partner increases or decreases her gestural activity and the other partner will respond, and this occurs with either the parent or the baby as the 'leader'. The implication that there is an *equal* parent–child partnership is not, however, shared by all researchers. Kaye (1982), for example, while agreeing that mother–baby interaction is characterized by turn-taking right from the beginning, believes that the mother is dominant in leading and managing the dialogue. Collis and Schaffer (1975) also believe that the smooth, apparently equal interaction is largely produced by the parents' skill and willingness in allowing themselves to be guided by the baby; thus the parent fits in with the baby's pattern of behaviour. Bruner (1982) has described this parental support as 'scaffolding'. Even if the relative contributions of parent and baby are not truly equal, the baby is still a very active participant in the interaction.

It might be useful to summarize the baby's knowledge at this point. She has some understanding of tangible objects in a three-dimensional world; she can fixate them visually and can follow moving objects with her eyes (providing they are within her range of focus). She can see and observe human beings and is able to identify similarities between herself and others and to engage in interactive behaviour with them.

Gaze

In their very early interactions or 'dialogues' with others, babies confine their attention to the interaction itself, looking and smiling at

Figure 1.2: Mutual gaze between father and 4-week-old daughter.

their partner (see Figure 1.2). Gradually, however, babies begin to turn away from these face-to-face encounters towards an exploration of objects in the wider world; yet, when they attend to these other objects, they show no inclination to share this interest with their partner. It is not until the age of at least 6 months that infants begin to look back and forth between an interesting object and the parent, as if to include the parent in the activity (Newson and Newson, 1975; Sugarman-Bell, 1978; Bates, 1979). And, according to a longitudinal study by Bakeman and Adamson (1984), this behaviour does not become routine until children are about 18 months old.

The emergence of the child's ability to engage the attention of a social partner in some activity with an object, sometimes called *co-ordinated joint engagement*, is often regarded as an important milestone in development (Werner and Kaplan, 1963). Whereas children eventually develop the use of gestures and words to communicate their interest, at this early stage they are very much reliant on *gaze* both to monitor where the parent is looking and to co-ordinate their own attention to their partner and to the object in question.

Early in the infant's first year it appears to be the *parent* who monitors the child's gaze (Collis and Schaffer, 1975; Collis, 1977) in order to see what she is attending to and what her needs might be; parents will name and talk about objects which the baby is already looking at. Babies of 10 months do not follow their mother's direction of gaze (Collis, 1977) and in order to gain their attention parents will use a variety of devices including the 'marking' of a target object by touching it, shaking it and naming it (Messer, 1983).

The nature of the tasks used in a number of research studies (e.g. Collis and Schaffer, 1975; Collis, 1977) may have predetermined their findings. Typically, a baby sat on her mother's knee and both were looking towards four toys positioned at one end of a small room. Since the baby was sitting in front of the mother and was facing away from her towards the toys it is perhaps not surprising that the mother should monitor the baby's gaze and not the other way round. Although the results are interesting they do not necessarily mean that babies *cannot* follow an adult's gaze. Indeed, Scaife and Bruner (1975) found that by 8 to 10 months infants are quite proficient, and by 11 to 14 months all of their subjects could follow an adult's gaze. The experimenter sat opposite the baby and mutual eye-contact was established before the experimenter moved her head and gazed 90 degrees to the right or left. Positive responses were recorded if the baby looked in the same direction as the experimenter but not necessarily at the same fixation point; in fact babies looked anywhere from 20 to 90 degrees away from the midline. In this study the baby was probably in a better spatial position to observe a definite and larger turn of the eyes and head than in the other studies. In addition the absence of toys removed the possibility of distraction and also the problem of deciding which toy the adult was looking at.

What the child is developing, according to Bruner (1975, p. 269), is a '*procedure* for homing in on the attentional focus of another: learning where to look in order to be tuned to another's attention'. Although the child may be in the process of this development there are objections to the notion that she is actually looking where someone else is looking. It may be that she is simply tracking the movement of her mother's head. It is also possible, as Piaget (1951) has suggested, that the child may be trying to recapture the moving visual image of the adult's head by moving her own when her mother's movement has stopped. Another possibility is that, although the older infant's gaze along the adult's line of regard may be terminated by the presence of an object, it may not have arisen in order to find an object. Butterworth and Cochran (1980) and Butterworth and Jarrett (1980) have carried out a series of experiments with mothers and their babies (aged 6, 12 and 18 months) which test these different explanations of the phenomenon of joint visual attention. These studies are also reviewed by Butterworth and Grover (1988) and an extended discussion of the implications for childhood egocentrism is available in Butterworth (1987).

Mother and baby were sitting opposite each other in the middle of a laboratory room. Targets were presented, either two or four at a time, at eye level at various locations around the room (see Figure 1.3). The mother was told to interact normally with her baby. When she had gained the baby's attention she was instructed to turn and inspect one of the targets in the room for 6 seconds before turning back to the baby. Video recordings enabled a subsequent detailed analysis to be made of the patterns of gaze.

These studies confirmed that babies certainly do change their line of gaze in response to the mother's change of gaze direction. The video analysis showed that the babies do not follow the mother's gaze *while* she is turning, but that they fixate the mother and turn to fixate the target themselves after she has located it. It seems that the baby is not simply visually tracking the mother as she turns, nor is the baby trying to recapture a moving visual image of her since her attention is immediately shifted on to the target. The baby can also ignore a target along her own line of sight and fixate a second target which the mother is actually looking at. This shows that it is the *mother's orientation* which the baby responds to and not simply the presence of any object along her own line of regard.

When the target was in the baby's visual field, she had no difficulty in fixating it (at 25 degrees, 40 degrees or 70 degrees from her midline). However, when the target was behind her she very rarely succeeded. After the mother had visually located the target the babies turned in the correct direction but terminated their search at 40 degrees from the midline, even though they were quite capable of fixating targets at 70 degrees. Although 18-month-old infants were more likely to make a response than 6-month-olds, they were not significantly more accurate to targets located behind them. Butterworth has suggested a two-step process to explain this rather curious phenomenon. First, the baby turns in the direction of the mother's gaze but only to the extent that the mother herself is kept

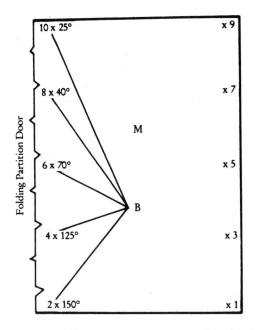

Figure 1.3: The laboratory layout and target positions used in Butterworth and Cochran's (1980, Figure 1, p. 256) study of joint visual attention. M = mother; B = baby. Approximate visual angles of targets with respect to the baby are shown. A subset of targets was presented on any one trial. (Reprinted with the permission of the authors and the publisher.)

within view at the periphery; this will be about 40 degrees from the baby's midline. If a target appears somewhere further on in the baby's visual field she will turn to fixate it. If no target appears she will not continue to turn. This suggests then that the baby needs to link the mother and the target within her own visual space in order to 'travel visually' from one to the other. Only at 18 months will babies turn to look behind them for a target fixated by the mother, but they will do this only when there are no other competing targets in their visual field.

In studies of the child's ability to follow another's line of gaze, the direction of gaze and the orientation of the head are normally complementary. Lempers, Flavell and Flavell (1977) have tried to assess the relative importance of these cues for the child. They used two observer conditions, one (*a*) in which the direction of the eyes and face coincided, and one (*b*) in which they diverged. In both conditions the experimenter and the child sat opposite each other and three toys were placed between them (a doll to the child's right, a dog to her left, and a car directly in front of her). The experimenter faced directly towards the child and then closed her eyes. In condition *a* she moved her head towards the right- or left-hand toy and then opened her eyes. In *b* she continued to face straight ahead, but moved her eyes under closed lids to the left or right before opening them. The child was asked to indicate (by pointing, showing or naming) which toy the experimenter was looking at. Condition *a* was easier than condition *b* in that *all* the 2½- and 3-year-olds chose the correct toy for *a* whereas only the 3-year-olds chose the correct toy for *b*. There was no significant difference between correct and incorrect choices for condition *b* among 2½-year-olds. At 3 years, then, children can use gaze rather than head orientation as the dominant cue. Although the correct response was the modal category for 1½- and 2-year-olds in condition *a* and for 2- and 2½-year-olds in *b*, some children did not respond at all, others refused to respond, and others simply looked directly at the experimenter. It seems that the younger children either did not understand the requirements of the task or, as is more likely in condition *b*, were confused by it. Lempers included similar tasks in his 1979 study. The results again show that nearly all 12- to 14-month-olds could correctly locate the object of the experimenter's gaze, if the child could see the head and eyes *together* turn towards an object. When these cues diverged, most children failed the task.

When the various cues for directing attention are used in combination, then children are likely to display successful performance at an earlier age than in some of the restricted conditions in experimental studies. The artificial manipulation in experimental work, while enabling the researcher to tease out the relative importance of different cues, may result in a rather bizarre task from the child's point of view, since cues which are normally congruent may be deliberately put in conflict. What is gained in experimental rigour may then be lost if children are confused and/or refuse to respond at all. In addition, studies which rely on verbal instruction may grossly underestimate very young children's abilities: not only are they required to organize and produce a response, but they must also attend to and comprehend correctly what is said to them. This seems to be a tall order. Experimental studies in this field should proceed with caution; at the same time I should like to see more carefully analyzed naturalistic studies.

Pointing

The importance of pointing for our discussion is in its use for directing another's attention to some object or event; in a sense, it is a way of sharing our own perspective of the world. It has been claimed that infants are able to follow another's point earlier than they can point themselves (e.g. Leung and Rheingold, 1981) and Bruner (1983, p. 75) has found that comprehension of an adult's point precedes the child's own pointing by about a month or two. Murphy and Messer (1977) found that with 9-month-old infants, mothers used pointing to divert the child's attention. These infants could follow the point if the mother's hand and the referent object were both within their visual field, but they failed to follow a point across their midline. In contrast, Grover (1988; Butterworth and Grover, 1988) found that her 9-month-olds did not understand the pointing gesture; they were equally likely to fixate the mother's hand as they were to fixate the target to which she pointed. By 12 months, however, 96 per cent of Grover's children responded to the target if it was within their visual field. But, like Murphy and Messer's infants, Grover's 12-month-olds still failed to locate targets which were behind them. These findings fit in with Butterworth's suggestion in relation to gaze, namely that the child needs to keep the two anchor points (the pointing finger and the target) within her visual field in order to link them up.

Both Murphy and Messer (1977) and Leung and Rheingold (1981) emphasize the verbal utterance associated with pointing. Most points by mothers, according to Murphy and Messer, are accompanied by vocalization; indeed, they found that only 5 out of 428 points were unaccompanied by some vocalization. It is clear that many of these utterances consist of naming and this is not surprising if the pointing activity is one of drawing the child's attention to a particular object (see Figure 1.4). Ninio and Bruner (1978), Murphy (1978) and Messer (1983) have found that mothers name objects which they themselves point to or which the child points to. By the time the child is about 22 months old, mothers can accompany their points with a *Wh*-question (e.g. 'What's that?') in order to elicit a name from the child; the correct name is provided if the child fails to respond or gets it wrong.

Tiedemann (1787, cited by Murchison and Langer, 1927) was probably one of the first to record the infant's deliberate pointing behaviour, but more systematic observations were made by Shirley

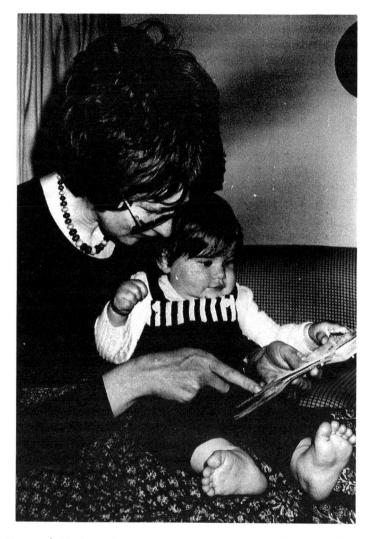

Figure 1.4: Mother points out a picture in a book to her 9-month-old daughter.

(1931–33) in her study of 25 babies. Generally, it is reckoned that the extension of the arm and index finger in a communicative pointing gesture occurs in most children early in their second year (see Figure 1.5a and b). Now, it has been considered by some writers, such as

Preyer (1896), that pointing emerges from the infant's desire to reach for or seize an object and Vygotsky (1962) has argued that the child's two gestures, the reach and the point, become differentiated through their differential treatment by the parent. If the mother routinely passes objects to the child when she (the child) happens to produce something which looks like a reach but names objects when the child happens to produce something which looks more like a point, then the child will learn to associate these different outcomes with the gestures and will distinguish the gestures themselves more clearly and learn to use them appropriately. And indeed, mothers do treat their children's gestures in different ways, more often producing object-naming words when the child points but not when she reaches towards an object or extends it towards the mother (Masur, 1982). We can also see from a number of studies that the child tends to use an open-handed reach to request an object beyond her grasp, but a point to indicate an object of interest (Bruner, Caudill and Ninio, 1977; Franco and Butterworth, 1988); furthermore, early object-naming vocalizations accompany points more than they do other kinds of gestures (Masur, 1982) and there are more visual checks to see if the adult is attending associated with points than with a gesture like the reach (Franco and Butterworth, 1988).

In contrast to the Preyer/Vygotskian view of the origins of pointing, Werner and Kaplan (1963) argue that, from the beginning, pointing is used by the child as a reference to an object of interest and is different from the reaching gesture. Unfortunately, the empirical evidence cited above cannot clearly distinguish between these two explanations. But, a possible way forward is to look at the *developmental ontogeny* of pointing and reaching in order to establish whether or not they are different.

There are two pieces of evidence which are particularly important. The first concerns the occurrence of something which looks rather like pointing in infants as young as 3 months of age when they are engaged in face-to-face interaction with an adult (Fogel and Hannan, 1985; Hannan, 1987). Although the index figure is extended, it is not accompanied by the arm extension; neither is there appropriate use of gaze and, until the age of 6 months, no particular object is singled out by the point. Nevertheless, the point is accompanied by vocalizations or mouth movements. It may be, as Fogel and Hannan have suggested, that this very early appearance of the specialized use of the index finger, in what eventually comes to be a communicative gesture,

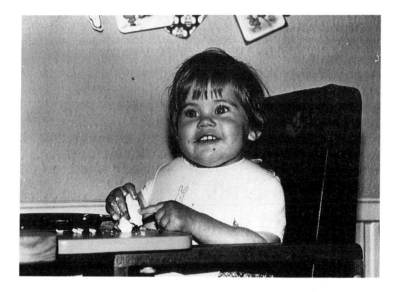

Figure 1.5(a) and (b): Pointing by a 1-year-old. (Photographs by G. Max Neal.)

is innate and that, later, it becomes integrated into a more co-ordinated and skilful act of pointing, involving the extension of the arm as well as the index finger.

The second piece of evidence which suggests that pointing and reaching have different origins is that the child's gestures, although often not clearly articulated, are nonetheless accompanied by different morphemes. In her case study of a little boy called David, Carter (1978) identified eight distinct classes of communicative behaviours between the ages of 12 and 16 months, each associated with different gestures and sounds. Whereas, reaching, for example, was accompan-ied by utterances beginning with *m*, directing an adult's attention to a particular object was accomplished by pointing or showing gestures accompanied by *l* or *d* sounds. Carter reports that, during David's second year, *l* sounds subsequently evolved into 'look', whereas *d* sounds evolved into 'there', 'this', 'that', etc.

There is reasonably strong evidence, then, that the act of pointing does not emerge out of reaching but is a separate, referential act from the beginning. Of course, we must not forget that the functions of pointing and reaching are not exclusive: as well as indicating a wish to possess an object, a reach also signals the location of that object; similarly, a point which locates an object for another observer can also be incorporated into a request for that object (e.g. 'Would you pass the salt?' + point), although such an intentional gesture as this may not occur until children are much older.

There is some disagreement among researchers regarding the defining components of a point. Although most agree on the necessity of the extension of the arm and the index finger, others (e.g. Leung and Rheingold, 1981) have wished to include a verbal utterance and a visual check that the other person is looking in the appropriate direction. Indeed, Bates, Benigni, Bretherton, Camaioni and Volterra (1979) regard the visual checking component as the *main criterion* of communicative pointing. (I take 'communicative' here to mean intentional on the part of the pointer.) There are some studies, however, which report very little visual checking by either adult or child and yet still regard the points as social and communicative (e.g. Murphy, 1978; Leung and Rheingold, 1981).

It is possible that in these studies the pointer did in fact check the observer but that this was done with a small rather than a large gesture such as a head turn. In other words, the level of analysis may not have been fine enough to detect rather subtle checks. On the other hand, it may be that the pointer did not check in these particular studies and only needs to check the visual gaze of the observer in certain circumstances. We would not expect visual checking in Murphy's (1978) task in which the mother and child were looking at a picture book, since the activity itself assumes that both participants are attending; indeed, visual checking was virtually absent in this study. In contrast, the infants in Anderson's (1972) study *always* made a visual check when they pointed and most of the infants in Franco and Butterworth's (1988) study did too; since these were older infants who had just begun to walk and were involved in looking at toys in a much larger space, they may have needed to check that the mother was actually attending. This suggests, then, that a circumstance when checking might be expected is when the pointer does not have her pointing hand, the referent object and the observer within her visual field.

It is unlikely, however, that this spatial factor would be the only one affecting visual checking. It is also likely that a delay in the mother's acknowledgement of a child's point would result in a visual check to see if the mother has attended. Leung and Rheingold (1981) note that mothers in their study responded very quickly to children's points thereby obviating their need for checking. In contrast, I have examples on video of my own daughter, aged 18 months 3 weeks, visually checking after a non-response on my part to her point; in all cases both the object in question and I are within her visual field. Observational studies might well demonstrate a relationship between observer-delay and pointer's visual checking; experimental studies could manipulate the delay interval.

In some circumstances in which the child cannot assume that the adult is already attending, it would make sense for her to check *before* she points something out, otherwise she may be wasting her time. And, in fact, Franco and Butterworth (1988) found that infants do make prior visual checks, but they are not made until the infants are about 16 months old; at 12 months, infants check that the adult is attending only *after* they have made the pointing gesture.

Although most researchers agree that children begin to point sometime in the early part of their second year, the onset and the extent of this pointing behaviour may vary according to different aspects of the task. Murphy and Messer (1977) and Lempers (1979), for example, found that a quarter of infants at age 9 months used points; similarly, half of Murphy's (1978) sample pointed at this age.

It has been suggested that the high frequency of pointing at this young age may have been influenced by the mothers' pointing behaviour. When Leung and Rheingold's study (1981) instructed their mothers not to draw attention to the objects only one child out of eight pointed at 10½ months and nine out of sixteen pointed at the age of 12½ months. The reason for the differences in the extent of pointing may also have been influenced by the particular task employed. In the picture-book activity used by Murphy (1978), for example, we might expect more pointing to occur in order that one particular item may be identified from others in very close proximity. In contrast, pointing is less likely to occur when the activity involves looking at more widely spaced toys in a room (Leung and Rheingold, 1981; Franco and Butterworth, 1988) when the body orientation of the participants makes it clear which object is being attended to. So, although we know approximately the age at which pointing begins to occur, we do not yet have a detailed and systematic account of the variables which affect the onset and frequency of pointing.

In Bruner's (1974/5) analysis of the young child's pointing gesture as a precursor to language, he seems to assume that the gesture occurs alone at first and is only later accompanied by a vocalization. We have already seen, however, that even at 3 months, infants are vocalizing or making movements with their mouths at the same time that they extend their index finger. Masur (1982) has also noted that children's points are often accompanied by early forms of object-names. And, from the video data of my own daughter it is also clear that pointing was almost invariably accompanied by a vocalization (ĕ or ă) from the beginning. It seems to me that the verbal and non-verbal elements are both very important and are used together from a very early age.

The busy time for pointing is around the age of about 12 to 18 months. Not only are the children engaged in this activity, but so are their parents. Even though mothers use more verbal directives when addressing an 18-month-old than a 10-month-old their use of pointing also increases (Schaffer, Hepburn and Collis, 1983). Although it would be possible for an adult to give sufficient detailed verbal information to specify a particular object for the child, in practice we rely very heavily on the pointing gesture. In fact, Shatz (1982) and Schaffer *et al.* (1983) found that the verbal utterance and the point do not convey exactly the same message; they are complementary but not equivalent. The gesture, then, should not be regarded as simply an optional extra, as Bruner implied; it carries its own message.

A number of researchers (e.g. Carter, 1978; Murphy, 1978; Zinober and Martlew, 1985) have noted that pointing declines after the age of about 20 months. A major reason for this general decline may be the decline in pointing as part of the child's response to the mother's points and requests and an increase in the child's use of object-names and direction of gaze (Carter, 1978). Although pointing does not drop out altogether and is of course available in the adult repertoire, the burden of communication originally carried by the pointing gesture is shifted more towards the verbal channel. Thus, the child finds other ways of drawing someone's attention to objects and events of interest and also learns when *not* to point. Pechmann and Deutsch (1982), for example, found that between the ages of 2 and 9 years the inappropriate use of pointing to specify an object declines and the use of verbal descriptions increases; when pointing *is* appropriate, however, both children and adults use it equally often.

Showing

Showing is an activity which aims intentionally to produce particular visual percepts in another person. It is closely linked with the activity of pointing. Thus, a child may manipulate an object or picture so that an adult can see it or see part of it; conversely, the adult may need to be manoeuvred into position in order to see a particular object or event.

Lempers *et al.* (1977) gave a number of 'showing' tasks to children from 1 to 3 years of age. The child and the observer sat opposite each other; the child was handed an item and was instructed to show it to the observer. The items used were a toy, a two-dimensional picture of a familiar object, and a picture pasted on to a three-dimensional block. Most children, even at 1 year, were able to show the toy to the observer by holding it up. Interestingly, the 1-year-olds did not orientate the object to *face* the observer; this shift began at age 1½ and was complete at age 2. Most children at age 1½ successfully showed the picture and the block picture; however, in both cases they held the picture horizontally between themselves and the observer. There was a shift at 2 years towards holding the picture vertically, and then a further shift at 2½ with the two-dimensional picture, and at 3 with the block picture, towards getting the image the right way up for the observer. Lempers *et al.* suggest that the younger children need to keep the object in sight themselves when showing it to another person. This also fits in with Butterworth's notion mentioned earlier that young children may need to keep an observer and a target within the visual field in order to link them up. The 2-year-olds in the Lempers *et al.* tasks were able to deprive themselves of the view of the picture while showing it to the observer. A further task made horizontal showing particularly difficult. A picture was pasted on to the inside base of a box. Two-year-olds had no difficulty in pointing the box-opening at the observer and away from themselves. Some 1½-year-olds also managed to do this; those who did not, tilted the box backwards and forwards as if trying to make the picture available to both participants. Again the younger children seem to be displaying a need to link up the object and the adult observer in their own visual field. Even if they do need to do this it nevertheless implies some knowledge of people as observers; complete egocentrism in contrast would lead to a disregard of others' needs altogether.

In other tasks, or variations of those tasks already mentioned, Lempers *et al.* wanted to see if the children would understand that the observer could not see an object because of a screen being in the way, and whether they would remedy the situation. All 2½- and 3-year-olds could move a screen so that the observer could see the object and most 2-year-olds could move the observer's hands from her eyes and show her the object. This shows that the children could diagnose and alter the observer's visual experience. The most difficult task was one in which the participants and the shown object could not be linked within the child's visual field – showing a hand or a picture to an unseen observer from behind a screen. Even 3-year-olds had difficulty with this task, particularly when showing a hand. Most younger children attempted to go round the screen or peep out from the screen when showing a hand.

I have not located any naturalistic studies in the literature which have looked at the child's ability to show objects to others. In my own data I have two examples of my daughter manipulating objects so that they presented a particular orientation to the observer. In the first case, at 2 years 1 month, she was 'speaking to granny' on her toy telephone; she replaced the receiver and turned the whole telephone to 'face' me so that I could use it. In the second case, at 2 years 5 months, on request she turned a toy duck so that it could see either herself or me (when I was sitting opposite her). This behaviour fits in with that of the 2-year-olds in the Lempers *et al.* study who could orientate a picture for someone else to see.

Searching

It is well known that babies below the age of about 4 months will not search for an object that goes out of their sight; this fascinating observation illustrated for Piaget (1954) that babies treat these objects as non-existent – 'out of sight, out of mind'. A number of researchers have subsequently cast doubt on this claim. Bower and Wishart (1972), for example, dangled a toy on a piece of string in front of the baby but out of her reach. When the room lights were turned off, the toy was literally out of sight. But, using an infra-red TV system to record the baby's movements, Bower and Wishart found that the baby would reach towards the toy even after a delay of 1.5 seconds. Hood and Willatts (1986) repeated this experiment with some modifications but came to the same conclusion that, by 2 months of age, infants do assume that an object continues to exist even when they can no longer see it. Not only does the infant assume that the object still exists but, according to Baillargeon (1987), by 7 months of age she also makes assumptions about the properties of the object – its height behind a screen and its softness or hardness, for example.

From these studies we know that very young infants assume that an object still exists when it goes out of their sight. Nevertheless, infants are not always successful in locating the object even when they have sufficient manual dexterity to search for it. A well-known case is the AB̄ error committed by infants between about 8 and 12 months of age. Having successfully searched a number of times for a toy at hiding place A, the child sees the adult hide the toy at B; but the child searches at A, not at B. The error is still made even when the occluders are made of clear plastic (Butterworth, 1977).

Piaget's explanation for this error is that the infant does not treat the object as independent of her own action; if she has successfully retrieved the object at a certain place she will repeat this action in order to retrieve the object again. The Piagetian task, however, confounds at least two variables. When the child searches at the old hiding place we do not know if she is simply repeating a manual action *relative to herself* or whether she is going back to the same location *relative to the environment*. Researchers have referred to these two strategies in various ways: *self-referent strategy* vs. *environmental strategy*, *egocentric strategy/code* vs. *allocentric strategy/ code*, *response hypothesis* vs. *place hypothesis*, and *egocentric strategy* vs. *spatial strategy*.

Bremner and Bryant (1977) tried to disentangle these two variables. In order to provide strong contrasting cues for the hiding places, they painted one side of the table black and the other side white; a hiding place was sunk into the middle of each half of the table and each place was covered by a grey cloth. There were two groups of infants, aged 8½ to 9½ months, and they successfully retrieved an object repeatedly hidden by the experimenter at the same hiding place. The infants were then moved round to the opposite side of the table. This time the object was hidden in a different location for half the infants (Group A) and the same location for the other half (Group B). The results were very clear: most of the infants searched in the different location and the object was retrieved by Group A but not by Group B. It is clear that these young infants defined the hiding place in *relation to themselves* rather than to the surrounding environmental cues.

Subsequent work by Acredolo (1978) supported Bremner and Bryant's findings in that environmental cues seemed to be ignored by infants at 6 months and were only beginning to be used by those aged 11 months; by 16 months most infants could make use of the environmental cues. Young infants' 'egocentrism', however, is not intransigent: Bremner (1978) found that they *are* sensitive to environmental cues if those cues are strong enough (e.g. making the hiding places themselves more distinctive). Furthermore, 'egocentric' responses are much less frequent when the rotation of the child is less than 180 degrees and when the experiment takes place at the child's home rather than in the laboratory (Acredolo, 1979).

These studies indicate that the developmental shift from locating objects relative to self and then to locating them relative to environmental cues is less clear-cut than had once been thought and it is perhaps more useful to think of the shift as a change in the infant's use of the same available information rather than a shift from one system to another separate one (Presson and Somerville, 1985). An important impetus for this change may be the increasing mobility of the infant (Bremner, 1980). Although a self-referencing strategy is adequate if the infant is usually in the same position for particular activities, such as feeding, it is not very useful when she is on the move, constantly changing her position relative to the environment. The child's increasing mobility, then, may lead to more reliance on environmental landmarks in order to retrieve toys and other objects which are out of sight. Support for this notion comes from Kermoian and Campos's (1988) study of infants aged 8½ months, showing that spatial search performance is greatly enhanced by the infant's ability to move about. In order to show that this performance is not simply the outcome of a maturational process, the researchers added a group of children who could not move about unassisted but who could use a baby-walker. There was no significant difference in search performance between these children and those who could crawl independently; both groups performed significantly better than a third group who did not move about on their own.

Towards the end of their first year and the beginning of their second, infants understand not only that objects which go out of sight also continue to exist but also that these objects can be retrieved. At first their attempts at locating objects seem to be governed by a self-referencing strategy but as they become increasingly more mobile infants make use of environmental cues. Having considered infants' ability to locate objects hidden by other people, I shall consider in the next section their ability to do the hiding for themselves.

Hiding

In a hiding task the child deliberately *deprives* the observer of a particular view. This can be achieved by moving an object under or behind a screen or by placing some obstacle between the observer and the object. The 'object' may be external to the child, may be part of her body (e.g. a hand), or may be her whole self. Similarly, the 'screen' may be a moveable or fixed barrier, or the child herself may act as a screen in order to block the observer's view.

Some of the earliest examples of hiding are the 'peep-bo' or 'peekaboo' games which are played early in the baby's first year. Bruner (1983) has described the development of these games as played by two boys, Jonathan and Richard, and their respective mothers. The game was first initiated by the mothers when these infants were 5 to 6 months old. Whereas Jonathan's mother played the game with a clown which was made to disappear into a cloth cone on a stick, Richard's mother used several different objects to cover her own face. The game was initiated and acted out by the mothers and the sequence of its constituent parts was highly predictable.

At about 9 to 11 months the frequency of the hiding game seemed to decline dramatically, only to re-emerge some months later. Interestingly, the infants now took a more active role and some negotiation would take place about who could take each part in the sequence; in Richard's case, for instance, he might be the one who is hidden or might reveal his mother's hidden face. There are parallels here with the study of imitation by Vinter (1986): after the early exposure and general reactions to the adults' modelling, the children's responses seem to drop out for a time but then re-emerge in a more specific form.

The peep-bo game appeared in my own daughter's repertoire at the age of 6¾ months. At first she pulled a nappy or a towel over her face and then laughed when she re-emerged. Later, she used a newspaper or clothes to play the game. When she could walk, she would hide herself behind a piece of furniture. At 15 months she became interested in repeatedly hiding a small figure underneath the sofa. Three days later she seemed to take account of other people's views, by picking up an object in her hand and putting it behind her back; she looked intently at the other person and then laughed as she revealed the object again.

These observations suggest that at first the child is concerned with depriving herself of a particular view. When she puts something over her face and then pulls it off again, she is probably more interested in her own contrasting visual percepts rather than in the effect on the other person's view. Only later can she hide an object from another person and, at first, this may only occur when that object is also hidden from her own view.

The child displays definite nonegocentric hiding behaviour when she can hide an object from another person but can still see it herself. Flavell, Shipstead and Croft (1978) found that nearly all 2½-year-olds could successfully hide a toy dog behind a screen from an observer; the same children, however, had much greater difficulty in moving the screen to hide the object. Lempers *et al.* (1977), on the other hand, found that 3-year-olds and most 2½-year-olds were successful in both of these tasks. Whereas in the Lempers *et al.* study the child had only to slide a screen along a fixed runner to block the observer's view, in

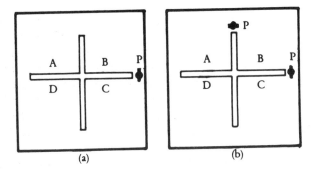

Figure 1.6: The cross-shaped configuration of walls and the positions of policemen (P) in the Hughes and Donaldson (1979, Figure 2, p. 135) study of hiding and co-ordination of viewpoints. In (a) only one policeman was used; in (b) two policemen were used. (Reprinted with the permission of the editors of *Educational Review*.)

the Flavell *et al.* study a portable screen was handed to the child to be placed on the table. A study by Hughes and Donaldson (1979) of slightly older children, aged 3½ to 4½ years, also demonstrated that children can successfully hide a boy doll from toy policemen who were positioned around an arrangement of intersecting walls (see Figure 1.6).

As well as manipulating the object or the screen, the child may hide an object by manipulating the observer in some way: in one of Lempers' *et al.* (1977) tasks some 2½- and 3½-year-olds turned the observer round so that her back was towards a large, immoveable object; one 2-year-old closed the observer's eyelids so that she could not see. In most of the tasks, though, the children acted on either the object to be hidden or on the screen; acting on the observer may be an individual preference and/or may only be resorted to when other possibilities are unavailable.

Although these studies of hiding demonstrate that quite young children can hide an object from an observer by placing it behind a screen, they cannot tell us whether young children's notion of hiding is the same as that of an older child or an adult. As Bridges and Rowles (1985) have pointed out, it may be sufficient for young children to place the hider on the opposite side of the screen from the seeker without even considering what the seeker might actually see. Even though their responses are counted as correct we know little of what actually counts as hiding for the young child. In a series of experiments with 3- to 7-year-olds, Bridges and Rowles found that it is not until the age of 4 years that most children really consider the seeker's view; although many 3-year-olds do realize that the seeker's viewpoint must be considered, many others interpret hiding to mean simply going behind an obstruction even when parts of the hider are not concealed. In their games of hide-and-seek, children of this age will often hide behind a chair but will fail to realize that their feet are still visible.

When my daughter first began to play hide-and-seek around the house, she repeatedly hid in the same place and shrieked with delight every time she was 'found'. She had not yet learned that as well as concealment another rule of hide-and-seek, as played by older children, is that the hiding place should be unpredictable. The hider must constantly think of new places to hide in order to outwit the seeker.

Yet further components to the notion of hiding may be added by older children, as Sacks (1980) outlined in his article on the game called, 'Button, button, who's got the button?'. There are many variations on this game, but the one I know best is where a group of children pass a ring from one to another along a circle of string. The 'it' child in the middle has to guess who has the ring. When we played this game at my daughter's fifth birthday party, it was chaotic: not only did the children in the circle have no idea how to conceal the ring without giving the game away, but the 'it' child in turn seemed to pay no attention to the movements of the children's hands nor to the expressions on their faces and simply guessed the whereabouts of the ring at random. By the age of 9 or 10 years, however, children have become extremely adept at suppressing cues which might lead to the discovery of the ring and also at laying false trails (manual, facial and verbal cues) to trick the 'it' child. The 'it' child, in turn, learns to be suspicious of the ostentatious passing of the ring from one child to another and to look for the leaking of involuntary cues which might signal the true hiding place.

Based on the evidence from the Lempers *et al.* study (1977) it seems that hiding may be a later development than showing. Whereas all the 2½- and 3-year-olds and two-thirds of 2-year-olds were able to turn the observer so that she could see a large object, only half of the 3-year-olds in a hiding task turned the observer away from the object. We cannot take this evidence alone as conclusive, however; we also need systematic comparisons of hiding and showing when the object itself or a screen rather than the observer need to be manipulated in the task. Unfortunately such comparisons are not yet available, although it is to be hoped that more studies will be forthcoming on the child's developing capacities within both these fields and that the relationship between them might be clarified.

Summary

The studies reviewed in this chapter demonstrate that during the preschool years the child develops a considerable understanding of other people's visual percepts. From the beginning the baby takes considerable interest in the human face and engages in 'conversations' with those around her. She begins to identify the body parts involved in adults' gestures and can produce imitative gestures herself. She can follow another's line of gaze or a point and can fixate the object or event the observer sees. Conversely, she can produce particular visual percepts in others by pointing out or showing objects to them. The child can search for and retrieve objects hidden by others and can hide objects from other people. She comes to understand that the observer may see an object which she herself cannot see, and vice versa.

It is clear that the ability to detect what another person is attending to emerges quite early even though it will develop into a much more sophisticated form later on. The importance of its emergence is made explicit by Scaife and Bruner (1975, p. 266): 'In so far as mutual orientation implies a degree of knowledge in some form about another's perspective then the child in its first year may be considered as less than completely egocentric.' From birth, the child enters a visual world in which objects in space are public and are jointly available to all observers. The child is not imprisoned by her own point of view, although she may use it as a starting point or reference from which to infer what another person can see.

The adults' role in this development is very active. In fact adults employ a number of devices to draw the child's attention to an object, an action or a relationship. As well as pointing and gazing, they may 'mark' a target object by touching it or shaking it; in addition, they tend to name and talk about the objects they themselves or the children are looking at. These behaviours are strongly related, and

Bates *et al.* (1979) have suggested that they form a 'gestural complex'. It seems to me that the combination of these verbal and non-verbal behaviours serves to minimise the potential ambiguity regarding the focus of attention. Conversely, by providing a number of cues, parents maximize the chances of success on the part of the child.

There is abundant evidence, then, that young children below the age of 4 years have a considerable understanding of other observers and other views. And yet Piaget and Inhelder dismiss as pointless (1956, p. 212, footnote) any attempt to study perspective-taking in children of about 4 years and below (Stage I) because these children do not understand the meaning of the questions put to them. The popular interpretation of this position has been to describe young children as totally egocentric and not able to understand anything at all about other people's points of view. For example, Bee (1975, pp. 185–6) says: 'It's not that the child knows that there are other ways of looking at things and just can't visualize them; rather she is actually a prisoner of her own point of view but doesn't know it.' In Chapter 2 I shall describe Piaget and Inhelder's study of perspective-taking, outline their findings, and then assess their claims regarding children's perspective-taking abilities in the light of more recent research.

2 Children's representations of different views

In Section II of their Chapter 6, Piaget and Inhelder (1956) tried to find out how the child represents *single* objects from particular points of view, and in Chapter 8 they went on to tackle the problem of the overall co-ordination of perspectives when the observer moves round a *group* of objects.

The *single-object* task will be described first. Children from about 4 to 12 years of age were asked to imagine what the apparent shape of a needle and a disc would be when placed in a number of different positions. Piaget and Inhelder anticipated that two problems might arise: first, to get the child to understand that the problem is about the *apparent* shape, not the actual shape; secondly, to find a suitable method of depicting the object. To overcome the first difficulty two methods were used in turn. To start with, a small doll was placed at right angles to the child, looking at the same object. The child was then asked to imagine how the needle or disc appeared to the doll. (A needle seen end-on to the child for instance would appear full-length from the doll's position). This method was supplemented with one in which the object was turned through 90 degrees or 180 degrees in front of the child and she was asked to imagine the shape of the intermediate positions; in addition, the object was also turned very gradually and the child had to predict the apparent shape of the final position. Figure 2.1 shows the successive presentation of the needle and the disc seen in perspective.

The second problem, that of finding out what the child sees, was also solved by using two techniques. The first of these was to ask the child to draw the shape. To counteract possible deficiencies in motor skills, especially among the younger children, the child was also asked to choose a shape from a selection of pictures; these included incorrect drawings containing typical errors found in children's spontaneous drawings.

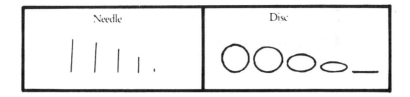

Figure 2.1: Successive presentations of a needle and a disc. Piaget and Inhelder (1956, Figure 19, p. 173) presented a needle (or a disc) vertically in front of the child and then tilted it backwards until it lay in the horizontal plane. The length of the needle appears to shorten and the disc appears to become a flatter ellipse and eventually a straight line. (Reprinted with the permission of the publisher.)

Now we move on to Piaget and Inhelder's well-known 'three-mountains' task which was used to study the child's representation of a *group* of objects seen from different viewpoints. They discuss this in their Chapter 8. A large model of the mountains was made, about one metre square and about 30 centimetres at the highest point (see Figure 2.2). From her position at A the child could see a green mountain topped by a little house in the right foreground. To the left was a brown mountain with a red cross on its peak. In the right-background was a high snow-capped grey mountain. The three mountains were of different heights and irregular shapes; there were also paths and streams marked on them.

A small wooden doll, about 2 or 3 cm high, was placed in a number of different positions around the mountains and the child was asked to imagine the different views that the doll would have. Three different methods of questioning were used, apparently given to each child in a fixed order. In the first method, three pieces of shaped cardboard[1] were presented and the child had to arrange them to duplicate her own view from position A. Then the doll was placed at position C and the child was asked to make the picture which could be seen from there. The procedure was repeated for positions B and D. The child then moved to other positions, was asked to construct the view with the pieces of card from those new positions, and was also asked to reconstruct views from positions occupied previously (e.g. position A).

In the second method, the child was shown a set of ten pictures each measuring 20 × 28 cm. These represented the mountains from differ-ent viewpoints, were painted the same colours as the model, and

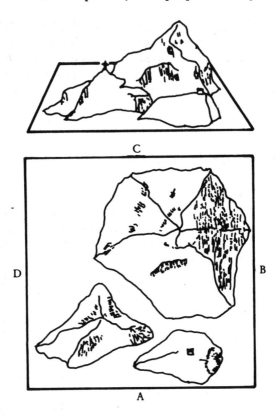

Figure 2.2: The three-mountains model used by Piaget and Inhelder (1956, Figure 21, p. 211) showing (above) the child's view and (below) a bird's eye view. (Reprinted with the permission of the publisher.)

showed the detailed features very clearly. The child had to select the picture which showed the doll's view. Piaget and Inhelder say (p. 212) that all ten pictures were usually shown at the *same* time. It is difficult to see exactly what is meant by this, since the size of the pictures would make it difficult to scan them easily if they were all spread out on a table; it is more likely that the pictures were presented in a pile and viewed successively.

In the third method, the child chose a picture and then placed the doll so that it could see that particular view of the mountains.

Piaget and Inhelder tested 100 children: 21 from 4 to 6 years 6 months, 30 from 6 years 7 months to 8 years, 33 from 8 to 9½ years, and 16 from 9½ to 12 years. It is not clear whether these children were the same ones who completed the single-object task. Although they do not explicitly say so, it is implied in Piaget and Inhelder's chapter that they tried, unsuccessfully, to test children below the age of 4 years.

Piaget and Inhelder's results

Piaget and Inhelder classify the results of their investigations according to a number of distinct stages. The stages are the same for both the single-object and the three-mountains tasks; these stages reflect general and fundamental cognitive functioning at different developmental levels. Before going on to outline these stages it is important to note a number of unsatisfactory aspects of Piaget and Inhelder's study. Although they mention the number and ages of their subjects they give no indication of the number and ages of subjects classified in each developmental stage. Furthermore, Piaget and Inhelder argue that in some cases different types of response may be indicative of the same basic way of thinking, and they give examples of these different response-types; yet we are not told which if any of the response-types is the most common. Indeed, overall, we do not know whether Piaget and Inhelder have accounted for all types of response made or whether they considered only the dominant responses.

The method of analysis is to give a general idea of the characteristics of each stage backed up by specific examples taken from individual children's protocols. No details of frequency are provided, only 'approximate' or 'average' ages for each stage. This kind of analysis has led some, such as Braine (1962, p. 42) to criticise Piaget – 'Instead of specifying his constructs in terms of evidence, he illustrates them with a wealth of suggestive observation.'

Stage I (below 4 years): Piaget and Inhelder reckon that these very
   young children do not understand the nature of the tasks, that it is
   pointless to attempt any consistent studies with them or to report
   their responses.
Stage IIA (4 to 5½ years): Children do not vary the shape or size of

the object relative to the observer. For instance a needle will be shown full-length whether it is actually seen that way or is seen end-on. The shape chosen to represent the object is its stereotypical shape (e.g. full-length needle or full-circle disc). A concession *may* be made to different perspectives in that the drawn figure may be orientated in different ways (e.g. vertical or horizontal on the page, in the case of the needle). Similarly, in the three-mountains task, each time the doll is moved to a new position, the child reproduces or selects her own view. These responses are considered to be *egocentric* in that the child fails to distinguish different views of the object(s) and represents the object with one stereotypical view. In the case of the three-mountains task, the child adopts her *own* view as the stereotype, but she remains unconscious of the fact that it *is* her own view.

Stage IIB (5½ to 7 years): The child at this stage *begins* to show signs of distinguishing between different viewpoints. She may respond egocentrically (in the manner of Stage IIA) when required to produce a drawing but may choose a more appropriate shape (e.g. an ellipse for the disc seen at an oblique angle or a dot for the needle seen endwise) when the selection method is used. In the three-mountains task she may select her own view of the model and then turn it towards the observer, or choose a picture on the basis of the dominant feature of the doll's view without considering the other relationships among the mountains relative to the doll's position.

This substage is regarded as an advance on substage IIA in that the child seems to be aware that the doll will see a different view but she does not realize that the internal relationships within the model (before–behind, left–right) will vary with different points of view; thus the child '. . . imagines that depicting one elementary relationship correctly (e.g. the dominant feature) will automatically elicit the remainder' (Piaget and Inhelder, 1956, p. 228). In practice, although the child *attempts* to represent another's point of view she does not know how to effect the necessary changes and usually ends up with her own view.

Stage IIIA (7 or 7½ to 8½ or 9 years): In this stage the child makes a clear distinction between different points of view but she has not yet developed a fully organized system of correspondence between viewpoint and view; Piaget and Inhelder regard this stage as one of genuine but incomplete relativity. In the single-object task the child

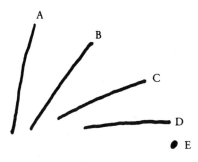

Figure 2.3: A Stage IIIA child's drawing of the successive presentations of the needle (Piaget and Inhelder, 1956, Figure 20, p. 174). (Reprinted with the permission of the publisher.)

realizes that the apparent shape of the needle or disc changes, and makes or selects different shapes accordingly but, as the child has not discovered the *quantitative* law governing the perspective changes, her responses show abrupt and qualitative changes in the apparent shape as the object is tilted (see Figure 2.3).

In the three-mountains task the child realizes that she must consider the relationships among the objects *relative* to the observer's point of view. However, the influence of her own view still persists in that when one relationship (e.g. before–behind) is correctly represented from the doll's perspective, another (e.g. left–right) will remain unchanged as seen from the child's position.

Stage IIIB (8½ or 9+): The child now understands that not only is the apparent shape of objects linked with the observer's point of view but that the law governing the transformation is quantitative and continuous. One boy, aged 9 years 4 months, 'draws a series of lines shorter and shorter, culminating in a point, to represent the series of positions of the stick between vertical and end-on. Likewise, he constructs a series of ellipses becoming thinner and thinner until they are simply a line, to show the successive inclinations of the disc.' (pp. 189–90).

In the three-mountains case, the child considers all relationships among the mountains simultaneously. She has now developed an overall co-ordinated system: for each position of the observer there corresponds a particular set of before–behind and left–right relationships among the objects.

The child understands that her own perspective is only one among many possible views; she has become conscious of her own viewpoint and can distinguish it from and co-ordinate it with others.

According to Piaget and Inhelder, the young child (below about age 4 years) progresses from having no notion of the problem at all to a stage where she understands that different observers are looking at the same object or groups of objects; but the views are not distinguished, they are all represented by the same fixed stereotype (which in some cases may coincide with the child's own perception). A breakthrough comes when the child realizes that different observers will have different views: at first she cannot imagine these correctly at all and only gradually masters the laws which govern the way the shape of objects or the relationships among a group of objects change as they are viewed from different perspectives. A full appreciation of the way views differ according to different viewpoints does not develop until at least the age of about 8½ years. Not only do children up to about the age of 7 years behave in an egocentric way, but below age 4 they are quite incapable of even understanding the task at all. The general picture is one of considerable pessimism about children's abilities well into middle childhood.

Even at only a few weeks old, babies understand something about other observers, and by the age of 3 years they know a good deal. To this extent at least, we cannot regard them as egocentric. It seems odd, then, that in Piaget and Inhelder's study children were regarded as egocentric even up until the age of 7 years. Were Piaget and Inhelder simply wrong or has the point of their argument been misunderstood? I think that in fact they have been misunderstood, and Piaget himself was aware of this problem: 'That term [egocentrism] has had the worst interpretation of any word I have used' (Piaget, in Hall, 1970, p. 28).

In Chapter 1 of *The Child's Conception of Space* (1956), and indeed throughout the book, Piaget and Inhelder make it clear that the young child, during the sensorimotor period (from 0 to 2 years), develops a considerable *practical* understanding of objects in space. She develops the ability to negotiate her environment and manipulate objects within it. She is not surprised when things look different from different positions. A major subsequent development for the child, and the one that Piaget and Inhelder are mainly interested in in their book, is the 'elevation' of this practical knowledge on to a representational plane; this representational ability only begins to emerge in the preoperational period (beginning at about 2 years of age) and is not fully developed until at least the concrete operational period (beginning at about 7 years of age). During the preoperational period the child's representations are static and inflexible, and it is this period which Piaget and Inhelder refer to as being egocentric. So, *egocentrism* does not mean that the child is totally self-absorbed and unable to appreciate that other people are observers and have different views; rather, it means that the child does not *represent* the views as other observers would actually see them. (Nevertheless, it may well be the case that the child has not learned all there is to know about other observers and their views.)

If this is a more accurate account of Piaget and Inhelder's position then it is not at all peculiar that we should find, as we did in Chapter 1, that children below the age of 4 have quite a considerable understanding of what other people can see. Most of this behaviour is *practical* and does not rely on representation.

When we turn to their study of the child's *representation* of perspectives, however, it seems to me that Piaget and Inhelder selected, albeit unwittingly, rather difficult tasks (the needle, the disc, and the three-mountains) in their study. Although their children between 4 and 7 years failed these particular tasks, they might have succeeded in others. Thus Piaget and Inhelder may have underestimated these children's ability to represent different perspectives. It will be useful here to introduce Flavell's (1974 and 1978) account of perspective-taking ability, partly in its own right, but mainly because it shows how the Piagetian task requires a very high level of perspective-taking ability for a correct solution. Rather than dwelling on the young child's difficulties with a complex perspective-taking task, Flavell has devised a sequence of graded tasks which he uses to demonstrate children's improvements in perspective-taking as they develop. Although Flavell's account is not without problems, as I shall point out, I think it helps in giving us a better understanding of why the young children failed Piaget and Inhelder's task and of why they responded in the way they did.

Flavell's account of the development of perspective-taking

Like Piaget and Inhelder, Flavell begins with a *practical* knowledge of space (*Level 0*) when 'Internal psychological processes like seeing are simply not yet objects of cognition' (1974, p. 94). At *Level 1*, the child starts to develop the ability to represent symbolically the visual experiences of herself and other observers. At first she can only represent *which* objects each person sees, but not which particular view of an object. If she sees a model cat, she will be able to select a picture (from a set portraying different animals) to represent this fact; but if given a selection of pictures with the cat in different positions she will not be able to choose the one which matches the way that she actually sees the model cat. It is at *Level 2* that the child can represent *how* different observers see objects, in terms of their orientation or arrangement *vis-à-vis* one another. In addition, at *Level 3*, the child is able to represent the apparent shape and size of the objects viewed by different people. Although 4-year-olds have some understanding of the projective size and shape of an object, such as a plate rotated before them (Pillow and Flavell, 1986), the ability to represent the projected image does not develop until the age of about 8 years and perhaps even much later.

Flavell is mainly interested in Levels 1 and 2, and these levels are perhaps the most pertinent to the responses observed in Piaget and Inhelder's study. As evidence for the levels, Flavell draws on the study by Masangkay, McCluskey, McIntyre, Sims-Knight, Vaughn and Flavell (1974). In their Experiment 2, Masangkay *et al.* used a *picture task* in which the experimenter held a card vertically between himself and the child; a dog was pasted on one side of the card and a cat on the other. After she had inspected both sides of the card, the child was asked questions such as 'Do *you (I)* see a cat or a dog?'. All children from 3 to 5½ years answered correctly. In contrast, in a *turtle task*, a profile picture of a turtle was mounted on a card placed horizontally between the observers. The child was asked 'Do *you (I)* see the turtle rightside-up (upside-down)?'. Children did not respond correctly until they were 4½ years old. Flavell's position is that the turtle task requires Level 2 ability; the question is *how* is the same object seen, not *which object* is seen. A problem with the contrast presented here is that the difficulty of the turtle task could be attributed as much to the relative difficulty or unfamiliarity of the linguistic terms ('dog', 'cat' *vs.* 'rightside-up', 'upside-down') as to the object characteristics (which object *vs.* view of object). (It would have been neater as well to have used the same objects in each task). Normally, terms such as 'rightside-up' and 'upside-down' occur later in a child's vocabulary than object terms such as 'cat' and 'dog'; but this lag may nevertheless reflect a conceptual difficulty. In fact, Flavell, Everett, Croft and Flavell (1981) subsequently attempted to sort out the confounding variables and still found evidence in support of the Level 1–Level 2 distinction.

The Level 1 picture task used is particularly clear-cut in that essentially a barrier is erected between the observers, and a different object is presented on each side. Now, other tasks which Flavell would claim can also be solved at Level 1 include a larger object occluding a smaller one from one person's viewpoint (although I have not come across an example in the literature) and a doll presenting, say, a frontal view to one person and a back view to another. Although the doll example appears to be a Level 2 task ('Which view of the doll do we each see? '), it can be solved by recasting the question at Level 1, 'Which sub-part of the doll do we each see?'. Ives (1980) used single object-arrays such as this and found that 89.5 per cent of 3-year-olds and 92.5 per cent of 4-year-olds could describe the experimenter's view correctly.

I do not know of any studies which have compared these tasks (1. two objects separated by a barrier, 2. one object occluding another, 3. doll) but they may reflect a developmental order of difficulty within Level 1.

One thing I find particularly problematic about Flavell's account is his idea of what constitutes *symbolic representation.* This is the main criterion which distinguishes the Level 0 child from the Level 1 child. Since Flavell says that a Level 0 child may be able to specify *verbally* which object the observer is looking at, but cannot represent the view visually, it seems that language is not accepted as a means of symbolic representation. Later, however, when he cites the work of Masangkay *et al.* as evidence for Levels 1 and 2 ability, the child is required to respond *verbally* to questions about what the observer can see! There seems to be some confusion, then, about what actually constitutes a representation of a visual perspective. This issue is important and has been taken up by Ives (1980), who compared a verbal and a visual response mode. Eighty-nine and a half per cent of 3-year-olds and 92.5 per cent of 5-year-olds could describe verbally which side of an object (front, back or side) could be seen from a particular position of a camera, whereas only 38 per cent of 3-year-olds and 51 per cent of 5-year-olds could select an appropriate picture. In a more complex task with 5-year-olds (Ives, 1983) using five possible views, the experimenter spoke the five possible verbal descriptions. Eighty-three per cent were correct with the verbal mode of response, but only 47 per cent with the visual response mode.

Ives (1980) says that these results imply that a linguistic response is more accessible than picture selection. Moreover, he says that children in the picture selection task first formulate the verbal label, often spoken spontaneously, of what the other person sees, and then search for the appropriate picture. It seems to me that language may function as a mediator, and may even be a necessary part of the process of locating the correct pictorial representation.

It may be that Flavell's levels and the sublevels that I have suggested in this section do reflect a developmental sequence, but it seems clear that this will occur much earlier when a child's verbal description of a view is considered rather than her representation using, say, a picture selection task.

Another problem with Flavell's account is that a verbal label such as *dog* or *cat* adequately describes which object each person sees in a Level 1 task; similarly, a child can select a picture of one animal or the other if a visual representation is required. But Flavell does not predict what kind of picture the Level 1 child would select if she had a choice nor which she would produce if asked to draw what the observer could see. (The material discussed in Part II will have a bearing on this question.)

Failure in Piagetian-type tasks

Despite the problems I have discussed above, Flavell's account helps us to see why children between about 4 and 7 years failed on Piaget and Inhelder's tasks. In these tasks (the needle, the disc, and the three-mountains) all observers can see the same objects (except, perhaps, that in Figure 2.2 the smallest mountain may not be visible from Position C). The question to the child, then, is not 'Which objects does each observer see?' but 'How does each observer see the objects?'. In Flavell's terms, this would require Level 2 ability for a correct solution. Thus we would expect the child who possesses only Level 1 ability to make errors in these tasks.

How will a child who possesses only Level 1 ability respond to a Level 2 (or Piagetian) task? As I mentioned above, Flavell's account does not allow us to make a specific prediction. Most of the literature on perspective-taking, however, reports that Piaget and Inhelder found that children select their own view in error. Because Piaget and Inhelder regard these young children as egocentric, the own-view error has become known as the 'egocentric error'. But this misrepresents Piaget and Inhelder's findings and their position. Children selected their own view in error only in the three-mountains task. In the needle and disc tasks their errors were different: typically, they selected stereotyped or 'best' views of the objects (full-length needle or full-circle disc). Piaget and Inhelder (pp. 213, 242 and 243) were not unaware of a possible contradiction here, but they argued that it is merely apparent. In all cases the child is responding with a stereotype or 'best view'. For the needle and disc this is a full-length needle and a full-circle disc respectively. In the mountains task, the three mountains do not have a familiar stereotype in the same way, so the child adopts her own view as the stereotype; in fact, the child's own view probably *is* her best view since the three objects can be seen very clearly.[2]

The point, then, is that young children who fail the Piagetian perspectives-tasks do so because they are imprisoned not by the view presented 'before their very eyes', but by their ideal view which they elevate as a 'false absolute' (Piaget and Inhelder, p. 213). Piaget and Inhelder make this very clear in their chapter and a more detailed discussion of the issue has been provided by Morss (1987). The child may be *aware* of different views of objects (see Salatas and Flavell, 1976) but she does not *represent* them; she only reproduces her stereotype. Liben (1978) and Liben and Belknap (1981) have shown that 3- to 5-year-old children will choose a picture showing all the objects in an array to represent their own view even though some are actually occluded in the array. Light and Nix (1983) have also found that 4- to 6-year-olds will select a *non*occluded view of two objects to represent her own or another's view, when in the array one object actually occludes another. These studies also show that the children do not respond with their own view but with a 'good view' of the array.

We can now outline the child's early stages in trying to represent another's view, based on the accounts of Flavell and Piaget and

Inhelder, and on the studies by Ives. Level 1 ability (beginning at approximately 2 years of age) concerns the child's ability to understand which object she herself sees and which object another person sees. When some form of visual representation is required the child selects a picture which shows the best view or stereotype of the object array. But this will underestimate what she actually knows of other views, since her ability to describe verbally what another person sees is much more advanced.

A Level 2 task is one in which the same object array is seen by both observers but they see it in a different orientation or arrangement. The child will be able to select a picture which shows the correct orientation of an object or the correct arrangement of a group of objects from a particular observer's point of view. Again, a verbal response may be in advance of the visual representation, and some very simple Level 2 tasks may be answered correctly by children as young as 4 or 5 years.

The development of Level 2 ability

When children begin to represent the way that objects are seen by different observers (Level 2 tasks) they may not be successful in all tasks. If a single object, such as a doll, is presented, it has easily discriminable sides which can be thought of as subparts. Thus, although both observers see the same object, they see different discrete parts of it, and this may enable the task to be solved with only Level 1 ability. Other objects, such as Piaget and Inhelder's needle or disc or Flavell's (1968) wedge-shaped block, which do not present such clearly different views, would require at least Level 2 ability for a successful solution.

Most studies have used multi-object arrays to study the way objects seen by two people are represented by the child. It is generally assumed that a multi-object array is more difficult than a single-object array, since the child has to work out the spatial relationship of at least two objects *vis-à-vis* an observer, and, if fronted objects are used, she must also consider their orientations. The research evidence is rather conflicting. Fishbein, Lewis and Keiffer (1972) used a single object with clearly discriminable sides and found it to be easier than a multi-object array, but Brodzinsky, Jackson and Overton (1972) found no difference. Flavell (1968) used a single-object with less easily discriminable sides and found it easier than the multi-object array, but Piaget and Inhelder (1956) found no difference. Ives (1983), using both verbal and a picture method, found only a marginal difference in favour of doll-like single objects *vs.* a three-mountains type array. Again a problem with a direct comparison of the findings is that different response methods (among other variables) were used.

Although a correct representation of another's view of a multi-object array would involve an understanding of the relationship among *all* the objects relative to that viewpoint, at first the child may only attend to part of the view, namely its dominant feature (cf. Piaget and Inhelder, p. 228). Elsewhere (Cox, 1978a and b) I have suggested that the 'dominant feature' might refer to the object nearest or in front of the other observer. In a picture selection task, children who correctly choose a picture to represent the other's view may do so solely on the basis of the object nearest the observer. That is, they decide which object is near her and then choose a picture in which the same object is at the forefront; they do not have to consider the position of the other objects, since these are normally correctly arranged. When the pictures included the correct one and other 'trick' ones in which the foreground object was correct but the positions of other objects were not, the same children chose these other views as often as the correct one.

When the child does consider the relationships between the objects, those arrays containing only one dimension should be easier than those containing two or more. Tanaka (1968) found this to be the case when one and two dimensions were compared. Such a comparison, however, may lead to problems: only two objects are needed for a one-dimensional array (see Figure 2.4a) whereas three are needed for a two-dimensional array (see Figure 2.4c). Thus, number of dimensions may be confounded with number of objects. One way of resolving this would be to line up three objects in the one-dimensional array so that number of objects is controlled (see Figure 2.4b).

Within one dimension one might predict that an increase in the number of objects should make the task more difficult so that the arrays in Figure 2.4b should be more difficult than those in Figure 2.4a. Although Nigl and Fishbein (1973) used arrays with two dimensions, they found nevertheless that performance was not affected when the number of objects was increased, and suggested that

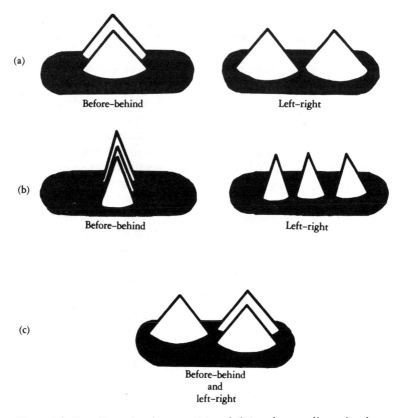

(a)

Before–behind   Left–right

(b)

Before–behind   Left–right

(c)

Before–behind
and
left–right

Figure 2.4: One-dimensional arrays ((a) and (b)) and a two-dimensional array (c).

additional objects above two for each dimension provides redundant information.

Some kinds of relationship may be more difficult than others. Piaget and Inhelder claimed that the before–behind relationship is amenable to perspective changes earlier than the left–right. The reason for this, they argue, is that 'there is a bigger difference between a background beyond the reach of immediate action and a foreground directly subject to it, than there is between a left and right which are equally near or distant' (p. 215); it is this greater asymmetry in the before–behind dimension which makes it easier to deal with.

Piaget and Inhelder were talking about the three-mountains array, and most of the research comparing the two sorts of dimensions has also used multi-dimensional arrays. These studies (Coie, Costanzo and Farnill, 1973; Nigl and Fishbein, 1973; Cox 1978a and b) have supported the claim that the before–behind dimension is represented correctly earlier than is the left–right dimension. Rather than reflecting any 'real' difference in psychological difficulty between the dimensions, the responses may simply reflect a particular order of processing of the two dimensions – before–behind first and left–right second. However, Tanaka (1968), Hoy (1974) and Minnigerode and Carey (1974) presented the dimensions separately in different arrays and still found that the left–right dimension was the more difficult.

In general it appears that left–right relationships are more difficult than before–behind relationships, as Piaget and Inhelder had predicted. And yet this conclusion seems to contradict that of other studies, such as Light and Nix (1983), which have demonstrated that children prefer a 'good view' (two objects are arranged side-by-side) rather than a 'bad view' (one object partially masks the one behind it). This issue cannot be sorted out simply by comparing the studies because there are so many differences between them:[3] not only are different kinds of objects used in the array, but the distance between them is not kept constant so that the amount of masking in a before–behind view may be greater in one study than in another. A further consideration is the selection of pictures made available to the child. It may be easier to select the correct picture if only two pictures are presented and both show a before–behind relationship and, conversely, more difficult to choose the correct picture if both show left–right relationships. The reason for this may be that the amount of overlap between the objects in the before–behind pictures may make it easier for the child to discriminate between them; in contrast the lack of any overlap between the objects in the left–right pictures may make it difficult for the child to distinguish them. This advantage for before–behind arrays, however, may be overridden when four pictures are presented to the child – two before–behind and two left–right arrangements – since the child may be tempted to choose a left–right, namely a 'good view', even when a before–behind picture is the correct one.

In trying to decide the order of difficulty of the two dimensions in a perspective-taking task, we must take account of other confounding variables and, in particular, the presence of masking, usually present in the before–behind arrangement but not in the left–right. Although the effect of masking/no masking has not been tested directly, there is some evidence which attests to its importance. For instance, Cox and Willetts (1982) eliminated the masking of one object by the other by using two flat discs in the array. The children chose their picture from a set of four (two before–behind and two left–right arrangements, with no overlap between the images in any picture). There was no difference between the left–right and before–behind arrangements for any of the positions occupied by the other observer. A further piece of evidence comes from a replication of Light and Nix's experiment. Suzanne Nawratil and I found, as did Light and Nix, that when children see one object partially masking another they tend to choose a left–right or good view instead of an overlapping before–behind picture. For another group of children, however, we moved the two objects farther apart so that there was no visual overlap and presented four pictures (two before–behind and two left–right arrangements) in which the images did not overlap; under these circumstances the children were less likely to choose a left–right picture.

Summary

In this chapter I have outlined Piaget and Inhelder's studies on perspective-taking and have discussed their findings, particularly with regard to their meaning of *egocentrism*. It seems to me that Piaget and Inhelder accepted that young children have a *practical* understanding of what others see, but that they have difficulty in representing those views. There are at least two main reasons, however, why Piaget and Inhelder found that children, even at 7 years of age, performed so poorly in their perspective-taking task. One is that the level of perspective-taking required for a successful solution was very high. As well as knowing which object(s) the observer could see, the child would also have to know *how* the object(s) looked to the observer. I outlined Flavell's work on the progressive levels of perspective-taking ability, which indicates that a knowledge of *how* objects appear to another observer is rather a late development.

The second reason for poor performance is that the pictorial response method underestimates the child's knowledge; as Ives' research has shown, children can describe verbally another's view at an earlier age than they can represent it with a picture. The pictures that young children do select tend to be stereotypes (also called 'best views', 'canonical views', 'ideal views', etc.); in some tasks the stereotyped view may coincide with the child's actual current view of the scene. It is these stereotyped views which Piaget and Inhelder took as evidence for the child's egocentrism, and it is important to note that an egocentric error is not necessarily an own-view error.

I have reviewed here some of the studies concerned with the *development* of the child's ability to represent different views, and indicated that this development progresses in a systematic fashion.

Notes

1. In much of the literature it is assumed that Piaget and Inhelder used *flat* pieces of cardboard, but the original report of the three-mountains task by Meyer (1935) on which Piaget and Inhelder's (1956) account was based talks about three *cartons* of similar shape and colour to the three model mountains. It may be that 'cartons' referred to *boxes* rather than to flat cardboard pieces.
2. Kielgast (1971) in fact suggested an idea, based on Gibson's theory (1950, p. 35), that an object or group of objects may have a 'unique orientation from which it is best viewed' and that the child may be searching for the most representative view.
3. There are a number of methodological variables, such as the method of response and the nature and position of the other observer in the task, which may affect the child's performance. I have not discussed them here because they are not essential to my argument. Interested readers might like to consult Fehr (1978) and Cox (1980).

Conclusion to Part I

It goes almost without saying that babies at birth, or very soon after, display considerable capabilities. In Chapter 1 I outlined a range of studies which have shown that babies can discriminate figure from ground, can follow a slow-moving object with their eyes, and know whether objects travelling towards them are on a 'hit' or 'miss' path. These kinds of abilities imply that babies already have some understanding of depth and three-dimensionality. They are not living in a 'flat', two-dimensional world.

Young babies also seem to treat people rather differently from other objects. Some researchers have claimed that babies are actually born with distinct social predispositions. Babies certainly prefer the human face to other complex patterns and there is some evidence that they can imitate parents' facial movements. In their 'conversations', parents and babies synchronize their contributions and take turns. This is probably due, however, in large part to the *adults'* skilful management of the interaction rather than to an equal contribution from the baby. Infants and young children can use a number of cues to find out what other people are attending to; particularly important are gaze and pointing. They also use these cues themselves along with showing and vocalizing in order to attract other people's attention and to refer them to objects of interest; conversely, children develop the ability to hide things from others and, in so doing, deprive them of particular visual percepts.

From a very early age, then, babies are not living in an isolated and private world. They are involved in interaction with a public world which they and others share. And yet the 'folklore' which surrounds the field of child development often presents the young child as egocentric, as being unaware of and unaccommodating to other people and other points of view. The debate about whether children really are or are not egocentric depends to a large extent on what is meant by 'egocentric'. Piaget and Inhelder's much cited study of visual perspective-taking involving the three-mountains task is probably largely responsible for the confusion surrounding the term.

In Chapter 2, after I described the study and outlined the findings, I summarized Piaget and Inhelder's claim: children below about age 7 are termed egocentric because they cannot represent the different views that observers will have of a particular scene. Now, just because children cannot represent a particular view, does this necessarily mean that they do not understand that it is possible to have different views and that different observers may have different views? Some of what Piaget and Inhelder say certainly implies this, but some of what they say does not! The evidence I presented in Chapter 1 showed that young children have considerable understanding of what other people can see, and I guessed that Piaget and Inhelder would not have disputed this. In Chapter 2 I suggested that perhaps the popular interpretation of 'egocentrism' misrepresents Piaget and Inhelder's position. I re-examined Piaget and Inhelder's meaning of the term and came to the conclusion that they accepted that young children do have considerable understanding of what others can see, but that children cannot *represent* what those views are like. (Many people may feel that I have been overly charitable and that Piaget and Inhelder really did believe that young children have no idea about other people's views.) I went on to qualify this, though, because it seemed to me that the tasks which Piaget and Inhelder used were particularly difficult ones and probably required both a high level of perspective-taking ability *and* representational skill for their successful solution.

Also in this chapter I outlined Flavell's ideas on perspective-taking which suggest that at first the child only understands which object(s) another person is looking at (Level 1) and not the particular way that the array is seen. Since the same objects could be seen from all different viewpoints, Piaget and Inhelder's tasks were really a test of *how* the objects were seen (Level 2). Children who have not yet attained Level 2 will only know that each observer sees the same objects; they will not appreciate how their views differ. But, even when children do know how the views differ, there remains the problem of how to communicate that knowledge. Piaget and Inhelder, and indeed most other researchers, asked children to represent the views pictorially. In Part II I shall show how children up to about age 7 or 8 years often draw (or choose) canonical views of objects, that is they draw a stereotyped or 'best' view rather than the particular view that they have at the time. Thus, in Piaget and Inhelder's tasks, children typically selected a full-length needle and a full-circle disc even though they could not see the objects like this, although they did choose a view of the mountains which corresponded with their own view. This pattern of responses indicates that the children were not trying to show what they could see from their viewpoint; they were simply selecting the picture which would best represent the scene *per se.* (It is argued that the child's own view of the three mountains also happened to be the best view. For Piaget and Inhelder, then, an egocentric error is not necessarily the child's *own view.*) Piaget and Inhelder regarded this as egocentric behaviour.

The pictorial mode of representation may have its own problems, and may lead us to underestimate drastically young children's knowledge about observers and what they can see. And, indeed, the work of Ives has shown that children can give a detailed verbal report of another's view at an earlier age than they can select a corresponding picture. Furthermore, Ives believes that children may first of all formulate a verbal account of another's view, and then search for an appropriate picture. Thus a linguistic response seems to be more accessible and may act as a mediator.

Do we as adults actually work out what other people see by picturing to ourselves the other's view? I suspect that in normal face-to-face interaction we do not; we probably use the same skills that infants do, albeit more skilfully. That is, we take account of the observer's direction of gaze, body orientation, and gesture. In addition, we can comprehend a detailed verbal reference to what the other sees. In normal face-to-face interaction this 'practical' strategy may be quite adequate. We may not need to have a mental picture of another's view. Neither do we need to experience another's emotion in order to understand what she is feeling (Chapter 9).

PART II   The Artist's Point of View

I began in Part I by asking questions about the young child's understanding of other people's views and her ability to represent those views. It turned out that although even very young infants have a considerable understanding of what other people see they have difficulty in representing these views, especially in a pictorial form. In fact, not only do they have problems in representing what someone else sees, they also find it difficult to represent their *own* view. The child's developing ability to draw what she herself sees is the topic I shall discuss in Part II.

In our society we are so used to seeing pictures, and even producing them ourselves, that we may not stop to wonder how we actually manage to interpret them. Although a picture *can* be simply an arrangement of lines, shapes or colours designed to produce pleasing or disturbing sensations in the viewer, we usually think of the marks on the page as representing or *standing for* objects in the 'real' world. If we wish to represent objects on a flat surface, we have a problem: in the real world we deal with *three* dimensions of space, but in a picture we only have two. In order to interpret correctly what another person has drawn or to draw a picture for others, we need a set of conventions or rules to avoid ambiguity and misunderstanding. (There are of course occasions when the artist may wish to create feelings of uncertainty in the observer or suggest to the observer that things *are* ambiguous, and she may do this by deliberately making aspects of the picture ambiguous.) As with language, if we are to communicate through pictures we must have agreed conventions about how they are constructed and what they mean, otherwise their communicative usefulness breaks down. We must also be aware that these conventions *are* conventions and will not necessarily be understood immediately by people from different cultures or by young children who have not yet had time to assimilate them.

There are many ways in which we can approach the study of pictures, and many aspects of them that we can discuss. I cannot even attempt to do justice to them all. In this section I shall deal mainly with the way that objects are spatially orientated and related one to another on the page. (The reader interested in other aspects of art, such as the appreciation of style, is referred to Gardner, 1972, and O'Hare and Westwood, 1984.) In Chapter 3 I shall introduce the system of linear perspective which is so dominant in the way we think we ought to represent a three-dimensional scene on the two-dimensional page. Also in that chapter I shall outline briefly Luquet's account of how children develop from a pre-representational scribbling stage, to a stage of intellectual realism in which they draw what they know rather than what they see, and finally to an 'adult' stage of visual realism in which they are assumed capable of drawing objects as they are actually seen.

In Chapter 4 I shall examine the evidence for the claim that young children cannot draw what they see but tend to draw rather rigid stereotypes which show too much. I shall show that young children often do rely on stereotypes and do not draw the object as it appears before them; however, a number of research studies have demonstrated that under certain conditions children as young as 4 or 5 years of age will draw what they can see. Chapter 5 deals specifically with 'how to draw an object in perspective'. Adults and even young children can draw *what* they see, but a problem arises over 'how' the object is seen. In particular, it is easy to show that one sees a cube rather than a ball. It is not too difficult to show that one sees only two faces of a cube and not three. It is very difficult, though, to get the depth lines 'right' in the picture so that the drawing matches how one sees the actual model cube. Children find this very hard indeed; it turns out that many adults do too!

Traditionally, it has been considered that young children are egocentric and confined to their own perspective. As they develop during childhood they are supposed to become aware of other points of view. What seems to be happening in the field of pictorial representation, however, is a development in the opposite direction; the struggle is towards adopting one's own perspective. It turns out that this contradiction is merely apparent.

3 How can we represent a three-dimensional scene on a two-dimensional surface?

In the real world we normally deal with three dimensions of space: up-down, near–far, and left–right. But a piece of paper has only two spatial dimensions. Immediately, then, a problem presents itself. Three into two won't go. So how do we deal with the third dimension? One way is simply to ignore it. In a map we can take a bird's-eye view of a scene, and draw only the two dimensions of the horizontal plane. The vertical dimension is not depicted; we must 'read in' our knowledge that buildings, for instance, have height (see Figure 3.1). We can, alternatively, take a different point of view and miss out the near-far dimension (see Figure 3.2); although the figures in the picture are rather 'flat' we know that in reality such figures are solid.

Sometimes different points of view may be juxtaposed in the same picture. Thus, in the fifteenth-century woodcut in Figure 3.3 the river is seen from above while the mermaids and landscape are seen from a frontal perspective. Although this Figure shows whole objects seen from different viewpoints, parts within the same objects were often shown from different perspectives. Commonly, in Egyptian art, (see Figure 3.4) the human figure is seen in profile but the eye is seen from the front.

It would be too simplistic, however, to regard this strategy as a primitive solution to the problem, and Hagen (1985) warns us against the adoption of a view of art as an evolutionary progression from a primitive to a modern, realistic style. Cubist painters in the twentieth century have deliberately shown objects or parts of objects from radically different perspectives in the same scene. For practical purposes, too, tourist maps often show the routes as seen from above but give a frontal view of notable buildings so that they can be easily recognized as landmarks (see Figure 3.5). This strategy is very similar to that used in the fifteenth-century woodcut.

What the pictures seem to do is to depict the typical or stereotyped

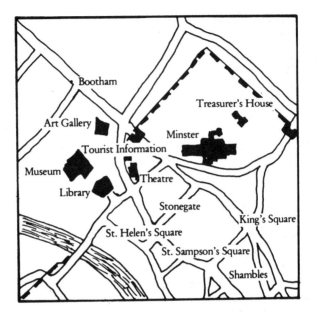

Figure 3.1: Map of York.

Figure 3.2: Taken from *Children Playing* by L. S. Lowry.

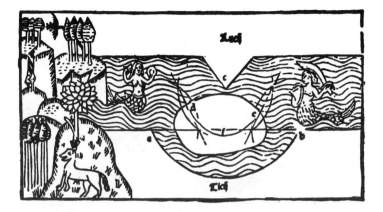

Figure 3.3: Woodcut by Bartolo da Sassoferrato, *de fluminibus*, Rome, 1483.

Figure 3.4: Figures in the sepulchral chamber of Sethos I, XIX dynasty, Karnak.

view of each object, often called the 'canonical' view. These canonical views are perhaps the least ambiguous *vis-à-vis* the identity of each object. But the scene as a whole would be impossible if considered as what the artist could actually see if she were viewing it from one particular fixed position.

Since the Renaissance the norm in Western art has been to adopt a

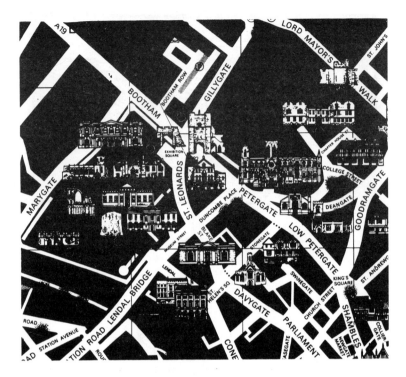

Figure 3.5: Tourist map of York.

particular viewpoint and to draw a whole scene from that perspective (see Figure 3.6). So the idea is that one looks *into* a picture as if looking through a window into a scene, and maybe beyond into the distance.

Generally, we regard the top of a page held vertically as 'up' and the bottom as 'down'; if the page is flat on the table, the part furthest away is 'up' and the part near to us is 'down'. The left–right dimension of the page corresponds to the horizontal–lateral dimension of the observer's space. Thus, the problem arises with the near–far or depth dimension of the real world: there is no equivalent on a two-dimensional flat surface. So how do we indicate that objects are solid and have depth, that one object is behind another and perhaps far away in the distance?

The solution proposed by artists in Northern Italy, notably Brunelleschi (1377–1446) and Alberti (1404–72), was the system

Figure 3.6: Leonardo da Vinci: perspective study for the *Adoration of the Magi*, pen, metalpoint, wash. (Reprinted with permission: n.436E, Gabinetto Désegni e Stampe degli Uffizi Florence.)

commonly known as *perspective*. (Actually, this system was not entirely unknown in antiquity.) The plane of the picture cuts across the rays of light travelling from the objects in the scene to the artist's eye, a single, fixed viewpoint. These points of intersection are traced on to the picture surface and reveal the apparent size and shape of objects seen from that particular position. In Leonardo da Vinci's (1452–1519) *Notebooks* there is a sketch which shows how an object in space is projected on to a flat surface (see Figure 3.7). A special piece of apparatus could be used by the artist to do this. In Figure 3.8 the artist has erected a grid and is viewing his subject through it from a fixed viewpoint marked by a sighting device. He observes the outline of the subject in each segment of the grid and draws it on to his picture, which is similarly marked out in squares.

An object near to the artist will appear larger than the same object placed further away; in fact, these size changes can be calculated precisely (every feature is halved in size as the distance doubles). The 'foreshortening' effect of perspective fixes a particular view of an object which may be radically different from its 'canonical' shape. Thus a disc known to be round may appear as a thin ellipse if it is depicted as being tipped horizontally away from the viewer (see Figure 3.9). The boundary lines of objects like tables and buildings are

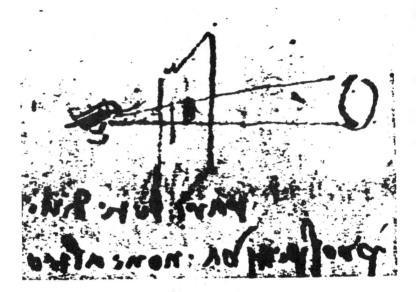

Figure 3.7: Leonardo da Vinci: sketch showing how three-dimensional objects appear on a flat surface.

drawn at such an angle that they converge towards a 'vanishing point' in the distance (see Figure 3.10). The artist can also achieve the effect of distance by varying the intensity of colour, the definition of the line, and the 'closeness' or 'openness' of texture.

These are just some of the characteristics of the perspective system which was further developed by artists such as Leonardo da Vinci. It became the ideal way of representation and was, and is, considered by many as more 'truthful' and closer to reality than any other projective system. And yet, even if we stand still, we do not normally see a scene in exactly this way. We do not see the world from *one* fixed point as through a fixed-lens camera. We have stereoscopic vision. Our eyes are constantly moving. Our perceptual size-scaling does not match a strict mathematical size-scaling, so we 'see' objects in the distance as larger than the size represented optically at the eye. Furthermore, colour and definition are not uniform across the field of vision. In fact, soon after the system of perspective had been established in the fifteenth century, modifications were already being made; many

Figure 3.8: Albrecht Dürer: *Der Zeichner des liegenden Weibes*, woodcut (B. 149). (Reprinted with permission of Kupferstichkabinett Staatliche Museen Preussischer Kulturbesitz, Berlin).

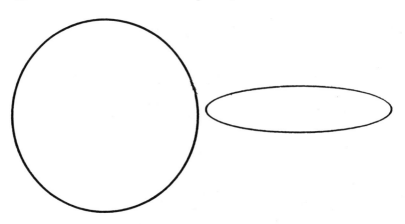

Figure 3.9: A disc known to be round (left) will appear as an ellipse (right) when it is tipped horizontally away from the viewer.

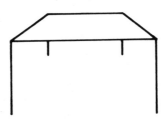

Figure 3.10: A table-top known to be rectangular will appear to be trapezoidal in shape.

artists have experimented with and adopted other systems of representation and, for practical purposes, designers and architects may choose among a number of different projective systems (Dubery and Willats, 1972). Nevertheless, the perspective system has been taught to students of art well into the twentieth century. Although the system is probably not the best one to use for all purposes (e.g. architectural drawings and maps) we are left with the popular assumption that it is the natural way of seeing things and the ideal method of representation.

The system of linear perspective is seen as the culmination not only of *historical* development, but also of ontogenetic development. It is

Figure 3.11: A bird drawn by Amy (aged 2 years 10 months).

often used as the yardstick against which the 'maturity' of a child's picture is judged.

Children's drawing ability was a serious topic of study as long ago as the 1880s – Ricci, for example, wrote a paper 'The art of little children' in 1887 – and had a prominent place in the study of child development well into the 1930s. From then on it lost its prominence and drawings were used mainly as 'tests' which aimed to reveal aspects of the child's personality and emotional difficulties (Machover, 1953) or mental maturity (Goodenough, 1926; Harris, 1963). It is only in the last fifteen years or so that interest in the cognitive aspects of drawings has been revived.

One of the most influential thinkers about children's drawing was Luquet (1913, 1927), and his ideas were later taken up by Piaget and Inhelder (1956, 1969). Essentially, Piaget and Inhelder adopted Luquet's ideas without revision; they simply incorporated them into their own theory of the child's developing concept of space.

Luquet postulated a series of three developmental stages of drawing. In the *scribbling stage*, from approximately 2 to 4 years of age, the child experiments with marks on the page. She comes to understand that these marks can represent real things. At first, this is *fortuitous realism*, since she interprets the lines she has already made; she does not intend to draw a particular object in advance. At 2 years 10 months, my own daughter drew a shape and then in a surprised voice said, 'Look! That's a bird!' She then said, 'He needs an eye' and put in a dot. After that she said, 'They have legs, don't they?' As she put in the legs she said, 'Five legs!' (See Figure 3.11).

Later, in the *preschematic stage*, from approximately 4 to 7 years, the child does have prior intentions about what objects she wants to draw. Nevertheless, she encounters many difficulties and her drawings are characterized by *failed realism*. Items may be placed near one another but may not be placed in the correct arrangement. Thus, facial features may be placed *outside* the contour of the head (see Figure 3.12). Piaget and Inhelder would regard this as an example of a mastery of topological *proximity* and *order* but not of *enclosure*.

Later, when these details are brought into the correct arrangement, each object is shown so that its criterial features are displayed. The child is said to draw what she knows rather than what she sees. Non-visible characteristics may be included, and the whole scene may contain objects and parts of objects viewed from radically different perspectives (see Figure 3.13). Pictures like these are reminiscent of those from earlier historical times (see Figures 3.3 and 3.4). This latter part of the preschematic stage is characterized by *intellectual realism*. It corresponds with Piaget and Inhelder's early projective spatial relationships: the child cannot successfully adopt a particular viewpoint, even her own, so there is no overall co-ordination of perspective for a whole scene.

After a transitional period, the child moves on to the *schematic stage,* at approximately 8 to 9 years, in which she attempts to draw a scene from a particular viewpoint and tries to show the depth of individual objects and the depth relationships between objects. This stage is the endpoint of the development and is characterized by *visual realism.* According to Piaget and Inhelder the child has developed an understanding of both projective and Euclidean relationships: a scene is drawn from a particular viewpoint, and distances, proportions, and relationships between objects are worked out correctly in relation to that viewpoint (see Figure 3.14).

Summary

The ideal, then, in Western conventional art is that a scene is drawn from a particular point of view. The artist draws only what can be seen from this viewpoint and omits everything that cannot. The system of linear perspective is generally accepted as the normal method of projecting aspects of the three-dimensional scene on to the

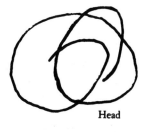

Head

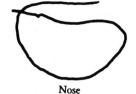

Nose

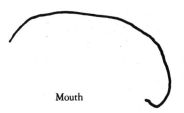

Mouth

Figure 3.12: Kate (aged 3 years) has drawn a nose and mouth separate from the head. (Reproduced with the permission of Charmian Parkin.)

two-dimensional surface of the picture. Children only gradually develop the ability to draw in perspective.

The general questions I want to consider in the following two chapters are: Why doesn't the young child generally represent a scene from her own actual viewpoint? Is she incapable of visual realism? Although older children and adults are assumed to be capable of drawing a scene from their own viewpoint, is this also what they generally aspire to do and, if so, how well do they do it?

Figure 3.13: A man and a cart (Piaget and Inhelder, 1956, Figure 23, p. 274). The man and the cart have been drawn from different perspectives. (Reprinted with the permission of the publisher.)

Figure 3.14: Objects on a table (Willats, 1977, Figure 7, p. 195). The whole scene is drawn from a particular viewpoint. (Reprinted with the permission of the author and the publisher.)

4 Draw what you can see, omit what you cannot

The linear perspective system has perhaps come to have a privileged place as the best or 'natural' way of representing the three-dimensional world on a two-dimensional surface. The essence of this system is that the artist draws what she can see from a particular, fixed viewpoint; everything which cannot be seen is omitted from the picture. Traditionally, it has been considered that young children do not, and perhaps cannot, draw visually realistic pictures; instead, as Luquet (1913, 1927) maintained, they draw 'what they know rather than what they see' [1], and in doing so may draw objects or parts of objects which they cannot actually see in the scene. The discussion in this chapter will be divided into two sections: (1) those studies which have concentrated on the total occlusion of a discrete part of one object, and (2) those studies which have concentrated on the total or partial occlusion of one object by another separate object.

Single-object scenes

Freeman and Janikoun (1972) asked 5- to 9-year-olds to imagine a cup and to draw it. All the cups in the drawings had handles. Each child was then asked to draw a particular cup which was placed in such a way that its handle was turned away and could not be seen by the child. There was, however, a flower design on the outside of the cup which was directly in front of the child and could be seen quite clearly. The younger children (5- to 7-year-olds) tended to include the handle in their drawings but omit the flower, whereas the older children (8- and 9-year-olds) tended to omit the handle but include the flower (see Figure 4.1).

Generally speaking, cups have handles. In fact a handle is probably a criterial feature of a cup; it defines it. So the younger children may

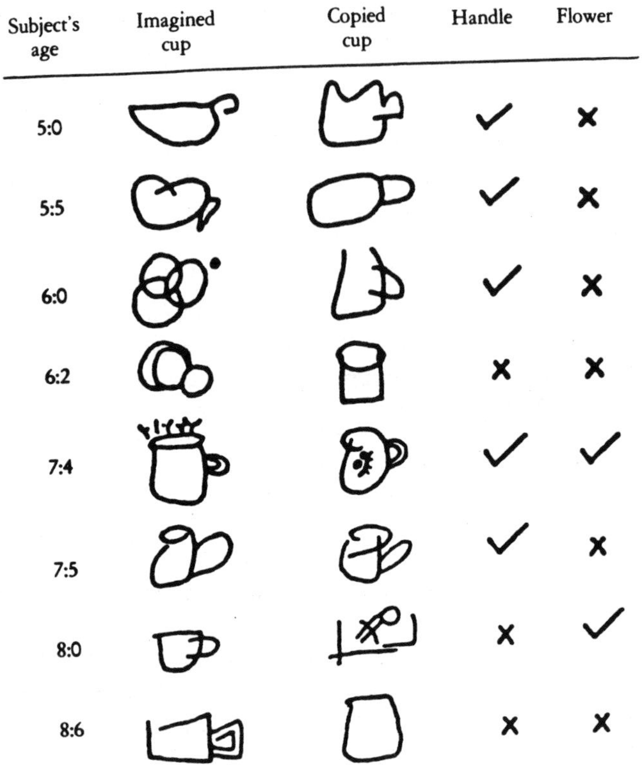

Subject's age	Imagined cup	Copied cup	Handle	Flower
5:0			✓	✗
5:5			✓	✗
6:0			✓	✗
6:2			✗	✗
7:4			✓	✓
7:5			✓	✗
8:0			✗	✓
8:6			✗	✗

Figure 4.1: Children's drawings of an imagined and then a copied cup (Freeman and Janikoun, 1972, Figure 1, p. 1119). (Reprinted with the permission of the publisher.)

have been drawing 'what they know about cups', namely that a cup has a handle. The flower, on the other hand, is not criterial: some cups may have such a design, but most don't. The younger children omitted the flower perhaps because it was not part of their mental image of a cup. The change from this *intellectual realism* to *visual realism* at around the age of 7 to 8 years is in line with the developmental pattern described by Luquet and outlined in Chapter 3.

Freeman and Janikoun pursued the issue of why the younger children included the handle in their drawings. They suggested that indeed the handle may have been included because it was part of the children's mental image of a cup. But it could also be the case that children feel that their cups will not be recognized as such unless a handle is included. One child, for instance, said: 'without the handle it looks like a pot. Shall I put it in to make it a cup?' (Freeman and Janikoun, 1972, p. 1120). The difference between these two hypotheses seems to be that in the first one, the child does not consider how the object *looks* but automatically 'tips out' her stored and static mental image of it, while in the second case the child may well consider how the object looks, but feels that a visually realistic representation may be ambiguous or inadequate.

This line of research has been taken up by Davis (1983). In Experiment 1 she asked 4- to 6-year-olds to draw a cup with its handle turned out of sight. Sixty per cent of the children included the handle in their drawings. They were then shown a pair of cups, one in its canonical orientation with the handle visible at the side and one with its handle turned away. All the children drew the visible handle on the canonically orientated cup and most of them (71 per cent) omitted the hidden handle on the other cup in their drawings. Of those who included the hidden handle in the first, single-cup drawing, over half (52 per cent) omitted it in the paired-cup drawing. Another group of children was given the paired-cup task first and then the single cup. Only 19 per cent of them included the hidden handle in the paired-cup drawings, and only 23 per cent included it in the single-cup drawings.[2]

Davis suggests that the reason why most children included the hidden handle when a single cup was presented first is that they did not realize that orientation was important. The juxtaposition of the two cups in different orientations made this more salient, and most children then omitted the hidden handle. Furthermore, there was a 'carry over' effect: those children who drew two cups first overwhelmingly omitted the hidden handle when they were then presented with a single cup. The paired-cup task seemed to cue the children into what they were 'supposed' to be doing, namely drawing only what they could see.

In Davis' second experiment, children from age 5 to 6½ years were given the single and paired-cup tasks, and then were asked to draw a cup with its handle turned away *and* a sugar bowl. These two objects *looked* identical even though the children knew that the cup had a handle and the bowl had not. Of most interest were those children who included the hidden handle in the single cup task but omitted it in the paired-cup task; there were twelve such children. Seven of them included the handle in the cup and bowl task; the other five did not include the handle but they did attempt to make the two objects obviously different (e.g. one was drawn much larger than the other, the bowl was given a rim whereas the cup was not, etc.). When the two objects present the same visual appearance, then, there is a tendency to make them look different in line with the children's knowledge of the objects; the inclusion of the handle may serve this function. Davis needed to check that this was the case, however, i.e. that the children simply wanted to express a difference between the objects. The alternative explanation for the inclusion of the handle could be that the children were particularly concerned to mark the cup as a cup.

So, in a third experiment, Davis put a black spot on the front of the sugar bowl in order to distinguish it visually from the cup. She predicted that the spot would be included and the handle omitted if her hunch was correct, but that the handle would be included if the children really did want to identify the cup as a cup. In fact, the children drew the spot and omitted the handle. Thus the visible spot was selected in preference to the hidden handle as a means of distinguishing the otherwise visually identical objects.

This neat series of experiments shows that children may indeed 'tip out' their mental image of a cup, but when this happens it is because the child does not realize that some other noncanonical orientation of the object is what is required. When this is made salient, by contrasting orientations in a paired-cup task, the child can draw what she sees and omit what is hidden. Nevertheless, she may be reluctant to do this if the final drawing does not show a known difference between the two objects (i.e. that one is a sugar bowl and the other a cup with its handle turned away). If she can find a visible feature to distinguish the two objects, like a spot on the sugar bowl, she will use this in preference to the hidden handle.

In most research studies the experimenter has named the object (*Here is a cup. I want you to draw the cup exactly as you see it*) and has generally allowed the child to examine it before being asked to draw it. Recently, Bremner and Moore (1984) have examined how the naming of the object to be drawn might affect the child's representation of it. In their Experiment 2, they presented a coffee mug with its handle turned away from the children (aged 6 years). No opportunity for prior inspection of the object was given. In one condition (A), the children were asked to name the object after they had drawn it; in the other condition (B), children named the object before drawing it.

In condition A, 13 out of 14 (93 per cent) omitted the handle; in condition B, only 2 out of 14 children (14 per cent) omitted the handle. It might be argued that perhaps all children, particularly in condition A, did not recognize the object as a mug. In fact, 12/14 in condition A and 11/14 in condition B did recognize it as such. And still 11/12 (92 per cent) in condition A omitted the handle, and only 1/11 (9 per cent) in condition B omitted it. There seems to be something, then, in the actual naming of the object prior to the drawing procedure which 'triggers' a canonical rather than a view-specific representation. It could be that the naming of the cup suggests to the child that she should make sure that her drawing is identifiable as a cup. An experiment by Nigel Simm and myself, to be discussed later, also shows, in a two-object task, that the way objects are named may influence the way the scene is interpreted by the child.

Research on single objects has shown that children often draw the canonical view of a particular object rather than their actual view. However, this may not be a general tendency, but may be the child's response only in certain kinds of task. In particular, the naming of the object for or by the child seems to elicit a canonical view, whereas the withholding of a name elicits a more visually realistic picture. Even when the object is named, however, children will sometimes forego the canonical view and draw what they can see; the particular circumstances under which this has been demonstrated are the paired-object tasks used by Davis. Most of the research has concerned children over 5 years of age. We know little of the behaviour of young children; it could be that canonical views are more prevalent and that visually realistic pictures are more difficult to elicit.

One object behind another

Total occlusion studies

Obviously, a handle is an integral part of the physical structure of a cup. Although young children *can* be induced to omit the handle from their drawings if it cannot be seen in the model, nevertheless they often include it. But what if two components are physically separated in a scene and one is not a necessary part of the other? If we place one object behind another so that it is completely hidden, will children draw only what can be seen (Luquet's stage of visual realism) or will they include the hidden object in the same way that they include a handle on a cup (Luquet's stage of intellectual realism)?

A study I carried out with Ann Martin (Cox and Martin, 1988) included a condition in which a small green cube was placed behind an opaque black beaker. This model was presented at eye-level, and 5-, 7- and 9-year-olds and a group of adults were asked to draw exactly what they could see.

Interestingly, most of the children (78 per cent at age 5 rising to 91 per cent at age 9) omitted the cube from their drawings as did all of the adults. Of those children who included the cube, eight enclosed it within the contours of the beaker, eleven placed it beside the beaker, and one placed it above the beaker. Nearly all of these children were in the two younger age groups.

Also in this experiment we included a model in which the green cube was placed *inside* the beaker. Again, most subjects omitted the cube in their drawings. Almost all of those who included it (14/15), placed it inside the contours of the beaker; only one child placed it beside the beaker.

These results suggest that when there is no necessary structural link between the objects most children, like adults, will omit the object they cannot see and draw only the one they can see. Perhaps it is because the cube is not part of the mental image or stereotype of the beaker that it is easier to omit it, whereas the handle is part of the stereotype of a cup. Those children who did draw in the hidden cube showed some sensitivity to the positioning of it: a cube placed *inside* a beaker was drawn inside the contours of the beaker, but a cube placed *behind* the beaker tended to be placed at the side of the beaker in the drawing. (This sensitivity to different spatial arrangements is examined further by Light and MacIntosh, 1980, Taylor and Bacharach, 1982, and Davis, 1984).

Partial occlusion studies

I want to turn now to studies of partial occlusion, that is, studies in which one object only partially masks the object placed behind it. When young children draw two objects in a scene they tend to separate them and draw the whole contour of each object. Freeman, Eiser and Sayers (1977) asked children from 5 to 10 years, and adults, to draw one apple behind another. With age there was a shift from a tendency to separate the objects in the drawing to a tendency to put them together, the cross-over occurring at about age 8 years. The way

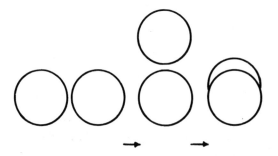

Figure 4.2: The developmental shift in the arrangement of objects found in a number of studies: horizontal-separate, vertical-separate, partial occlusion.

the two apples were united is what I have called partial occlusion (Cox, 1981c and 1985a) and what Freeman (1980, pp. 214–17) calls 'hidden line elimination' (see Figure 4.2).

Freeman also found a shift from a horizontal-separate arrangement of the objects to a vertical-separate arrangement at about age 7 years. It should be pointed out, however, that no model was presented in the Freeman *et al.* study; the younger children (aged 5 years) in particular may not have known what a 'behind' relationship meant. When I presented children with a model of one ball behind another (Cox, 1978c and 1981c, Study 2) I also found that children below age 8 years separated the objects in their drawings whereas older children and adults used partial occlusion. In contrast to Freeman *et al.*'s findings, though, I found that most children as young as 5 years drew a vertical-separate arrangement and only at age 4 was a horizontal arrangement used to any great extent. The model, then, shows the children what kind of arrangement they are supposed to be drawing.

This predominantly vertical-separate arrangement has not been found in all studies; for instance, Light and Humphreys (1981) found that only about a third of their 'separate' drawings had a vertical arrangement. An obvious explanation of this apparent discrepancy is the angle from which the subject views the scene. In my research studies, the subject looks down at the model which is placed on a table; the farther object is visible 'over' the nearer one. In the Light and Humphreys study, on the other hand, the model is raised up on a platform to the subject's eye-level. The farther object cannot be seen over the nearer one (unless the subject actually stands up), but can be seen 'round the side' if the subject moves her head to the right or left.[3]

Now why do children below about the age of 8 years draw more than they can actually see? Is it that they do not understand the partial occlusion device? Apparently not. Hagen (1976) asked 3- to 7-year-olds to match a partial occlusion picture to the appropriate scene (given a set of four scenes). Almost all the children interpreted the picture as a complete object partially occluded by another. More recently, Granrud and Yonas (1984) have shown that even 7-month-old infants seem to be sensitive to depth information provided by partial occlusion pictures. These infants will reach out to the 'nearer' part of the figure, whereas, on control figures, they do not show a preference for any one part of the figure. This finding indicates that these infants interpret spatial occlusion in pictures as a device for portraying depth, and their ability to do this develops somewhere between 5 and 7 months of age.

Could it be that the partial occlusion configuration is simply too difficult for children to produce? To check this, I asked 5- to 7-year-olds to copy the configuration in Figure 4.3 (Cox, 1985a). Eighty-one per cent of the 5-year-olds, 91 per cent of the 6-year-olds, and 92 per cent of the 7-year-olds drew the figure in exactly the same way that older children and adults draw one ball behind another, i.e. they drew a full circle first, and then attached an arc to it. A further 14 per cent of 5-year-olds, 6 per cent of 6-year-olds and 7 per cent of 7-year-olds drew less accurate but perhaps passable copies (see Figure 4.3). The high rate of accurate copying shows that at least the children do not lack the motor skill to produce a partial occlusion.

But, of course, a copying task such as this (from two dimensions to two dimensions) is not the same as drawing from a model (from three dimensions to two dimensions). The arc in the copying task need not necessarily represent part of a whole circle, whereas the arc in the drawing-a-model task does represent the visible part of a round object. Maybe, then, the young children's difficulty is in inhibiting a tendency to draw a full contour. Freeman *et al.* suggested that this might be the case. They postulated a developmental accretion of drawing rules in which the child progressed from (1) a side-by-side arrangement giving minimal depth information, to (2) the addition of an 'up the page means behind' rule, to (3) overlapping circles, to (4) a deletion instruction which would inhibit the completion of the farther circle (see Figure 4.4).

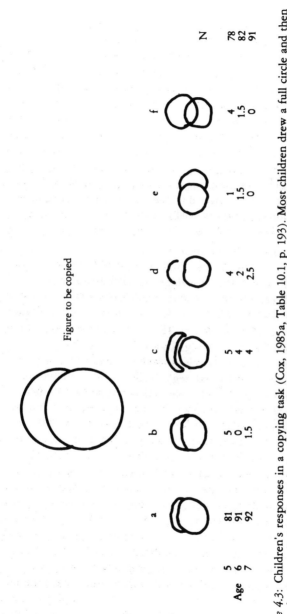

Figure 4.3: Children's responses in a copying task (Cox, 1985a, Table 10.1, p. 193). Most children drew a full circle and then attached an arc to it (a). (Reprinted with the permission of the publisher.)

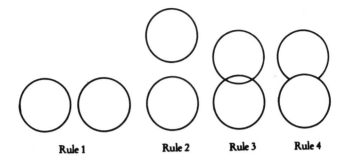

Rule 1 Rule 2 Rule 3 Rule 4

Figure 4.4: A predicted order of representations of one apple behind another based on the developmental accretion of drawing rules (Freeman, Eiser and Sayers, 1977, adapted from Figure 1, p. 307). (Reprinted with the permission of the authors and publisher.)

If the young child's problem were simply a failure to eliminate the hidden part of the farther circle, we would expect to find many overlaps (Rule 3) in her drawings. But there were in fact very few of these in Freeman *et al.*'s data. Children seem to progress from separating the two whole circles (Rule 2) directly to producing the partial occlusion configuration (Rule 4). If the younger children *are* unable to inhibit the drawing of a complete circle, they also take great care to place the second circle quite separate from the first one. There seems to be a deliberate strategy to depict two complete and separate objects. This strategy is not confined to a drawing task either. When I asked children to draw one ball behind another *and* to select an appropriate picture from a predrawn set (Cox, 1981c, Study 3), children below 8 years both drew and selected pictures in which the two objects were complete and separate.

It seems to me that when an object such as a cube is completely hidden by another object placed in front of it (as in the Cox and Martin study described above), most children assume that the cube is not meant to be drawn. Unlike a handle on a cup, the cube is not part of the mental image of the nearer object, so the tendency to include it is much less. When a farther object can be seen, albeit only partially, the child may assume that she is supposed to draw what she can see, namely two objects. After all, the instructions usually say, 'Draw exactly *what* you can see'. In other words, she may not realize that what the experimenter is getting at is that it is *how* each object appears, rather than whether it is visible or not, which is the salient issue. In Chapter 2 I outlined Flavell's model of perspective-taking in which young children are at first sensitive to *which* objects can or cannot be seen by an observer, and only later take notice of *how* each object is seen.

Now, is it the case that children *cannot* draw a scene 'how it looks' or are we simply failing to get the message across to them that that is what we want them to do? From the work done with single objects like cups, we can say that in some circumstances children of 5 years and above *can* draw a view-specific picture. Research using two-object arrays has gone on in parallel with these studies.

The 'cops and robbers' task

It may be the case that children do not attend carefully to the details of the verbal instructions to 'draw a scene as it looks' in a drawing task. Barrett, Beaumont and Jennett (1985) asked children to draw one ball behind another, and varied the emphasis on *visual* realism in the verbal instructions. This had no effect on children below age 6½ years; they did not draw view-specific pictures. The more detailed instructions did however have some effect on the older children; more partial occlusions were produced.

Donaldson (1978; McGarrigle and Donaldson, 1974) has argued that young children seem to be attuned more to the non-verbal aspects of a task than to the verbal instructions. I have devised a task in which the idea that part of the scene should be omitted in the drawing would easily suggest itself to the child, and this message should be carried not only in the verbal instructions but somehow be incorporated into the task itself. It seemed important to incorporate the notion of 'hiding' in the task, since this is essentially what is involved in a partial occlusion; a part of the scene is hidden from the observer by an intervening object. And hiding is well-known to children from a very early age (see Chapter 1). The task (Cox, 1981c, Study 5) involved a robber who was chased by a policeman. The robber hid behind a wall, but the policeman knew where he was hiding because the top of the robber's head was visible over the wall. This game was enacted using models on a table in front of the child. In one condition, a toy policeman was used; in another condition, the child pretended that *she* was the policeman. In both cases, the view was essentially the same. The child was asked to 'draw what the policeman can see' or 'draw what you can see'. (See Figure 4.5.)

No significant differences were found between the two 'policeman'

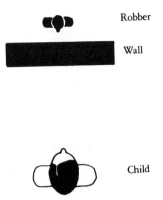

Robber

Wall

Child

Figure 4.5: Layout of the 'cops and robbers' task.

conditions, and there were no significant differences when the children were asked to draw the view as opposed to selecting a picture from a predrawn set. The majority of children from age 6 and above represented the scene with a partial occlusion (86 per cent at age 6 years, 94 per cent at age 8 years, and 95 per cent at age 10 years), as did all adults. Interestingly, even 44 per cent of the 4-year-olds did so too. (See Figure 4.6 for examples of the partial occlusions drawn at each age level.)

We have here a task which demonstrates that young children, at least at age 6 years and to some extent at age 4, *can* draw a view-specific picture. They can inhibit any tendency to draw the whole contour of the occluded object and any tendency to separate the two objects on the page.

Why do children produce a view-specific picture in the 'cops and robbers' task but not in the 'ball behind a ball' task? There are many differences between these two tasks, not only in the materials used but also in the way they are presented. We need to find out which ones are important. First of all, I compared directly the two sets of task materials: children from 4 to 10 years and adults were divided equally between a ball–ball and a man–wall condition. Within each of these, half the subjects were told that one object was 'behind the other' whereas the other half were told that one object was 'hiding behind the other'. Although there was a tendency especially among the young children for the 'hiding' condition to elicit more partial occlusions, there was no significant difference between these two sets of

Age 4 years

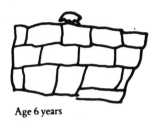

Age 6 years

Age 8 years

Age 10 years

Adult

Figure 4.6: Examples of the partial occlusion of a man by a wall in different age ranges.

Table 4.1: A comparison of ball–ball and man–wall materials and two types of instruction.

| Age | One object behind another | | One object hiding behind another | |
	1. Ball–Ball	2. Man–Wall	3. Ball–Ball	4. Man–Wall
4	13	36	13	57
6	21	64	31	64
8	67	87	100	93
10	93	100	100	100
Adults	100	100	100	93

Note: Percentage of subjects using partial occlusion.
Source: Cox, 1985a, Table 10.2, p. 195.

instructions. There was, however, a significant difference between the two sets of task materials: the man and wall elicited far more partial occlusions than did the two balls (see Table 4.1).

The important finding, then, is that it is not necessary to present the materials in the form of a game and it is not even necessary to talk about 'hiding' at all; simply placing a man behind a wall is enough to elicit partial occlusions, at least for most 6-year-olds, whereas placing a ball behind a ball is not.

My next task was to look at the task materials themselves to see why they produced such different rates of partial occlusion.

The task materials

Can *any* object be placed behind a wall and still elicit high rates of partial occlusion among young children, or is there something special about a *man* being placed there? To test this, I presented a series of different objects placed behind a wall-like rectangular block. I also wanted to find out if there is something special about the occluding object being rectangular, so to check this I varied the objects used as occluders.

I did not simply choose objects at random but decided to vary them systematically. Table 4.2 gives the pairs of objects presented; the occluded object is named above the occluder in each pair. I placed two identical (except for colour) wall-like blocks one behind the other; these were the same in terms of depth and shape. I then varied depth

Table 4.2: Percentage of children drawing a partial occlusion in each condition.

Age	a	b	c	d	e	f
	block	cube	disc	ball	bottle	man
	block	block	block	block	block	block
4	0	0	0	0	13	21
6	8	6	38	68	70	75
8	52	19	63	80	100	94
	cube	block	ball	disc		man
	cube	cube	cube	cube		cube
4				3		10
6	11	20	31	62		62
8	42	52	68	96		92
	ball		cube	block		man
	ball		ball	ball		ball
4				7		10
6	7		27	52		62
8	48		37	92		92
	disc	ball	block	cube		man
	disc	disc	disc	disc		disc
4				7		10
6	14	30	26	52		62
8	46	48	41	96		92

but not shape by placing a cube behind a block. The disc placed behind a block varied shape but not depth. When a ball was placed behind a block the two objects were different in both shape and depth. More complex shapes and additional features distinguished the occluded object from its occluder in the bottle and the man conditions. This same idea of the manipulation of the degree of difference between the two objects in the scene was extended to other object-pairs in which a cube, a ball, and a disc were the occluders.

The object-pairs listed in Table 4.2. were actually presented in random order to 4-, 6-, and 8-year-olds. The children had at least two separate testing sessions, and some children, particularly the younger ones, had more. As usual, the objects were placed one directly behind the other so that the child could see part of the occluded one over the top of the nearer one. The occluder was always red and the occluded object was blue (except that the bottle and the man were mainly blue and yellow). All objects were 8 cm high.

As the results in Table 4.2 show, not all objects placed behind the block elicited the same rate of partial occlusions; the rate increases towards the right of the table. The man, as an occluded object, does seem to elicit high rates even when placed behind a variety of different occluders.

What seems to be happening is that the more similar the two objects in the scene (Table 4.2, column a) the less likely the children are to use partial occlusions; instead, they tend to separate the two objects on the page. If either depth (column b) or shape (column c) is altered the partial occlusion rate rises (although the cube behind a block may be a special case where it does not!) When both depth and shape are different between the two objects (column d) the partial occlusion rate rises even more. The bottle (column e) and the man (column f) conditions also elicit high partial occlusion rates. I have suggested elsewhere (Cox, 1985a) that it is asymmetry between the objects in the scene which leads children to use partial occlusion whereas similarity leads them to separate the objects on this page. This pattern seems to hold for the 6-year-olds and the 8-year-olds, the percentages being higher in the older age group. Among the 4-year-olds, however, the percentages of partial occlusion are very low indeed; even in the man–block condition, only 21 per cent produced a partial occlusion. I shall come back to this younger age group later on.

It is one thing to chart the task materials which will or will not elicit partial occlusions from young children and it is interesting to discover this similarity/asymmetry phenomenon. But we also need to know why similar objects in the scene prompt children to separate them on the page and why scenes in which the objects differ are the ones which elicit partial occlusions. The suggestion I put forward in the first edition of this book is as follows.

Perhaps children scan the scene first and note the two objects they will have to draw. If the two objects are very similar perhaps they are drawn without the child having to refer back to the scene. Thus, two separate and complete mental images (or a repeat of the first one, if the two objects are actually the same shape) are accessed and then drawn without consideration of how they should be united on the page. In order to know how the second image should be modified the child would need to look again at the scene.

When the two objects are rather different perhaps it is more difficult for the child to 'hold on' to the mental image of the second image while the first one is being drawn. After she has drawn the first one she may need to look back at the scene in order to see what to do next. Not only does she see the object she must draw but she is also likely to notice how much of it she must draw. So the chances of her producing a view-specific picture are increased. It would be very difficult to draw the scene as it looks without looking back at it during the drawing process. One would have to note the two objects to be drawn, access two mental images, hold on to one while the first was being drawn, and then modify the second image according to some visual memory of the scene which can only have been formed on the initial viewing. This would be a very daunting task indeed.

Recently, Martin Nieland and I have investigated this idea by manipulating young children's scanning behaviour experimentally. We used two age groups of children: 5- to 6-year-olds and 7- to 8-year-olds. All the children saw a scene of one ball partially masked by another placed directly in front of it. Within each age group there were three conditions. In the first, the children were simply asked to draw the scene. In the second condition, at the beginning of the session the experimenter discussed the appearance of the scene with the children, asking them to point out exactly which parts of the occluded ball could and could not be seen from their particular viewpoint. In the third condition, this discussion took place after the children had already drawn the nearer ball but before they had started the occluded one.

We predicted that the discussion of the appearance of the scene (conditions 2 and 3) would increase the incidence of partial occlusions in the children's drawings and that this would be particularly marked when the discussion took place immediately before the children drew the occluded ball (condition 3). As it turned out, these manipulations had no effect: regardless of experimental conditions, the younger children drew the two balls separately and the older ones drew partial occlusions. So, we still have no clear explanation of this intriguing phenomenon!

I want now to turn back to the youngest children being studied in this work, that is, 4-year-olds. In general, it is only materials like the man and the wall which have elicited view-specific pictures from these very young subjects. Furthermore, if we look at the results over a number of different studies the highest percentage of partial

Table 4.3: Partial occlusion responses made by children in a study by Cox and Simm (unpublished manuscript).

Age	ball block		ball wall		man block		man wall	
	×	√	×	√	×	√	×	√
4 to 5 years	14	1 (7)	15	1 (6)	10	5 (33)	5	10 (67)
7 to 8 years	7	8 (53)	3	11 (79)	8	7 (47)	4	11 (73)

Notes: The percentage of children drawing partial occlusions is given in brackets. × = other responses. √ = partial occlusion.

occlusions have been found when the wall has been referred to as a *wall* and not as a *block*, and also when the child has been told that the man is *hiding* behind the wall as opposed to being simply behind it. Could it be that very young children will omit from their drawings parts of the scene which they cannot actually see only when presented with contextually very powerful scenes, that is, scenes in which the occluded object is obviously hiding from the viewer? Nigel Simm and I (unpublished manuscript) asked the children to draw the man–wall materials, one behind the other; for half the children, we described the objects as 'a man behind a wall', and for the other half, 'a man behind a block'. We also added a ball–wall and a ball–block condition, and again exactly the same pair of objects was used in both conditions.[4]

We found quite dramatic differences between these two descriptions (see Table 4.3). Among the children aged 4 to 5 years, the ball was almost always drawn separately from its occluder, whether the latter was called a wall or a block. Far more partial occlusions were drawn when the man was the occluded object but, interestingly, more so when he was behind a wall rather than behind a block. With age, the partial occlusions increased in all conditions as one might expect, but either object (man or ball) placed behind a wall elicited more partial occlusions than when placed behind a block.

What may be happening here is that calling something a *wall* implies that the object behind it is hiding. After all, people may hide behind walls. Calling something a *block* does not convey this notion so powerfully. However, this works for the youngest children only when the occluded object is something which can sensibly hide behind a wall, i.e. a person. A ball behind a wall will not produce the same result. This idea takes me back to my original cops and robbers task in which I tried to make the notion of *hiding* an inherent part of the task materials. It may turn out that only heavily contextualized tasks such as this will prompt young children to draw 'how a scene looks'. Indeed this may give us a lead as to *how* this ability develops. That is, it may begin with this kind of task and may then gradually, but systematically, be extended to others until, eventually, older children and adults will use the strategy routinely with all scenes regardless of the relationship of one object to the other.

Summary

Young children seem to draw stereotyped pictures which may include more features of the object than can be seen if an actual model is present. For example, if asked to draw a cup with its handle turned away, children below about 7 years of age tend to include the handle in their drawings; older children and adults will omit it. This kind of observation led Luquet (1913, 1927) to say that 'children draw what they know, not what they see'. Children in this stage of *intellectual realism* appear unable to draw things as they see them; they seem unable to adopt a particular point of view, namely their own.

The research studies reviewed in this chapter certainly show that children often do 'tip out' a stereotyped or 'canonical' view of objects. This may not necessarily be their *general* tendency, but a function of the kinds of tasks researchers have used.

In most studies the objects to be drawn have been named. This naming process may affect the way the child interprets the task. If she is asked to name an object, say a cup, *before* she draws it rather than afterwards, she is more likely to draw a handle even though the model cup has its handle turned away. Presumably the way that the scene is described cues the child as to how it should be drawn. The naming of the cup perhaps 'calls up' the stereotyped mental image of a cup. Or it may even suggest to the child that the experimenter wants her to make the drawing clearly identifiable as a cup. Children will draw a more visually realistic picture if a man is described as being behind a *wall* rather than a *block*. The man behind a wall perhaps suggests that the man is hiding and therefore that a part of him should be hidden from view; the man behind the block may not convey this notion so powerfully and therefore the children are less likely to produce a partial occlusion.

Features of the objects in the array itself may also influence the child's choice of a canonical or a more visually realistic picture. For instance, if the children are asked to draw a pair of cups, one in its canonical orientation with its handle at the side and one with its handle hidden, 5-year-olds can draw what they see, and omit what they cannot. It seems, then, that the contrast between the two objects in the scene prompts children to draw what they see. This also appears to be the case in other studies in which one object is partially occluded by another: children are more likely to draw what they see if there is a definite contrast between the two objects in the scene; conversely, the more similar the two objects the less likely children are to draw a visually realistic picture.

The idea, then, that children draw what they know rather than what they see cannot be accepted unconditionally. It clearly does describe much of what young children normally draw, but it grossly underestimates what they are capable of.

Notes

1. A maxim perhaps more accurately attributable to Kerschensteiner.
2. Melanie Hoff and I replicated the design of Davis' first experiment, but we used dolls instead of cups. Our results were very similar.
3. In this study, if a fixed, single viewpoint could have been maintained the children's actual view should have meant the *total occlusion* of the farther object by the nearer one. Thus a view-specific drawing would show only one object. However, the low rates of single objects in the drawings (17 per cent at age 5 years 8 months rising to 52 per cent at age 7 years 8 months) suggests that *both* objects could in fact be seen without much difficulty.
4. Although in this experiment it was the verbal description of the scene which was varied I want to point out that its nature was rather different from the verbal manipulation performed by Barrett, Beaumont and Jennett, 1985. In Barrett *et al.*'s study, the instructions concerned the way that the child should tackle the drawing process; in this present study, in contrast, the verbal description cued the child as to how the scene itself should be interpreted.

5 How to draw 'in perspective'

To be able to draw in perspective can be interpreted as meaning that the object shall be depicted as it appears from a particular viewpoint, *any* given point of view. If we imagine that the page intersects the rays of light between the object and the artist's eye (see p. 57), then the perspective drawing is produced when these intersection points are joined up. Clearly, a different picture will result if the object is rotated slightly or if the artist shifts position (see Figure 5.1).

Although each of these 'snapshots' shows a particular way that we see the object (i.e. the projection at the eye) we may not feel that they are all equally good representations. Indeed, if presented with these pictures in isolation, in many cases we may fail completely to identify the object. What we perceive an object to be may be built up over a continuous period of experience with it (or objects like it) in the real world (Gibson, 1979; Kellman, 1984); and some particular views may appear idiosyncratic and not at all representative of what we actually know about the object.

In Chapter 4 I discussed various studies which have shown that very often children produce canonical views of objects like cups. That is, they include the defining feature and orientate the object so that this feature can be seen clearly. Thus, typically a cup has its handle drawn at the side. Presumably, this canonical view is the least ambiguous as to the object's identity. But canonical views are not peculiar to children; adults also share these 'best' views. When I asked 26 undergraduates to draw a cup, all of them produced a canonical orientation. Although there were *some* attempts to show the depth of the cup (by making an ellipse at the top and a curved edge at the bottom) apparently the depth of this object is not a necessary property of its adequate two-dimensional representation.

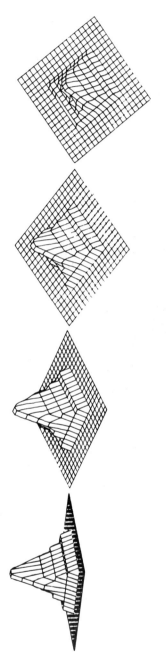

Figure 5.1: The rotation of an object. (Computer graphics by Dr Rob Fletcher, University of York.)

Adults' drawings of tables and cubes

When we turn to objects like tables and cubes, however, adults do attempt to depict depth. In fact, a very important property of these objects is their depth. In the case of the cube, the square shape of each side is of course defining; but so is the fact that it has surfaces in all three spatial dimensions. Among tables, perhaps the most typical example is a rectangular surface supported by four legs; the important thing about it is that the top surface is in a horizontal plane stretching both across and along the viewer's line of sight. So, with both cubes and tables one might expect that subjects will attempt to depict their depth. In fact, 25/26 of my undergraduate sample drew a table in oblique perspective; 15 of these drew the front edge parallel to the horizontal axis of the page. One person drew a frontal view (see Figure 5.2.) All 26 drew a cube in oblique projection (see Figure 5.3). Sometimes the 'hidden' edges were drawn with solid lines or with dotted lines.

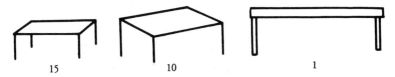

Figure 5.2: The responses of 26 adults who were asked to draw a table.

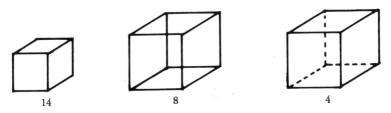

Figure 5.3: The oblique view of a cube drawn by 26 adults.

When asked what 'drawing in perspective' means many adults will say that it means producing a drawing such as one of those shown above in which the object is depicted 'in depth'. Now this is rather different from saying, as I did at the beginning of this chapter, that it involves the ability to depict an object from any particular point of view. First, the oblique projections shown in Figure 5.3 above are not accurate copies of what an artist could see; they are in fact impossible views. The only way that an artist could see a face of the cube as a square would be if she saw it from the front at eye-level, in other words if the front face only was visible. If a cube is seen from a corner angle, no face will 'squarely' confront the viewer and no angles will appear as right angles. A more accurate drawing of the projection at the eye is shown in Figure 5.4.

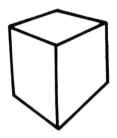

Figure 5.4: A perspective projection of an oblique view of a cube.

Nevertheless, all 26 of my undergraduates drew the front face as a square as in Figure 5.3 above. Hagen and Elliott (1976) asked adults to choose the most natural pictures of a cube seen in depth. Most of them preferred an oblique projection with only a very small degree of convergence of lines (see Figure 5.5).

Figure 5.5: Preferred drawing of a cube. Most adults in Hagen and Elliott's (1976, Figure 1, p. 481) study preferred an oblique representation of a cube with only a very small degree of convergence of the lines. (Copyright 1976 by the American Psychological Association. Adapted by permission of the author.)

Secondly, if 'drawing in perspective' means that the drawing shows what can be seen from any particular given viewpoint, then we can find some viewpoints from which the depth of the object is not clearly evident. For example, a square *is* the real view of a cube seen frontally, at eye-level. Yet, even though this is a possible view of a cube, adults generally do not judge it as a cube drawn 'in perspective' because it does not indicate the depth of the object. Perspective, then, to ordinary people has something to do with the depiction of depth.

It is probably the case, as Phillips, Inall and Lauder (1985) have suggested, that very few children discover how to draw 'in perspective' for themselves simply by looking at the object. In fact, by the end of their first year in secondary education (i.e. by the age of about 12 years) children have been taught the 'trick' of how to draw 'in perspective' (see Figure 5.6).[1] Teachers normally draw a square first; this represents the front face of the cube. Then they draw the left-hand edge of the top face, followed by the right-hand edge, followed by the lower edge of the right-hand face; all these 'depth' lines are the same length and at the same angle. These 'free' ends are then joined up by the final two lines. In their training study, Phillips *et al.* have found that the most important feature of the teaching is that the children should see or draw for themselves the *sequence* of lines making up the final form.

The oblique view which is taught is not strictly a possible view as I mentioned before. Yet it has certain virtues. It conveys the idea of depth. It also shows that a square shape and parallel lines are important features. And it also solves many production problems for us. Once we have constructed a square, which even most 4-year-olds can do fairly successfully, the only major decision we have to take is at what angle we should attach the first of the 'depth' lines. Thus, the drawing itself provides many cues to guide the artist from one step to the next. Even so, even adults may not be very skilful at carrying out their intentions!

If a cube were to be drawn as it would actually be projected to the eye (see Figure 5.4), although all the vertical lines would be parallel they might all be of different lengths. Furthermore, except for the vertical lines, none of the other pairs of opposite lines would be parallel. Thus it would be a very difficult configuration to draw.

According to Luquet (1913, 1927) adults are in a stage of visual realism, and should be able to draw what they see. So, what would happen if we presented adults with an actual cube so that they have a

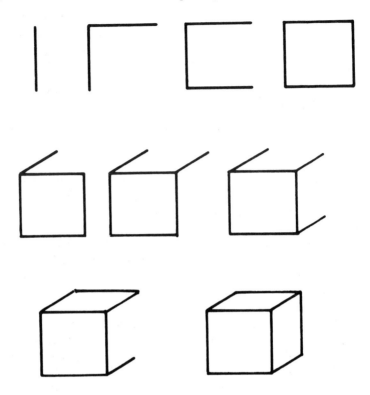

Figure 5.6: 'How to draw a cube'. This sequence of steps in the drawing of a cube shows the order in which teachers add each line.

model to draw from? If the cube were presented in a non-oblique orientation, adults should be able to modify their stereotyped oblique drawing in order to represent their actual view.

I presented adults with a cube placed in front of them on a table (Cox, 1986); only the front and top faces of the cube could be seen. In Condition 1 they were simply asked to draw what they could see. Eighty-eight per cent drew two faces of the cube; only 12 per cent drew the three faces of an oblique view. In Condition 2 the instructions actually drew attention to the fact that only two faces of the cube were visible. Ninety-six per cent drew two faces and only 4 per cent drew an oblique view (see Table 5.1). So, if the criterion of a 'view-specific' picture is simply a match between the number of faces in the drawing

Table 5.1: Adults' drawings of a cube placed in front of them on a table.

	2 faces drawn	3 faces drawn
Condition 1	45	6
	(88%)	(12%)
Condition 2	48	2
	(96%)	(4%)

and the number seen on the model, then adults are very good at drawing what they can see. The more specific instructions given in Condition 2 did not improve the view-specific responses significantly; these were already high in Condition 1.

One of the tricky things about drawing cuboid objects in depth is getting the angles right. And this seems to be a major problem for adults, let alone children. Of the adults who drew the two visible faces of the cube, only 42 per cent actually converged the lines of the top face and made the more 'distant' edge shorter than the near edge. A few adults tried other 'angled' solutions, but most drew rectangular solutions. The pattern of response types was rather similar in both Condition 1 and Condition 2 (see Table 5.1). (Strictly speaking the front face should not be drawn as a square, but should converge slightly towards the lower part. No drawing showed this convergence and, since it would be extremely slight, it is perhaps unrealistic to expect adults even to be aware of it let alone to draw it.)

These data suggest, then, that adults generally draw what they can see, in terms of the number of faces visible, but fewer than half of a sample of adults will draw *how* these faces are seen. This is perhaps because it is difficult to override our 'natural' tendency to see an object, such as a cube, as three-dimensional and made up of parallel lines and right angles. The oblique view we are taught may serve us well in some circumstances, for example when we are simply asked to draw a cube. But when this solution will not do we apparently do not have much to fall back on. The artist, though, is taught to override her knowledge of the object's structure and to draw what she sees (see Pratt, 1985), and she does not then need to rely on a very limited repertoire of well-learned but rigid representations. Maybe adults *should* be capable of drawing a scene as it looks, but without specific artistic training most cannot.

Children's drawings of tables and cubes

I have spent a good deal of space discussing the way that adults draw 'in perspective' and have concentrated particularly on drawings of a cube. There seems to be a conventional stereotyped way of drawing a cube, namely an oblique view. However, adults can modify this stereotype if they are asked to draw a cube in a rather different orientation. Nevertheless, they may still have difficulty in getting the angles 'right'.

Well, what of children? How do they tackle the problem? What are their solutions? And can they modify their stereotyped forms if asked to draw an unusual orientation? First of all I shall simply describe studies which have looked at children's drawings of a table and those which have looked at their drawings of a cube.

Willats (1977) obtained a perspective projection of a scene (see Figure 5.7), a group of objects on a table, by placing a vertical sheet of clear plastic between the subject's viewpoint and the table. The outlines of the scene were then traced on to the surface of the plastic, keeping the viewpoint fixed with the aid of a small ring sight. Thus, this drawing was obtained using the same method as the fifteenth-century artists (see p. 57). Children's attempts at drawing the scene were then graded from a simple Stage 1 drawing, in which no coherent projective system was used, through to Stage 6 which approximated the perspective system in the 'canonical' picture. This series of six kinds of drawing was seen by Willats as progressively more complex and was related to the children's chronological age, 5 to 16 years (see Figures 5.8 to 5.13).

In Stage 1, the table top is drawn as a rectangle and the objects are drawn above it and separated from each other. In Stage 2, the table top is represented by a straight line and the objects are arranged along it. In Stage 3, the surface is again shown as a rectangle, but this time the objects are arranged along the 'far' edge. In Stage 4, the artist has drawn an oblique view of the table. The sides of the table are at an angle to the front edge and are parallel to each other. In Stages 5 and 6 the artist succeeds in varying degrees in making the sides of the table converge, and the nearer edge is longer than the far edge. The arrangement of the objects is much the same in Stages 4 to 6.

Clearly, children do not imitate what they see directly from nature, nor do they simply imitate the perspective representations in pictures they see around them. Willats argues that in the early stages, at least,

Figure 5.7: The perspective projection of a scene (Willats, 1977, Figure 1, p. 192). (Reprinted with the permission of the author and the publisher.)

Figure 5.8: Stage 1: No projection system (Willats, 1977, Figure 2, p. 192). (Reprinted with the permission of the author and the publisher.)

the drawings show the children's own invented solutions to the problem of depth; they are not solutions which are taught to them nor are they common in pictures which they normally see. The latter stages, however, may reflect an interaction between the level of the child's own graphic skills, what is formally taught, and the child's cognizance of the perspective solution common in Western art. Jahoda (1981) has essentially confirmed Willats' findings.

Although Willats describes the subject's view of the scene as the 'canonical view', in fact most people would not represent a table in this way. If asked to draw a table from memory or to choose the best

Figure 5.9: Stage 2: Orthographic projection (Willats, 1977, Figure 3, p. 193). (Reprinted with the permission of the author and the publisher.)

Figure 5.10: Stage 3: Vertical oblique projection (Willats, 1977, Figure 4, p. 194). (Reprinted with the permission of the author and the publisher.)

picture of one, most adults and children (aged from about 9 years) draw or choose an oblique view (see Figure 5.11).

Willats' task is actually rather complex. Not only did the children have to tackle the problem of how to draw the table, but they also had to place the objects on top of it, and this in turn involved partial occlusion. Freeman (1980, pp. 256–8) asked 20 children aged 10 and

Figure 5.11: Stage 4: Oblique projection (Willats, 1977, Figure 5, p. 194). (Reprinted with the permission of the author and the publisher.)

Figure 5.12: Stage 5: Naive perspective (Willats, 1977, Figure 6, p. 195). (Reprinted with the permission of the author and the publisher.)

11 years to draw a table only, and gave them a doll's table as a model. The results are shown in Figure 5.14.

These results are similar to those of Willats. When Freeman went on to ask the 'vertical-oblique' drawers to copy a picture of a table drawn in oblique projection, only one child managed to do it; the others produced their usual vertical-oblique style.

According to these data, then, children below about 9 years of age

Figure 5.13: Stage 6: Perspective (Willats, 1977, Figure 7, p. 195). (Reprinted with the permission of the author and the publisher.)

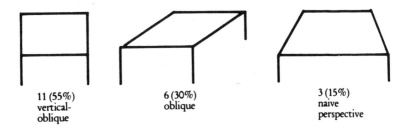

| 11 (55%) vertical-oblique | 6 (30%) oblique | 3 (15%) naive perspective |

Figure 5.14: Drawings of a table by 10- and 11-year-olds in Freeman's (1980) study.

represent the table top with a single horizontal line or with a rectangle. Only later do the angles deviate from right angles. Typically, the first departure is the oblique projection in which the sides of the table are parallel. Later, in the naive perspective and perspective systems the sides converge into the distance.

Now let us see how children draw a cube. If asked to draw a cube or a block with no model present children below about 9 years of age will draw various kinds of rectangular configurations. By age 11 to 12 years 79 per cent of children tested drew an oblique view and by age 14 to 15 years 91 per cent drew an oblique view.[2]

Mitchelmore (1978) presented children with an actual model cube in an oblique orientation. Most of the 7-year-olds drew a single square (see Figure 5.15); Mitchelmore called this Stage 1. Piaget and Inhelder (1956) suggested that these very early drawings are based on topological rather than projective relationships: a closed figure represents the volume occupied by the object rather than a particular view of its outer surface; more recently, Moore (1986) and Willats (1985) have provided data in support of this notion. A single square, then, represents the volume occupied by the cube. At the same time, it does give some indication of the shape of the object. Mitchelmore found that the single square was still a common response at age 9 and at 11 years. At Stage 2 children added further squares or rectangles and thereby produced a rectangular configuration.

From age 9 years, attempts were made to show the oblique orientation of the cube seen from a particular viewpoint (Stages 3A and 3B), but very few realistic perspective drawings (Stage 4) were produced, even at age 14 years. In other words, children were not very skilful at getting the angles 'right'.

In drawing an oblique view, were children actually responding to the particular view of the cube in front of them or were they merely 'tipping out' their stereotype of a cube? In order to see whether children can modify their stereotyped cube, I asked 7- and 12-year-olds to draw a cube which was presented directly in front of them on a table so that only the front and top faces were visible (Cox, 1986). As with the adult sample discussed above, they were divided into two conditions. In Condition 1, they were simply asked to draw what they could see; in Condition 2, their attention was also drawn to the fact that only two faces of the cube were visible. Now, if children of about 7 years of age are in a stage of intellectual realism they will not be concerned with drawing a cube as it looks from a particular orientation; rather, they will try to capture the essence of a cube *per se*. We would not expect more specific verbal instructions about what can be seen to affect their drawings.[3] We might expect 12-year-olds to be in an intermediate stage. That is, we might expect that they would draw a stereotyped view in Condition 1, but that the more specific instructions of Condition 2 might lead them to draw what they could actually see.

In Condition 1 (see Figure 5.16), 29 per cent of the 7-year-olds produced a single square, 43 per cent produced drawings with two sections, and 27 per cent produced configurations with three or more sections. At age 12, 46 per cent produced two-section drawings and 50

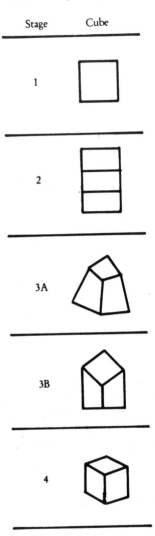

Figure 5.15: Developmental stages in the drawing of a cube (Mitchelmore, 1978, Figure 2, p. 235).

per cent produced three-section configurations. So, fewer than half the children drew two-section configurations, and there seems to be a shift with age from drawing only a single square towards drawing the stereotyped three-section oblique view (more or less skilfully executed).

Now let us look at the responses in Condition 2, when it was pointed out that the children could see only the front and top faces of the cube. Only 16 per cent of the 7-year-olds now drew a single square. The percentage of two-section drawings rose to 70 per cent. The remaining responses are distributed across the three- and four-section categories. Among 12-year-olds, the dominant response is a two-section configuration and 87 per cent of the children produce it.

What seems to be happening, then, is that most children as young as 7 years of age can produce a drawing of a cube which matches the number of faces that are actually seen, provided that this requirement is pointed out to them. By the age of 12 years, children have learned 'how to draw a cube' and there is a tendency to produce this stereotyped oblique view; again, however, this tendency can be curbed if it is made clear that only two faces of the model cube can actually be seen. Specific verbal instructions from the experimenter, then, are effective in eliciting view-specific drawings from children even as young as 7 years. Adults already produce view-specific drawings and are not reliant on the more detailed instructions.

Very few children even at the age of 12 years produced converging lines on the top face of the cube. Most drew the edges parallel. As with the adult data, I have taken a rather liberal criterion of view-specificity, namely a two-section drawing irrespective of the way the sections were drawn. Even so, a developmental trend in the way that the top face is drawn can be traced: perpendicular parallel lines at age 7, oblique parallel lines at age 12, and converging lines among adults.

The perpendicular bias

Probably the most noticeable difference between younger children's drawings of objects in depth and those of older subjects is that objects like tables and cubes are shown as rectangular forms. In other words, younger children emphasize vertical and horizontal lines and right angles whereas older ones can draw oblique lines and acute angles (although by no means all older subjects are very skilful at this).

Now, perhaps the younger children simply have difficulty in drawing obliques. It has long been observed that children can draw a

	Age	Condition 1			Condition 2		
		7	12	Adults	7	12	Adults
(drawing)		2			2		
(drawing)		1	3		2		
(drawing)		2	16	4	2	2	1
(drawing)		5	18	2	1	4	1
(drawing)		4			4		
(drawing)		4	19		3	9	22
(drawing)		6	14	7	6	22	4
(drawing)		1	1	1	5	4	4
(drawing)		15	5	13	12	6	12
(drawing)		5	7	5	21	12	10
(drawing)		18			11	2	

Figure 5.16: The responses of children and adults who were asked to draw a cube.

circle by about age 3, a square at age 4, a triangle at age 5, and a diamond at age 7 (Piaget and Inhelder, 1956). Thus, figures involving obliques appear at a later age. Various studies have looked at the background shape of the paper on which the figure has been drawn. Pieces of paper are usually rectangular and provide horizontal and vertical cues. It should be fairly easy, then, to draw a vertical or a horizontal line, since either one can be drawn parallel to an existing edge of the paper. There are no oblique edges though, so an oblique line will be rather difficult to draw. Berman (1976) showed 3- to 4-year-olds square cards on which were drawn a horizontal, a vertical, or an oblique line. When the child had seen a card, it was removed, and she had to reproduce the line on another square card. Horizontals and verticals were easy, but obliques were difficult. In fact, the errors tended to be horizontals or verticals.

Berman, Cunningham and Harkulich (1974) presented this same task but the lines were drawn on circular cards instead of square ones, and were presented on a circular table. In this case, the vertical line was the most accurately reproduced; there was little difference between the horizontal and the oblique. Both these studies relied heavily on memory since the stimulus cards were removed before the child began to draw.

Brittain (1976) allowed the child to observe the stimulus design while she was drawing it. He found that circles, squares and triangles were all easy to draw for 3- to 5-year-olds if the shape of the paper matched the figure to be drawn. So, basically, the child can draw lines parallel to the edges of the surrounding frame. Naeli and Harris (1976) also found that a compatible frame facilitated the task and an incompatible frame hindered it (see Figure 5.17); they found a similar result whether the child had to draw the figure or had to place a cut-out shape on the frame.

What these studies suggest is that oblique lines are not that difficult to draw, particularly if there is a cue available in the shape of the surrounding frame. Of course, in the table and cube pictures there is no oblique cue in the frame. So, this is perhaps why children do not draw the 'depth' lines as oblique. But, there are typical 'errors' in children's spontaneous pictures in which obliques are routinely drawn even though the frame is rectangular (see Figure 5.18).

The sides of the chimney should be vertical and parallel with the sides of the house and the paper. Similarly, the trees on the mountain should be vertical. Yet, in both cases the lines are oblique and are not

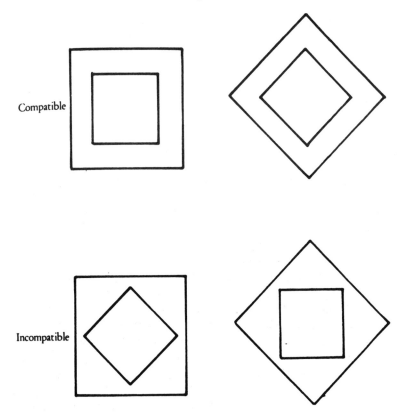

Compatible

Incompatible

Figure 5.17: Shapes surrounded by a compatible or an incompatible frame.

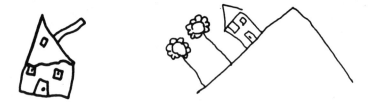

Figure 5.18: A chimney perpendicular to the roof, and house and trees perpendicular to the mountainside (Piaget and Inhelder, 1956, Figure 26, p. 383). (Reprinted with the permission of the publisher.)

parallel with any nearby cues. Piaget and Inhelder (1956) explained these errors as a lack of understanding of the Euclidean concepts of the vertical and the horizontal. If this were so, one would expect that errors would be random. Yet, what is most striking about these pictures is that the chimney and the trees are drawn *perpendicular* to their baselines. The errors are quite systematic. Furthermore, the errors occur in production tasks but are much less marked in selection tasks (Perner, Kohlmann and Wimmer, 1984), indicating that young children recognize that vertically drawn chimneys are correct but perpendicularly drawn chimneys are not. Could it be, then, that it is not so much a difficulty with drawing obliques *per se*, nor a difficulty with drawing an oblique in a rectangular frame, nor the lack of conceptual knowledge about verticals and horizontals, but a tendency towards drawing perpendiculars on to a 'local' baseline which accounts for the kinds of drawings in Figures 5.8, 5.10 and 5.15?

Ibbotson and Bryant (1976) wanted to find out if this bias was present in decontextualized tasks. They asked children aged 5 to 6½ years to copy a series of figures made up of a shorter line drawn on to a larger baseline. The angle between them was 90 or 45 degrees and they were presented in a number of different orientations, so that the baseline could be horizontal, vertical or oblique (see Figure 5.19). The baseline was already drawn on the response card and the child had to draw in the second line.

The results showed that the 90 degree figures were copied more accurately than the 45 degree figures. There was a strong perpendicular bias in the errors of the 45 degree figures. That is, the shorter line was drawn more perpendicular to its base than it ought to have been. This error was quite strong with horizontal and oblique baselines but not with vertical baselines. Ibbotson and Bryant called this the 'vertical effect'. In subsequent experiments, Ibbotson and Bryant found the same pattern even when the motor response was changed (children had to place a straight wire on to a baseline) and also when the line to be copied was inside a rectangle (see Figure 5.20).

Bayraktar (1985) has found that the perpendicular bias is very stubborn indeed; even when strong cues were provided, such as making the edge of the paper parallel to the target line to be drawn or placing a red line parallel to the target line, the perpendicular bias persisted. The bias begins to fade at about age 7 years but is still there to some extent even among adults.

It is difficult, then, for children to draw a line at an acute angle to

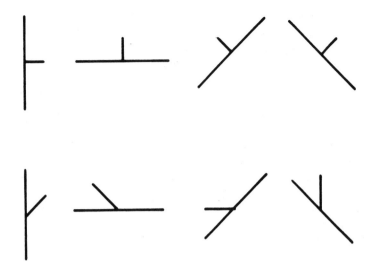

Figure 5.19: Figures made up of a short line drawn at 90 degrees or 45 degrees to a longer baseline, and presented in a vertical, horizontal or oblique orientation.

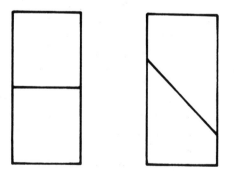

Figure 5.20: Rectangles containing a line drawn at 90 degrees or at 45 degrees.

another line, especially if the baseline is horizontal or oblique; the tendency is to draw it perpendicular to the base. Bremner and Taylor (1982) have argued that the perpendicular bias found by Ibbotson and Bryant may not be a tendency to draw a line perpendicular to a baseline but rather a tendency to *bisect* the baseline and so create two equal angles. To test this idea they presented 'dog-leg' baselines subtending an obtuse angle. In some cases a central, intersecting line bisected the angle (see Figure 5.21a, upper part); in others the intersecting line created a right angle and an acute angle (see Figure 5.21b, upper part). Bremner and Taylor also presented figures with straight baselines, and with intersecting lines drawn either perpendicular to or oblique to this baseline. All the figures were presented in a variety of different orientations.

Each baseline was drawn on a card in black and the intersecting line in red. The children had another card with an identical baseline and they had to draw in the red intersecting line. If the error is a perpendicular error, then the intersecting line should be drawn to form a right angle. On the other hand, if the tendency is towards bisection, then children should draw the intersecting line so as to bisect the angle of the base. The results provided clear support for the notion of bisection. Children copied bisected figures more accurately than nonbisected ones, even though these contained a right angle.

But how do these findings of Bremner and Taylor and of Ibbotson and Bryant relate to the problem of how children draw the 'depth' lines on to the horizontal front edge of a table or on to the front face of a cube? When these depth lines are drawn, they are not drawn on to the middle of a baseline; they are joined on to 'corners'. Bremner (1984) pointed out that the bisection tendency could not occur if the line to be copied joins a baseline at its end, since children will be constructing one angle only and not two. When he compared 'middle' and 'end' figures, 3- to 4-year-olds tended to make errors towards the perpendicular in both. A bisection bias, therefore, cannot be the sole explanation of the perpendicular error; there does seem to be a genuine perpendicular bias.

Still, however, the 'end' task does not really seem to be the same kind of problem as the adding of a 'depth' line to a table or to a cube. In these examples, the line is not drawn on to the middle of a baseline, nor strictly speaking on to the end of a line; it is attached to the origin of an angle (see Figure 5.22). I do not know of any study which has looked at children's ability to copy an 'outside' line rather than the

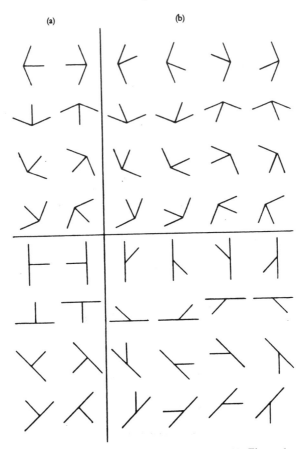

Figure 5.21: Figures used by Bremner and Taylor (1982, Figure 1, p. 164). Those on the left contain a central line which bisects the angle, whereas those on the right contain an intersecting line which creates (above) a right angle and an acute angle or (below) an obtuse angle and an acute angle. Those in the upper part involve a 'dog-leg' baseline, whereas those in the lower part have a straight baseline. (Reprinted with the permission of the authors and the publisher.)

intersecting line in such a configuration. A child could, I suppose, treat the task in the same way as an 'end' task. That is, she could ignore the vertical left-hand line and simply attach the 'depth' line on to the end of the horizontal line. In this case, the perpendicular bias should operate. Alternatively, the child might treat the depth line as a continuation of the left-hand 'baseline' and view the horizontal line as the intersecting one. In such a configuration the bisection bias should operate to produce two equal angles. Either way, the child will produce a line perpendicular to the horizontal line of the table or cube. Of course, we must not forget, also, that there may well be yet another cue influencing the child's drawing – the edge of the paper. All in all, the biases operating and the cues available in this task, either separately or together, seem to work against the child drawing an oblique 'depth' line, and towards drawing a perpendicular. Even so, no adequate explanation of the bias exists. Ibbotson and Bryant (1976) suggested that it arises from the carpentered world we live in, but Bayraktar (1985) argues that this is unsatisfactory as an explanation, especially as she has found the bias to be just as strong among rural Turkish children, who presumably do not live in a highly carpentered environment.

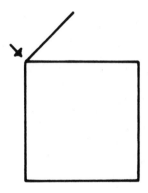

Figure 5.22: A 'depth' line drawn onto a square.

The studies discussed above suggest that powerful production biases may be at work, at least in these essentially two-dimensional, decontextualized tasks. Although it is useful to decontextualize a task and use abstract figures in order to demonstrate a production bias, it does not follow that a particular way of drawing a 'real' object is solely explicable in terms of that production bias. It merely indicates that there is a tendency towards a production bias irrespective of the child's knowledge of the characteristics of the object to be drawn. Furthermore, the tendency towards the perpendicular in these decontextualized tasks *is* only a tendency and, as Crook (1983, 1985) has argued, is not substantial enough to account for the very definite perpendicular errors found in many spontaneous drawings. The chimneys jutting from roofs at alarming angles and the trees almost toppling off the mountainsides do not merely *tend* towards the perpendicular; they are very obviously perpendicular.

It seems to me much more likely that the child's knowledge about the objects she is drawing leads her to make certain choices of line. Children know, for instance, that chimney pots normally rest on and are parallel to the ridge of the roof and that, except in hilly areas, trees grow up perpendicular to the horizontal ground. They also know that the surface of a table and the faces of a cube are rectangular. Maybe, then, these features are preserved, wittingly or otherwise, in the children's drawings. Indeed, this seems to be the implication of the results of a study by Phillips, Hobbs and Pratt (1978). They gave children line drawings of a cube to copy and also another design unlikely to be seen as representative of any particular object (see Figure 5.23). The cube was copied much less accurately than the other design by children aged 6 years 9 months to 7 years 9 months. Presumably the knowledge that cubes have square faces led the children to draw a number of squares even though only one square was present in the model. The children had no such 'real-world' knowledge about the other design and so there was no comparable interference in the copying process and they had more freedom to make a more visually realistic copy. Other more recent studies (e.g. Cox, 1989; Lee, 1989) have also shown that children as young as 7 years can copy trapezoidal shapes reasonably accurately, but when the shapes are described as tables or cubes, etc., children tend to draw rectangular forms.

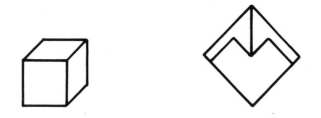

Figure 5.23: Line drawings presented as stimuli in a copying task (Phillips, Hobbs and Pratt, 1978, Table 1, p. 19). (Reprinted with the permission of the authors and the publisher.)

Although there is considerable evidence, then, for a production bias – children tend to make angles more perpendicular than they ought to be – this bias in itself is not compelling enough to be accepted as a sole explanation for children's perpendicular errors in their spontaneous drawings. Children's knowledge of the structure of the object itself or its relation to its supporting surface is very important in the way the child depicts the scene. This suggestion that the child's knowledge of the objects influences the way they are drawn is reminiscent of, if not the same as, Luquet's notion of intellectual realism. It must be emphasized, though, that this notion does not specify whether children *intentionally* draw what they know of an object or whether their knowledge gets in the way and that they can't inhibit it sufficiently in order to draw what they see. This issue has been discussed by Crook (1985).

In the same way that the production bias may not be a complete explanation, neither may Luquet's. The question really is not which of these two explanations can best explain children's errors, but how do they work together in a range of different contexts to influence the child's drawing.

Summary

By 'drawing something *in perspective*', people generally mean showing the depth of an object. In this chapter I have looked at the way that adults and children draw objects like a table and a cube. Children draw these as rectangular forms: the table-top is drawn as a rectangle and the cube is represented with a single square or a configuration made up of a number of rectangles. By about the age of 12 years, children have been taught how to draw things, particularly cubes, in perspective. Typically, they draw an oblique view of a cube, and if adults are asked to draw a cube, they also produce an oblique view. Interestingly, this 'stereotype' is actually an impossible view!

If we present an actual cube in front of an adult she will modify her stereotyped drawings and draw only the number of faces of the cube that she can see. Young children will do this only when the instructions are made very explicit. Not surprisingly, they find it very difficult to get the angles 'right'. Surprisingly, though, adults do too. Although most of them draw *what* they can see, in terms of the number of faces, fewer than half draw them *how* they are seen. Thus, they tend to draw rectangular rather than oblique forms.

One of the difficulties, particularly for children, may be the powerful production biases which operate in this kind of task. These biases militate against the child drawing an oblique line, and favour perpendicular forms. As well as these production biases, children may have a great deal of difficulty in suppressing what they know about the scene they are drawing. For instance, they know that tables and cubes are rectangular forms, so it is perhaps rather difficult and 'unnatural' to have to inhibit drawing them in that way. Exactly the same problems may confront adults, although to a lesser extent, and this may explain why many of us, especially if we have no artistic training, find that drawing is a very hard and often frustrating task. There seems to be a very large gap between what ordinary adults are thought capable of, in the theories of Luquet and of Piaget and Inhelder, and what they actually do.

Notes

1. I am grateful to Jennifer Cobley and to David Cox for their careful observations made in secondary and primary schools.
2. I am grateful to Jennifer Cobley for collecting these data.
3. Although he used different models, Barrett (Barrett and Bridson, 1983; Barrett, Beaumont and Jennett, 1985) did find that to some extent 7-year-olds, but not younger children, were sensitive to the verbal instructions and could produce a more visually accurate picture.

Conclusion to Part II

The notion that an artist should draw what she sees from a particular point of view became dominant during the Renaissance, and aids and devices were developed to help her towards this goal. This method of representation, and in particular the projective system of linear perspective, is today still considered by many to be a true reflection of how we see the world about us. The juxtaposition on the page of different views of an object, for instance in Egyptian painting or among some Cubist painters, is often regarded as quaintly primitive in the former, or eccentric and 'experimental' in the latter. It has long been observed that young children also typically draw a scene from 'a medley of different viewpoints'. Piaget and Inhelder's explanation for this is that these children have not yet developed a co-ordinated system of perspectives; they cannot successfully adopt a particular viewpoint, even their own.

The research studies discussed in this section do indeed show that young children often seem to ignore what they see and draw stereotyped or 'canonical' forms of the objects. But they do not always do this and sometimes they do produce visually realistic pictures. We are beginning to chart the variables which will elicit these different kinds of response. The occurrence or non-occurrence of the naming of the object seems to be particularly important, as is the way that the scene is described. Furthermore, the extent of contrast or similarity between two objects in a scene has also been shown to influence the kind of picture the child draws. These findings hold with children as young as 6 and possibly 5 years of age. But there is actually very little research on children younger than this. What is available indicates that very young children will modify their stereotyped forms only in very heavily contextualized tasks.

It is possible, then, for young children to draw *what* they can see. It is generally much more difficult for them to show *how* objects look.

(We have already encountered this what/how distinction in the discussion of children's perspective-taking ability.) So, for example, children will draw two faces of a cube if they can see only two, but they have great difficulty in getting the angles 'right' so that the drawing reflects the shape projected to the eye. It turns out that this is a problematic task even for adults. Strong production biases militate against the drawing of oblique lines and favour perpendicular forms. There is also the problem of overcoming one's knowledge about the object in order to draw it as it looks. So, if it is known that a cube, for example, is made up of rectangular surfaces, it is difficult to suspend this knowledge and draw shapes which are radically different. Unless we have artistic training to overcome these biases, even adults have difficulty in drawing a visually realistic view of a scene. So the ability to draw something from our own point of view turns out to be quite a struggle, not something that we 'naturally' do.

PART III   Conversational Role-taking

Language is a very powerful symbolic system. In Chapter 2 I presented research evidence that shows how children can describe verbally another's view much earlier than they can represent that view pictorially. In this section I want to examine the child's use of language not as a means of representing overtly her knowledge about a cognitive task but in the communication process itself, in the context of ordinary conversations, which nevertheless reveals the child's cognitive understanding.

Even before they can talk, babies have learned a great deal about 'having a conversation'. They understand and use various non-verbal gestures and devices for directing attention, and their 'dialogues' with adults display synchronized turn-taking sequences. These features are all part of what a conversation is about. Some research studies imply that the baby is as skilful as the adult in regulating the dialogue. I am inclined to agree with others, though, who maintain that the baby's skill is limited, and that it is the adult who is skilful in allowing herself to be paced by the baby. Nevertheless, the baby is not oblivious to the adult; she *is* taking account of the adult's contribution.

First of all, in Chapter 6, I shall pursue the issue of how adults' talk might be adapted to help young children to have a conversation. It is well known that adults use baby-talk when addressing young children, but it is not clear what function this might serve. I shall go on to discuss *children's* ability to adapt their speech to the characteristics of the receiver: for instance, whether the receiver is very young and linguistically inexperienced, or conversely, is older and fluent. Finally in Chapter 6, I shall discuss children's ability to adapt their speech *within* a particular interaction – when, for instance, the receiver does not acknowledge what the child has said or indicates that the child's utterance is problematic in some way.

In Chapter 7 I shall consider the area of deixis. The deictic features of a language include terms such as *I* and *you, here* and *there*, etc.; the person or place referred to can only be known by reference to the identity of the speaker (and listener) and her place in time and space *vis-à-vis* other people and objects. Take, for example, the utterance '*I want that one there*, not this one *here*'. For a correct interpretation, one must know that *I* refers to the speaker and also that *here* and *there* refer to locations near to and farther from the speaker. Misunderstandings would occur, for instance, if one did not appreciate the distinction between *here* and *there* and, crucially, that they have meaning relative to one particular person's point of view rather than another – in this case, the speaker's. I shall discuss children's acquisition and development of these deictic terms.

The relevance of this section on language to the general theme of *The Child's Point of View* is that a speaker must have an appreciation of another's viewpoint in order to adapt her speech to that person's needs and, thereby, to communicate effectively. The 'folklore' of egocentrism claims that young children do not have such an appreciation and that they do not communicate effectively. But even Piaget, in *The Language and Thought of the Child* (1926), estimated that at least 50 per cent of young children's speech is communicated effectively, and Garvey and Hogan (1973) found a much higher rate (66 per cent) in free play activity between preschool children who were already acquainted. If it can be shown that children do adjust their speech when speaking with people of different ages or in response to the other speaker's difficulty in understanding a particular utterance, then this implies that they are sensitive to other people's characteristics and needs and can adapt their behaviour accordingly. Furthermore, since deictic terms are intrinsically related to the particular points of view of conversational participants, a correct use and understanding of these terms also implies considerable knowledge on the child's part about the shifting roles of speaker and listener.

6 Taking account of the listener's needs

Baby-talk

Adults speak rather differently to young children than they do to each other (Cross, 1977 and 1978; Garnica, 1977 and 1978; Snow, 1977b; Jacobson, Boersma, Fields and Olson, 1983; Durkin, Rutter and Tucker, 1982; Durkin, Rutter, Room and Grounds, 1982). This speech, often called 'baby-talk', 'motherese', or 'CDS' (child directed speech) has certain noticeable characteristics. Utterances are shorter, slower and syntactically simpler than in adult–adult speech. There are frequent repetitions, recasts (in which the adult retains the child's meaning but puts her sentence in a syntactically different form) and expansions (in which the adult slightly changes both semantic and syntactic aspects of a child's sentence). Adults' pitch to younger children is generally higher, the intonation is more exaggerated and the speech is very clear. There are more special words like 'doggie' or 'bunny' and more use of nouns instead of pronouns, e.g. 'Mummy do it' instead of 'I'll do it', or 'Amy have it' instead of 'You have it'. The content of speech is very much limited to the here and now or to events only just past or about to happen. Non-verbal gestures accompanying speech are more frequent and exaggerated.

Although this talk is often referred to as 'motherese', in fact fathers, other adults and older children address young children in a similar way (Jakobson, 1960; Snow, 1972; Golinkoff and Ames, 1979; Kavanaugh and Jirkovsky, 1982). It also occurs in all languages and cultures (Jakobson, 1960; Ferguson, 1977; Harkness, 1977). As children grow older the extent of the adult's use of baby-talk grows less. Snow (1977a) and Sylvester-Bradley and Trevarthen (1978) have studied the changes which occur in the mother's speech during the child's very early months, and Snow (1972) and Garnica (1977) have also looked at differences in the mother's speech to 2-year-olds and older children. In general, it seems that baby-talk is much less marked with older children. For instance, Garnica (1977) found no difference in the incidence of rising terminal pitch in speech addressed to 5-year-olds compared with adult–adult speech. As the child gets older and becomes more linguistically and cognitively mature, baby-talk is phased out and speech to children approximates speech to other adults. It is important to note, also, as did Brown (1977), that adults do not use baby-talk all the time, but that children are addressed with 'normal' adult speech too, particularly as they get older; children also hear adult–adult conversations around them. As well as baby-talk, then, children also have an adult model of speech available to them.

We know that adults use baby-talk when talking to young children and we can describe some of the characteristics of it. It is not clear, however, why it occurs. It may be that adults temper their language in order to teach young children syntactic forms. We find little evidence, though, of a *direct* and *explicit* teaching role by parents. Brown and Hanlon (1970) and Hirsh-Pasek, Treiman and Schneiderman (1984) found that parents will correct or question the *truth* of a child's utterance, but will rarely correct its grammar. An example given by Hirsh-Pasek *et al.* is of a child saying, 'That broken', followed by the parent's response, 'Yeah, that's true'; here, the parent confirms the truth of the utterance even though a morpheme is actually missing from the sentence. So adults do not generally give direct feedback on the grammar of a child's utterance, at least not in the overt form of 'picking up on errors'. And, intuitively, one feels that constant interruption and correction of grammar would both disrupt and inhibit communication. What parents may do, however, in responding to the child, is to recast part of the child's utterance into a correct, grammatical form, thereby supplying a good model. Hirsh-Pasek *et al.* found that mothers repeated about 20 per cent of their 2-year-olds' ill-formed sentences, correcting the error, whereas they repeated only 12 per cent of the children's well-formed sentences.

A further consideration for the specific-teaching hypothesis of baby-talk is that if parents were concerned primarily to teach young children, they would surely use syntactic forms a step ahead of the child's current level of complexity. And, this, according to Newport (1976) and Newport, Gleitman and Gleitman (1977), they do not do. In fact, in producing utterances like 'Mummy do it' or 'Amy have it', adults actually use *ungrammatical* sentences which, presumably, children have to 'unlearn'.

It seems to be more profitable to think about baby-talk in terms of its usefulness in *communicating* with an immature listener. Many researchers (e.g. Brown, 1977; Newport *et al.* 1977; Furrow, Nelson and Benedict, 1979) take this view. Although baby-talk is more a response to the child's cognitive and linguistic level rather than a routine strategy for changing it, that is not to say that parents never try to teach their children. We might expect, then, that parents' baby-talk should be finely tuned to the child's level of language development. The data from Cross (1977), who studied sixteen mother–child pairs in which the children were aged from 19 to 32 months, and Furrow *et al.* (1979), who recorded seven mothers and their 18-month-old children, show that this relationship is very strong. Utterances are delivered one proposition at a time and are short and syntactically simple; they are well-formed and clearly spoken, and may be repeated for maximum effectiveness. Their high pitch may mark them out specially for the child's attention, and her attention may also be solicited by other means such as using her name. Newport *et al.* (1977), however, argued from their findings that baby-talk is not *finely* attuned to the child's linguistic needs, but only grossly adapted to the child's age. And the ways in which it is adapted are not in terms of syntactic simplicity, but in terms of brevity of utterance. The problem they point out is that sentence length and syntactic complexity are often confounded, so it is difficult to decide which variable is more important. *Deletions* are a case in which a syntactically complex utterance can also be quite short. An example would be 'Want to go out? ' instead of 'Do you want to go out? '. Such utterances are quite common when directed to children but virtually non-existent in adult–adult speech. So it seems that adults are more concerned with shortness of utterances than syntactic simplicity when speaking to young children. As Snow (1986) points out, it may be that syntactic simplicity is actually an artifact of semantic simplicity.

When we say that baby-talk is used by adults to communicate effectively with an immature listener, we must remember that parents are engaged in a variety of different activities with their children at different times and will wish to communicate different things in different ways. These different activities and intentions may be related to different features of baby-talk. Bakker-Renes and Hoefnagel-Hoehle (1974) found that caretaking activities such as dressing, bathing and feeding elicited the stereotyped forms of baby-talk (short utterance length and paraphrase) whereas play and book-reading elicited more complex speech from the adult. McDonald and Pien (1982), in their study of 2½- to 3-year-olds and their mothers, found that imperatives were used to control behaviour whereas open questions were used to encourage participation. Furthermore, they found that individual mothers could be characterized as mainly directive or mainly conversation-eliciting. In my own video data, parents frequently repeat a child's utterance in a questioning intonation and rising terminal pitch and/or by using a tag, like 'isn't it? ', at the end of an utterance. This questioning form may serve a number of functions: it may be a means of checking what the child has said; it may also serve as a device to mark the end of the adult's turn; and, further, it may be a means of soliciting the child's participation. So the different features of baby-talk may function to get the child to engage in a variety of activities; included in these activities is that of having a conversation, at taking turns at contributing information on a particular topic.

Even if baby-talk, from the adult's point of view, is used primarily for communication purposes rather than specifically to teach the child, it may still serve as a model for language learning useful to the linguistic novice. We need to find out, then, how the child makes use of the particular features of baby-talk. Whereas those studies cited above are correlational and therefore cannot be used to establish a causal link, some experimental studies have considered the effect of parental input on the child's language development. Such studies have concentrated on parental expansions (Cazden, 1965) and expansions and recasts (Nelson, Carskaddon and Bonvillian, 1973; Nelson, 1976), and on the way that these might affect the child's acquisition of syntactic structures. Expansions and recasts are thought to be important for language development for a number of reasons: they provide a correct model of what the child is trying to say, they do so immediately after the child's own utterance, and they provide moderately discrepant information. The general format of the experimental studies is to match two groups of children who lack certain syntactic forms. One group is then exposed to expansions and recasts of their utterances. Comparisons are made between the groups' subsequent level on various syntactic measures; any significant differences between the groups can then be attributed to the experimental manipulation. Cazden's study (1965) failed to accelerate the child's level of syntax, but later studies (Nelson *et al.*, 1973; Nelson, 1976) were more successful; in particular, Nelson (1976) found that children's use of negative *wh*-questions or complex verb constructions increased as a result of experimenter recasts into these forms.

These positive results from some of the experimental studies, even though they have concentrated on the development of syntax, suggest a way in which feedback may operate in normal adult–child interaction. That is, by recasting and expanding the child's utterance, the adult provides a good model without the need for direct corrective feedback of the child's own utterance. The child *is* given feedback but in a positive and supportive way. Of course, in concentrating on the development of syntax, the experimental evidence deals with only part of what is involved in being a skilled language user; whether other features of baby-talk function to facilitate other aspects of the child's role as conversational participant, and in what ways they might do so, remains to be conclusively demonstrated.

Before I move on to a discussion of *children's* speech I must mention a particular problem with most of the studies of baby-talk. Most of these studies cited above concentrate on *frequency* of use by adults of various constructions. Newport *et al.* (1977, p. 136) are aware that frequency may not be the appropriate variable to measure. This worry is emphasized by Kuczaj (1982) who suggests that once a minimally sufficient amount of exposure to a particular construction has occurred, additional exposure is not necessarily helpful to the child's acquisition of it. Kuczaj also maintains that although adult input is important to some extent, it is the child's *use* of the input which is important. Thus he wants to make a distinction between *input* and *intake*. Gleitman, Newport and Gleitman (1984) also stress that the child herself may be selective in what she uses and when she uses it. She may be biased towards noticing a word or construction which is stressed or which occurs in initial position, and these preferences may change over time. While the adult input is important, then, what the child makes of it, and when, may also be extremely important considerations. I might add that one variable influencing the *intake* might be the particular purpose for which a construction is used. Most studies have either looked at the total frequency of a given construction in the adult speech or have divided them into question forms *vs.* declaratives, but they have not considered whether the utterance is used to praise the child, chide her, etc.; different practical uses of the constructions may have a bearing on the extent to which the child notices or attends to the input at all.

In summary, then, it appears unlikely that parents use baby-talk for the sole and explicit purpose of teaching language to their young children. They use it as an effective means of communicating with a cognitively and linguistically immature listener. This speech, though, contains a variety of features which may facilitate the child's understanding of what is being communicated, may help her own acquisition and development of language, and may also facilitate her skill as a conversational participant.

It has become evident more recently that the kinds of parental speech adjustments we see in Western cultures are not universal and that in some cultures, such as the Kaluli of Papua New-Guinea, parents not only model an appropriate utterance for a young child but also give specific instructions for the child to imitate it. These parents adopt for themselves a direct teaching role and believe that, if the child is to become a competent speaker, she must hear and repeat the fully-grammatical adult form. It does not matter that the child cannot understand all the grammatical intricacies of the utterance; the point is that she will learn the context in which it is appropriate to make that particular kind of utterance. Kaluli children, like children all over the world, develop into competent speakers and appear to do so as quickly as children in other cultures. It is clear, then, that the kinds of speech adaptations made by adults in Western cultures are not actually essential for children's successful language development; parents with very different beliefs and practices produce children who are equally successful language users.

Children's speech to others of different ages

I have spent some time examining how adults in Western cultures adapt their speech to a greater or lesser extent when addressing young children, and how this might facilitate children's own language learning. In what ways do children, if at all, adapt *their* speech to others, particularly to younger children with limited linguistic skills?

By the end of the 1960s and the beginning of the 1970s there seemed to be conflicting evidence. Whereas the observational studies of Brown and Fraser (1964), Jakobson (1968) and Cazden (1970) revealed that children do 'talk down' to those younger than themselves, the results of a number of specially designed research tasks (e.g. Piaget, 1926; Glucksberg, Krauss and Weisberg, 1966; Flavell, 1968) suggested that children are very bad at adapting their communications to the needs of their listeners. Piaget (1926), for instance, found that 6-year-olds were unable to explain to another child the workings of a tap or a syringe, and Glucksberg *et al.* (1966) showed that preschoolers do not describe an object precisely enough for listeners to identify it among several others. A problem with these kinds of studies is that instead of concentrating on the way that the language is used, they have focused on the children's ability to communicate information they themselves may not have grasped. It seems inappropriate, as Shatz and Gelman (1973) have also pointed out, to judge children's ability to communicate information about a cognitive problem, such as the workings of a tap, when their own understanding of it may be inadequate. If we are interested in how children communicate, then we need to be sure when that process is being complicated by their lack of knowledge and understanding about the content of the message.

Shatz and Gelman (1973) studied the speech of 4-year-olds to adults and to 2-year-old children. In their Study A, the child was presented with a toy, was encouraged to play with it and to talk about it with the experimenter. She was then asked to tell the experimenter how to work the toy. After that, the child was told that a younger child was to join them and would need to be told how to work the toy. Two things strike me as rather odd in this study. First of all, it seems peculiar to ask a child to tell you how to work something when she may well assume that you already know. Secondly, although there were good reasons in this study for fixing the order of the sessions, the experimenter always interacted with the child before the younger child was brought in. These problems aside, there *were* differences in the ways the 16 children treated their listeners. They all reduced their utterance lengths to the younger children compared with the adults; they used fewer complex constructions and more attention-getting devices like *see, look* and *watch*. The tendency to treat the two age groups differently was not affected by the child's sex or sibling status (i.e. whether or not they actually had a younger sibling). Shatz and Gelman also analyzed tapes of spontaneous speech to see if similar effects would be observed. The mothers were asked to make tapes of themselves in conversation with their 4-year-old children. These were compared, in Study B, with tapes in which the children were playing with a 2-year-old, and, in Study C, with tapes in which the children were interacting with a peer. In both cases, the mother was present but was instructed to refrain from entering the conversation. The peers and younger children were not related to the 4-year-olds but we do not know if they were strangers or not to the participants before the study began. The results showed that peers and adults were treated in a very similar fashion, whereas 2-year-olds received shorter and less complex utterances. Interestingly, in Study B, there was no significant difference in the use of attentional utterances directed to adult listeners or to 2-year-old listeners. The percentage of attention-getting devices to younger listeners was comparable to that in Study A (22 per cent and 21 per cent, respectively); the adult percentage was much higher in this study (16 per cent) than in Study A (4 per cent).[1]

Sachs and Devin (1976) also analyzed speech samples from four children, aged 3 years 9 months to 5 years 5 months, interacting with various listeners. As in the Shatz and Gelman study, the children spoke with an adult (the mother), a peer and a baby (aged between 1 year 2 months and 2 years 5 months). As well as real listeners they asked the child to talk to a doll which of course gave no feedback. Sachs and Devin suggested that if baby-talk was used to a doll, it would show that children have some 'abstract' appreciation of a speech style which is appropriate and that is not reliant on direct cueing.

All four children spoke to younger listeners in a different way than to peers and to their mothers. In particular, with younger listeners they used shorter utterances, more names and endearments and more imperatives. They used fewer questions, but those they did use were requests for information about internal states rather than relating to the 'external world'. There were slight differences between speech to peers and to mothers; in particular, the mean length of utterance (MLU) was shorter for peers than for mothers. Modifications were also made for baby doll listeners along similar lines. When these children acted *as baby*, the MLU and frequency of some syntactic constructions were reduced. However, none of the children used utterances that were entirely like those of a younger child. One problem was that these children, particularly the younger ones, found it very difficult to maintain their role-playing. Nevertheless, even when they produced quite complicated utterances, they did so with the pitch and intonation characteristic of baby-talk.

This study, then, showed that children are not dependent on direct cueing from a listener; they speak in an appropriate way to a doll as well as to a real baby. When they themselves pretend to behave like a baby, pitch and intonation are the consistent adjustments made.

Dunn and Kendrick (1982) found that systematic adjustments were made by even younger children (2 years 10 months to 3 years) when talking to their infant siblings (aged 1 year 2 months). An important feature of *this* study is that as well as analyzing the child's speech to the mother, the mother's speech to the sibling is assessed too; thus, we can see whether the child's speech to the baby was similar to the mother's way of addressing the baby. In fact the child's MLU was shorter to the baby than to the mother, but interestingly it was significantly shorter than the *mother's* utterances to the baby. Similarly, the child used far more attentional utterances and repetitions to the baby than to the mother, and these were used significantly more than in the mother's speech to the baby. The frequency of partial or full imitations of maternal utterances was very low indeed – only 3.6 per cent of the total child–baby utterances. When the contexts were examined, repetitions and attentional utterances were used by the child to restrain, prohibit, or direct the baby's actions, whereas a much lower proportion of maternal repetitions and attentional utterances occurred in this kind of context. Mothers used a much higher frequency of questions to the baby than did the children, and to a large extent these questions were enquiries about the baby's internal state, wants, or needs.

If young children are aware of listeners' characteristics then we would expect them to adjust their language accordingly; in particular, we would expect them to speak in a simpler way to even younger children who are cognitively and linguistically limited. We know from the three studies outlined above that children do speak differently. Their utterances are much shorter and less complex and are delivered in a higher pitch; more names and attention-getters, more repetitions and imperatives, but fewer questions, are used.

One problem occurs again which Newport *et al.* (1977) raised regarding adults' use of baby-talk. And that is the possible confounding of brevity of utterance and simplification of syntax. Gelman and Shatz (1977), in a discussion of their 1973 data, point out that although 4-year-olds' speech to 2-year-olds is often syntactically simple, it is not always so; it may contain some syntactically complex constructions. Gelman and Shatz argue, a point also made earlier in this chapter, that what is considered appropriate speech for younger listeners is not necessarily speech that is syntactically simpler, but speech which will *communicate* effectively with an immature listener. And what the 4-year-olds considered appropriate to communicate was to *show and tell* the 2-year-olds about a toy. Sentences were short and simple. In the process of transmitting information about the toy to adults, 4-year-olds talked about mental states, modulated their assertions, and requested information or confirmation. These involved more complex utterances. Similarly, in Dunn and Kendrick's study (1982), children directed and restricted the infant, whereas, in contrast, the children's interaction with their mothers (and indeed the mothers' interaction with the infants) was much more participative.

These differences in what kinds of communication take place between child and infant and child and adult are of interest in themselves. To 'show and tell' something to someone, for instance, is to treat that person as uninformed; to request information or confirmation, on the other hand, is to propose oneself as the 'inferior' party and the other as the more knowledgeable. By behaving selectively to listeners of different ages children show that they regard younger children, in particular, as immature and in need of special treatment.[2]

What the three studies discussed above do not show clearly, however, is whether or not the child can alter the complexity of an utterance to different listeners when the *same kind of communication* is involved. When a child tries to restrict the person's behaviour in some way, for example, does she simplify her speech if she is addressing an infant, but not a peer or an adult?

From my observations of my own daughter's speech at age 2 years 1 month to babies and to dolls, it was pitch and intonation which were the obvious features; the syntax did not alter compared with her speech to adults. It would not be surprising if very young children cannot make specific modifications of syntax, since they themselves will still be in the process of mastering basic syntactic forms. And, indeed, Andersen's study (1984) of role-playing by 4- to 7-year-olds confirms this hunch: when role-playing a young child with the aid of a puppet, Andersen's younger children from time to time effected a higher pitch and a baby-talk overtone; the older children not only managed to maintain these prosodic markings throughout their role-play but, in addition, managed to make occasional modifications of syntax, e.g. 'Mama, I not going that.' Gleason (1973) has also noted that 5- to 6-year-olds sometimes modify their syntax when speaking to younger children; characteristics like recasts and expansions, however, seem to be used only by adults (Brown, 1977).

We should expect, then, that as speakers themselves develop, they will become more adept at modifying their speech to younger listeners. Clearly, a developmental study is needed in order to chart the precise changes in the use of baby-talk as child-speakers grow up. Andersen's study (1984) goes some way to providing such evidence, although the age range is limited – 4 to 7 years – and the data are frequently collapsed across the age-range, thereby masking any developmental trends.

If children's talk to infants does indeed exhibit baby-talk characteristics, it is difficult to know if the child actually appreciates that infants are cognitively and linguistically limited, or if the child is simply imitating the way she has heard adults speak to them. Even if she does understand that infants are cognitively and linguistically immature, this knowledge in itself will not tell her *how* to address a younger listener. It seems likely, then, that imitation does play a part. Dunn and Kendrick (1982), however, found that children actually imitated directly very few of the mothers' utterances. A problem here, though, is that in their study, as with others, the mother's speech to the infant was related to promoting reciprocal interaction or turn-taking whereas the child was concerned to direct or restrict the infant. It is not surprising, then, that the child did not imitate the mother's utterances. It may be, however, that some of the child's utterances *were* imitative, but of the mother's directive speech heard at other times and in the relevant context.

Since there are no differences between the way a child *without* a young sibling, compared with one *with*, uses baby-talk (see Shatz and Gelman, 1973), it seems that children may not need actually to experience an adult's talk to a younger child. It may be that children can generalize to the infant the way that their own parents speak to *them*. If they can do this, it is a considerable achievement in itself. But it is very difficult to be sure that only children have not heard their parents speaking to other younger children or indeed have not overheard other parent–child conversations. Children may need only minimal exposure to adults' baby-talk in order to understand that this is an appropriate way to address a younger child.

Children's conversations

The research discussed above represents what might be called a *sociolinguistic* approach. That is, researchers study the ways in which children's speech varies according to different categories of *listener*. I have concentrated on listeners of different ages. Another approach is to look at the adjustments children make *within* a particular discourse involving the same listener; adjustments in these circumstances should provide evidence that children are responding to the demands of the immediate interaction and are not merely addressing the listener in some generally appropriate form. I shall discuss the research on establishing a topic in discourse, and on clarification requests.

Establishing a topic
Keenan and Klein (1975), drawing on the ideas of Sacks, argue that conversations do not just happen; participants must 'work' to achieve coherence. For example, in order to talk about a topic sensibly it is necessary to ensure that the listener knows who or what is being spoken about. A number of devices are used to do this. The speaker may introduce a new name in a rising and questioning intonation and may pause for the listener to indicate by a nod, 'uh-huh', etc. that she understands what or who is being referred to. This kind of construction is called a 'try-marker' by Sacks and Schegloff (1974). They illustrate the way that speakers may offer further try-markers if listeners do not at first respond.

A: . . . well I was the only one other
   than the uhm tch *Fords*?, Uh
   Mrs Holmes Ford? You know uh //
   the the cellist?
B: Oh yes, She's she's the cellist.
A: Yes
B: *Ye//s*
A: Well she and her husband were
   there . . .

Speaker A assumes that the referent (Mrs Holmes Ford) may be problematic to start with and introduces the name in a questioning form. She is reluctant to add new information until the listener has identified the referent. When the listener does acknowledge that she has understood, this shared knowledge can then become the basis of further comment and elaboration.

I discussed in Chapter 1 how very young babies use the direction of the adult's gaze to determine what is being attended to. Babies also respond to other devices such as pointing, showing, touching and shaking of the object, as well as naming of the object. By the age of about 2 years children have developed considerable skill in using these devices themselves to get adults to attend to particular features of the environment. As they develop language they master linguistic devices too for establishing co-reference. But this will take time. Keenan and Klein hypothesize that it will be more difficult for young children than for adults to establish a discourse topic. They do not make a *direct* comparison between adult and child speakers, but analyze the ways in which twin boys, aged 2 years 9 months, handle the interaction. They look at the way in which the speaker makes an assertion and the kinds of response he accepts from the addressee as an acknowledgement of it. Keenan and Klein isolate three types of assertion: self-description (e.g. 'I got feathers', 'I got big one', 'I rip it now'), actual-world assertions (e.g. ' "A" "B" "C" in there', 'moth' + point, 'some in there', 'lots in there') and fantasy-world assertions (e.g. 'Oh house broken', 'all very quiet'). They also identify five types of relevant response. The first one is direct *repetition*:

A: big one/no/
   big one/
B: big one/

The second is *affirmation*:

A: got feathers/
   got feathers/. . .
B: oh yes/

The third is *denial*:

A: Jack and Jill/
B: no Jack and Jill/

The fourth is *matching* in which the second speaker claimed he was performing a similar action:

A: I find feather/
   I find feather/
B: Yes/I find/
   I get one/now I get
   good one/I get good
   one/a big one/[3]

And the fifth is *extension*:

A: flower broken/
   flower/. . .

B: many flowers broken/

Keenan and Klein argue that coherence is achieved to a large extent by 'tying one's utterance to the speaker's prior assertion'. Repetition is one way the child can fulfil his role as conversational partner, by acknowledging that he has understood the topic introduced by the speaker and, in fact, Keenan and Klein found that 57 per cent of relevant responses were actually repetitions of the speaker's utterance. Later the child will be able to use syntactic devices, such as pronouns, to accomplish the same task. (The child's understanding and correct use of pronouns will be discussed later in Chapter 7.) An example from my own daughter, although at a younger age (2 years 2 months) than the twins mentioned above, is as follows:

M: Would you like some chocolate?
Amy: Where's it!
M: It's here.

The use of the pronoun *it* indicates that both participants are still referring to the topic introduced at the beginning, namely the chocolate.

Although Keenan and Klein do not discuss the issue, a question arises whether the children's assertions are *constructed* so as to elicit particular kinds of response from the other participant. In Keenan and Klein's second example ('got feathers'), although speaker B affirms speaker A's claim, he does so by saying 'oh yes' rather than simply 'yes'; he seems to treat speaker A's utterance as news. Now, speaker A may have constructed his utterance initially in order to point out something interesting and previously unknown to speaker B. Similarly, in the third example, speaker A's assertion ('Jack and Jill') may have supposed that speaker B possessed the information to confirm or deny it. If it could be demonstrated that the speaker can construct utterances so as to elicit such different kinds of response, then this would imply that speakers can attribute different knowledge states to the addressee.

What happens if the listener does *not* give the appropriate acknowledgement? What kind of 'work' does the speaker have to do to elicit it? Keenan and Klein give an example in which the speaker (B) repeats his utterance about a moth until the other twin (A) eventually does acknowledge what he's said with, in this case, a repetition of the word 'moth'.

A: goosey, goosey gander. . .
B: moth/moth/
A: goosey, goosey gander, where shall I wander/
B: moth/moth/moth/moth/
A: upstairs downstairs in the lady's chamber. . .
B: moth/moth/moth/
A: moth/
B: gone moth/all gone/
A: two moths/
B: many moths/
A: mmm/many moths/many moths/
B: he goed/on the ceiling/
A: gone/

In the 'adult' extract above (p. 126), the speaker gradually provides more background information about 'the Fords' to enable the listener to identify the topic. In the 'twins' extract, speaker B repeats the 'moth' utterance until he gets a relevant response. It's as if the adult speaker assumes that the adult listener is already trying to identify the referent and that the speaker's job is to supply helpful clues. In the children's case, the speaker's main task is simply to get the listener to respond, and repetition is one strategy that can be used for this purpose. (It may have been this child's only available strategy.) This may be a particularly difficult job when the listener is a sibling or peer and is not as co-operative and skilful in managing a conversation as an adult.

Whereas Keenan and Klein have focused mainly on the use of repetition as a means of establishing a topic, Wootton's work on address terms (Wootton, 1981) identifies another way in which a speaker might solicit a response from the addressee. In this work the conversations are mainly between 4-year-old children and their parents. It is often assumed that the use of a listener's name functions as an attention-getter. Thus, children use more names when speaking to children younger than themselves than they do to peers and adults; it is assumed that the child has to work hard at gaining and maintaining the attention of the infant. Wootton shows, however, that names are not always used in this way; indeed, the *positioning* of the address term in the utterance is indicative of the work it is doing. I shall take examples of what happens following a parent's non-response to a child's utterance, in order to demonstrate the different functions. When an address term occurs at the beginning, it *does* act as an attention-getter.

Child: Is it yours?
         (Pause)
Child: Mummy is it yours?
Mother: Yes sweetheart

In this example, the mother does not respond to the child's first utterance. The child then uses the address term and a repeat of the utterance. The child treats the mother as having not attended to the first utterance. By using 'Mummy' in an initial position she instructs her mother to attend to or monitor what she has to say. By repeating the whole utterance, she treats her mother as not having attended to it before.

In contrast, the final positioning of an address term suggests that this item serves a different function.

Child: Have to cut these Mummy
         (Pause)
Child: Won't we Mummy?
         (Pause)
Child: Won't we?
Mother: Yes

Wootton argues that the final position of the address term is not an attention-getter, since the main part of the utterance has been completed at that point. Furthermore, after the mother's non-response, the child does not repeat her utterance; she treats the mother as having attended to it the first time. The address term, then, at the end, seems to be used to solicit a response from the mother. Wootton suggests that this kind of construction is used in a similar way to tag questions (e.g. 'We *are* going to the cinema, aren't we?').

At present there is little *developmental* work which traces the different devices used by the speaker to elicit a response. It may be, for instance, that the use of repetition as seen in Keenan and Klein's example may decline in frequency as other forms, such as address terms in final position, are acquired.

The use of the two devices, repetition and the positioning of an address term, show that children can take an active role as speakers in maintaining a conversation. The way they construct their utterances indicates that they can assess the state of the listener; for example, they may need to gain the listener's attention before delivering their message. They develop an appreciation that the listener may find their utterance problematic in some way, they can assess the nature of the problem, and they can take steps to remedy it. However, it is unlikely that any one of the devices available to the child at a particular time is completely superseded by another one appearing later. No doubt each type may be appropriate on some occasions. Furthermore, simply because gestures such as gaze and pointing are devices used at an earlier age than linguistic terms (see Chapter 1), this does not mean that they will fade out of the child's repertoire. These gestures may be used along with the initial statement, or, in the same or modified form, to pursue the topic if the addressee does not respond appropriately.

Clarification requests

A clarification request, or contingent query (Garvey, 1977), as its name suggests, occurs *within* a discourse and is directly related to what has gone before. Typically, the first speaker says something. The second speaker indicates that the utterance is troublesome in some way. The first speaker responds by clarifying the problem. The second speaker may then indicate that the utterance is no longer troublesome.

Garvey and BenDebba (1978) presented adults with tape-recorded utterances, each followed by a contingent query, and asked them to select 'the most natural response' from a set of three written alternatives. They found that a rising intonation (↑) in the contingent query signalled that the first speaker should repeat all or part of the utterance; specifically, the use of 'what? ↑' signalled complete repetition whereas 'where? ↑' or 'who? ↑' signalled partial repetition. Thus:

A: Joe Glick knows a friend of yours
B: What? ↑
A: Joe Glick knows a friend of yours

A: Jo Glick knows a friend of yours
B: Who? ↑
A: Joe Glick

A falling intonation indicated that the first speaker should give specific information about some particular aspect of the utterance:

A: Joe Glick knows a friend of yours
B: Who? ↓
A: That Greek fellow

Contingent queries were also used to invite confirmation of some aspect of the speaker's utterance:

A: Joe Glick knows a friend of yours
B: A friend of mine? ↑ or He does? ↑
A: Yes

BenDebba and Garvey (in Garvey, 1977) recorded conversations of 3-
to 4-year-olds talking with an experimenter in a nursery school. The
experimenter was instructed to put different types of contingent
queries to the children. They found that all types of query were
responded to appropriately, that is, in line with the examples above.
An example of one conversation is as follows:

Child: I have a bean bag dolly
   but not that color. I have
   a all different color one
Adult: What? ↑
Child: I don't have that color of
   a bean bag doll
Adult: You don't? ↑
Child: No, not that color
Adult: What color?
Child: A different color
Adult: What different color?
Child: All these different colors
Adult: Oh I see

Garvey (1977) also looked at the use of and response to contingent
queries in pairs of children aged 2 years 10 months to 5 years 7
months. She found that most sorts of query were used and generally
responded to appropriately, especially by the older children. About 74
per cent of responses to all queries were appropriate, about 6 per cent
were of some relevance, and about 20 per cent failed to elicit a reply.
The use of the queries indicates a developing capacity to locate as
problematic various aspects of what is said to them. Since the queries
are 'tied' to the speaker's utterance, they also demonstrate that the
listener is indeed a co-operative partner in the conversation. In fact,
adults may use the contingent query as a device to keep the
conversation going, particularly with young children.

 Garvey suggests that the contingent query, or request for clarification, will pinpoint for the first speaker precisely what was troublesome about her utterance. For instance, she maintains that 'What?↑'
and 'Pardon?↑' request repetition of the whole utterance. Corsaro
(1976) also argues that the reason for such questions is that the first
speaker's utterance was not heard clearly. Now, although these forms
can be followed by a complete repetition, this is not always what

happens. The child may recast the utterance in some other form. It is as if the adult has indicated that the utterance was problematic, but in fact does not specify precisely in what way, and the child must determine the difficulty for herself. Her recast utterance reveals the way in which she perceives her first utterance to have been problematic for the listener. We need only look back at BenDebba and Garvey's data (p. 132) to find a case in which the adult's 'What?↑' is not followed by an exact repetition:

Child: I have a bean bag dolly
        but not that color. I have
        a all different color one
Adult: What? ↑
Child: I don't have that color of
        a bean bag doll

Langford (1981), in a detailed analysis of some of Wootton's data, gives a number of examples in which 4-year-olds take the mother's 'What?' or 'Pardon?' query to indicate some problem *other than* a failure to hear the utterance. An example is as follows:

Child: Is Derek a nice boy?
Mother: Pardon?
Child: Is Derek a bad boy?

Here the child assumes that the evaluative term 'nice' is problematic, and changes this to 'bad' in the next utterance.

Child: Mummy who built the one we
        seen on Sunday?
Mother: What?
Child: (   ) Is this the one we
        (after) the roo:dboat?

In this reformulation the child attempts to specify what he meant by 'one' in the first utterance.

Langford argues that when it is clear that the adult has not heard the child's utterance, a specific form like 'What did you say?' rather than 'What?↑' or 'Pardon?↑' is used. I have an example from a conversation with my own daughter (aged 2 years 2 months) which does show a complete repetition after this specific query, but it is then followed by a reformulation when I still fail to understand what she is saying. (We were sitting at a table in a café and she was tucking into a toasted teacake. Nothing had been said for a while and I was gazing elsewhere.)

Amy: I'm puttin lots in
M: What did you say? (turning towards her)
Amy: I'm puttin lots in
M: I don't understand (shaking of head and
        puzzled expression)
        What did you say?
Amy: I got too *much*
M: Oh yes, you must be careful not to put too much in.
        You might choke.

Amy may reasonably have assumed that my first query indicated that I had not attended and needed to hear her utterance again. So she repeated it. My next statement and gestures made it clear that I *had* heard her second utterance but that I still did not understand. Nevertheless, I still asked, literally, for a repetition ('What did you say?'). But she did not repeat herself again; instead she recast the utterance into a different form which I then indicated that I understood and elaborated on. Clearly, Amy recognized that my problem was not simply a failure to hear her and she then revised her hypothesis about the nature of my problem. So, exactly how did she come to understand my difficulty? It seems to me that it was not my words themselves nor the way they were intoned, but the *sequence* of what had gone before which was crucial.[4] And such sensitivity to sequential information over a number of turns is very impressive.

I have so far suggested that the clarification request directs the child's attention to some difficulty with the *form* of the first utterance, i.e. that it needs to be repeated or reformulated. Hustler (1981) raises the possibility that a query such as 'Pardon?' could also indicate to the child that her proposition is being refused. He reviews an extract from Langford's paper:

Child: Come and see Captain Flack
         (Pause)
Mother: Pardon
         (Pause)
                          (F)
Child: I see Captain (V)lack
Mother: Huh, Huh.

Hustler argues that the child may interpret the pause followed by 'Pardon' as 'refusal-implicative', and further suggests that the child's pause and subsequent reformulation in terms of a statement indicates that the child has avoided putting the parent in a position in which she might give an explicit refusal. If this interpretation is correct, then, Hustler says, quite a sophisticated negotiation has taken place.

The clarification request or contingent query is not always presented in such a way as to identify precisely what is troublesome about the speaker's utterance. The child is placed in the position of having to decide among a variety of possibilities. And, indeed, they and adults do not *always* interpret the clarification request correctly, but have to have a second or even third 'stab' at locating the problem. My own daughter's misreading of my query in the café example above indicates this. Also, in Wootton's data, there is an example of the child's initial misinterpretation of her mother's problem with the utterance:

(Playing some sort of fishing game, involving the dangling of a piece of rope out of an upstairs window.)
C: Hey
     (Pull up) the ro:pe with thi:s do:wn
     (Pause)
M: I beg your pardon
C: Plea:se
M: No: I don't understand what you're saying
     What d'ye mean
C: Could ye'hh
M: Close the *win:*dow with the r(he)o-'hh
C: Rope down on
M: Well watch your fingers

The child treats her mother's 'I beg your pardon' as a politeness request and then says 'Please'. Her mother then indicates that this was not the issue; she simply had not understood the child's meaning, which turns out to be an instruction for helping her to close the window on to the rope. This kind of exchange leaves us with the intriguing research question, 'What procedures do children use in order to pinpoint the problems that others have in interpreting their utterances?'

Summary

In this chapter I have reviewed the work on baby-talk which shows that adults' speech is adapted in a number of ways for the purpose of communication with a cognitively and linguistically immature listener, and I have considered the possibility that the various features of baby-talk may facilitate the child's development of language and her skill as a conversational participant. I examined some of the evidence which indicates that children, in turn, adapt their speech when talking to listeners of different ages. It is not clear, though, whether this is independent of the kinds of activity the child engages in with parents, peers and younger children. Furthermore, even if children really do use baby-talk to younger listeners, it is not clear whether this indicates a knowledge of the listeners' cognitive and linguistic immaturity or whether children are simply imitating adults' baby-talk.

I went on to examine evidence from a rather different approach to conversation, namely the way that a child might respond to the listener's difficulties with specific utterances. The examples in the two areas discussed (establishing a topic and clarification requests) seem to me to provide good evidence that young children can and do construct their utterances with direct reference to the other person's turn. The child expects the listener to show signs of understanding and to respond relevantly to what she has said. She can understand that others may find her utterances problematic and can determine what the difficulty is and take steps to clarify it. Even very young children between 2 and 3 years of age, do make conversational adjustments.

Notes

1. However, Shatz and Gelman found that, in fact, one child used *Mommy* repeatedly and contributed half of the total number of adult-directed attention-getters. A general tendency to treat the listeners differently in this way may have been masked by this individual case.

2. I have the feeling, though, that these studies may have artificially exaggerated the different kinds of exchanges between mother and child and between child and infant. Normally, a child may need to use more proper names and attention-getters in order to attract the attention of an adult who might be busying herself with household chores; while being recorded, the adult is already engaged in interaction with the child. Also, while being recorded, adults may see it as their job to promote conversation and activity, and therefore they may be less inclined than usual to restrict and prohibit the child.

3. It will be seen that it is often difficult to separate these categories. For instance, B's response 'Yes/I find/' etc. could be affirmation, matching *and* extension.

4. I am grateful to Dr A. J. Wootton for this suggestion.

7 Deictic expressions

Although the written word has become extremely important in recent historical time, presumably language was first used and is still used predominantly for *face-to-face* communication. Written language, if it is to be effective, has to be more explicit and 'elaborated' than normal spoken language because it cannot rely to such a great extent on the context of the utterance, including gesture. Take an example from Levinson (1983, p. 55): suppose we find a message inside a bottle in the sea and it reads, 'Meet me here in a week from now with a stick about this big'. We do not know who *me* refers to, where *here* is, when *now* is or was, or how big is *this big*. We *would* have known this information if we had heard the message direct from the sender. *Me* would have referred to the person speaking, *here* would have referred to the location she or we occupied or, perhaps, a place that she indicated by gesture either in the environment or on a map, and *now* would have referred to the time at which the utterance was delivered. *This big* would no doubt have been indicated by gesture, either by 'miming' the length with the hands or by drawing the hearer's attention to some object of an appropriate length. The referents (person, place, time) of these deictic terms (from the Greek word for pointing and indicating) will change as the speaker changes. Thus, the persons referred to as *me* (or *I*) and *you* change when another speaker takes over; similarly, the locations referred to as *here* and *there* by one speaker may become *there* and *here* for someone else. Deictic terms, then, shift referents depending on the identity of the speaker. Thus, the point of view shifts from speaker to speaker. This is problematic enough, but it is further complicated in a number of ways. The speaker may not always speak for herself: she may for instance use *we* to indicate to the addressee that she is speaking on behalf of herself *and* another body or to indicate that the addressee is also included in the term *we*. In some languages there are distinct pronouns for each of these uses. The speaker may also adopt the addressee's viewpoint instead of her own. Some languages do this when referring to location: instead of writing in a letter 'How is the weather there in Singapore?', the writer says 'How is the weather here in Singapore?', thus adopting the recipient's spatial perspective.

Similarly, for time, Levinson (pp. 73–4) points out that the utterance may encode the *coding time* (e.g. 'This programme is being recorded today, Wednesday, April 1st, to be relayed next Thursday') *or* the *receiving time* (e.g. 'This programme was recorded last Wednesday, April 1st, to be relayed today'). Another complication is that many deictic expressions may also be used in nondeictic ways. For example, in 'The ball is in front of the doll' the expression *in front of* is used nondeictically if it means that the ball is located near the doll's face regardless of the doll's orientation *vis-à-vis* the speaker. However, if the expression is used deictically it means that the ball is located between the speaker's face and the doll, whether the doll faces the speaker or not. In the nondeictic sense the description can be used by any speaker regardless of viewpoint. In the deictic sense, it can only be used if the ball intervenes between the speaker and the doll; a speaker in a different location will describe the relationship differently (see Figure 7.1). It is not difficult to imagine the dilemma a person may face in trying to interpret such utterances, especially if they are unaccompanied by gesture.

In this chapter I shall discuss the development in children of some deictic terms in English within the categories of person and place. I realize that the pattern of this development will not necessarily be the same in all languages and cultures, since the adult use of deictic terms does not have a universal pattern. I shall have space to include only a few examples; for a fuller coverage, although not a developmental one, the chapter on deixis in Levinson (1983) is recommended. The reason why I am especially interested in the *child's* acquisition of deixis is that these expressions provide an excellent opportunity to study the child's ability to decentre and take account of different points of view. In fact, as Elliot (1981, p. 59) implies, the correct use of deictic terms '*depends* on the ability of both speaker and addressee to work out each other's point of view. . . .'

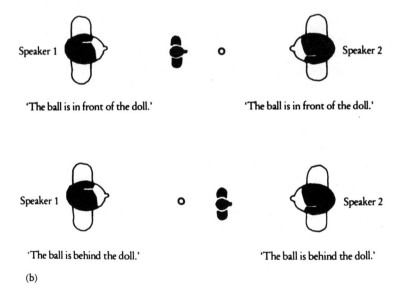

Speaker 1

'The ball is behind the doll.'

Speaker 2

'The ball is in front of the doll.'

Speaker 1

'The ball is behind the doll.'

Speaker 2

'The ball is in front of the doll.'

(a)

Speaker 1

'The ball is in front of the doll.'

Speaker 2

'The ball is in front of the doll.'

Speaker 1

'The ball is behind the doll.'

Speaker 2

'The ball is behind the doll.'

(b)

Figure 7.1: (a) Deictic and (b) nondeictic uses of *in front of* and *behind*.

Person deixis

English speakers generally refer to themselves as *I* or *me* and to things belonging to themselves as *my* or *mine*. Similarly, *you, your* and *yours* refer to the addressee(s). (I shall not discuss the literature connected with third-person pronouns; the interested reader is referred to Wykes, 1981, 1983; Brener, 1983.) How do young children manage to grasp the notion that the referents change when another speaker 'takes the floor'?

With a proper name like *Fred* or a noun like *chair*, the referent can remain the same no matter which speaker uses the term. A child could simply imitate the adult's word and associate it with the person or object. But, if a child imitated the adult's *I* and *you*, she would use *I* to refer to the adult and *you* to refer to herself. In fact, some autistic children do misuse the terms in this way: Roger Brown (in Brown and Herrnstein, 1975, pp. 444–7) cites the case of 'John', a 10-year-old autistic boy; and Macnamara (1982), the case of Ken, a 4-year-old. Failure to use pronouns correctly is one of the language disorders taken into account when diagnosing autism (Kanner, 1949; Rutter, Greenfield and Lockyer, 1968; Ricks and Wing, 1975). But it is not only in these abnormal cases that pronouns are misused. Although most normal children have learned the adult use by age 2 or 2½ years there are a number of cases in the literature of children with otherwise normal linguistic development who do make errors; Cooley (1908) gave examples from one child and, more recently, Chiat (1981, 1982) has presented data from some 2-year-old children. An important point about normal children is that the terms are not consistently misused: correct use and errors co-exist. Furthermore, correct adult use eventually takes over.

Let us look first of all at the developmental pattern of what is acquired in normal children before we consider how the child might alight on the correct hypothesis that *I* and *you* depend on the shifting roles of speaker and addressee.

At first, parents tend to use proper names (*Mummy, Baby*, etc.) to refer to themselves and to the child; they may use pronouns in conjunction with these and they *may* also indicate the referent by gesture, such as pointing, although gesturing is not very common when only two people are involved (see discussion by Wales, 1979, pp. 253–5, of data from Cross). Children at first use proper names to refer to themselves and to others (e.g. *Amy do it, Mummy cake gone*).

Strayer (1977) video-taped four parent–child pairs for half an hour every two weeks from the child's age of 22 months up to age 32 months. Initially, the children responded correctly to commands which included a proper name (the parent's or the child's) over 80 per cent of the time. Parents used commands involving *you* over six times more frequently than those involving *me*, and, in the early recordings, the children responded appropriately to about 40 per cent and 10 per cent of these respectively. At the end of the study, appropriate responses rose to over 80 per cent for both types of utterance. Both Strayer (1977) and de Villiers and de Villiers (1974) have given comprehension tests involving first- and second-person pronouns. Both found that children performed better with *your*-type commands (e.g. 'Point to your head') than with *my*-type commands (e.g. 'Point to my head'). When we look at the child's *use* of these pronouns, the first-person pronouns (*I, my, me*) are used earlier and more frequently than second-person pronouns (*you, your*) (McNeill, 1963; Huxley, 1970; de Villiers and de Villiers, 1974; Strayer, 1977; Wales, 1979; Macnamara, 1982). Strayer found that very few errors were made in her study. What seems to be happening, then, is that a child first *understands* the pronouns used by others which refer to herself (*you, yourself*, etc.); later she understands the pronouns used by others to refer to themselves (*I, me*, etc.). When the child comes to *use* pronouns herself, it is those which refer to herself (*I, me, my*)[1] which she uses first, and then later those which refer to others (*you, your*, etc.); in the meantime, she uses proper names to refer to other people.

Well, how do children come to learn the correct use? If the child only ever interacted with one adult and did not witness conversations between the adult and another person, she would have no way of discovering that *I* and *you* were not 'tied' to a particular person as are proper names. The parent would always use *I* to refer to herself and *you* to refer to the child. So it is highly likely that the child would misuse the terms when she did start to speak. No doubt the parent would then point out the error and take steps to correct her. Of course children are not normally brought up in this restricted way; other people (another parent, grandparents, siblings, friends, etc.) also interact with the child *and* with each other. Perhaps it is in this way that the child discovers it is not only herself who is called *you*; others can be called *you* as well. (It is reasonable to suppose, however, that the child may at first believe that *you* refers only to herself, and may not attend to the fact that it is used to refer to other people too.) *You* can be anyone, including the child herself, when she is the recipient of a message. When people speak to the child or to each other they call themselves *I*; so *I* can be used by anyone who is speaking. Thus the child can learn that *I* and *you* are not associated with a particular person, but they shift according to the role a person occupies. Because the young child hears people referring to each other as *you* and to herself as *you* she has a very direct way of knowing that she can be included in the 'recipient' category. It may be that she responds appropriately to *you* commands before *I/me* commands because, in speech directed towards the child, *you* refers to herself, a single referent, whereas *I* may be used by different speakers, and therefore has multiple referents. However, it could be a result of the frequency with which the terms are used; Strayer found that considerably more *you* commands were used by parents.

Interestingly, the child has never heard herself referred to as *I*, so she does not have a direct means of learning that she can be included in the speaker category. Yet she does include herself in this category and uses the first-person form. Not only that, but she acquires this form before the use of *you* to refer to addressees. The earlier acquisition of the *I/me* form is clearly not directly related to adult frequency since adults use far more *you* forms to children. The reason would seem to be that when the child uses *I*, she is the only referent; many people can be addressed by the child as *you*, so this second-person pronoun has multiple referents. My explanation, then, for the child's understanding of *you* before *I/me* but use of *I/me* before *you* is in terms of the restricted set of possible referents. In speech directed at her, the child herself is the only referent for *you*, but many speakers will call themselves *I/me*. When the child herself speaks, she is the single referent for *I/me*, but many people could be called *you*. The tasks in which the set of referents is limited should be easier to master.

There is a problem, however, which may complicate the conclusions regarding children's understanding and use of *I* and *you*. And that is, that most studies have looked at the child's interaction with her mother. It may be that children are reluctant for some reason to use a pronoun (*you*) to refer to their mothers, preferring to use a proper name, whereas they may use one to refer to another person. Charney (1980) has certainly found that children were reluctant to call their mothers *her* when speaking with a third person; they preferred to use the proper name *Mummy*. This raises the problem more generally of children's production data. Production data show what children *do* say, but not necessarily what they *can* say. There may be good reasons why children do not use a particular word or construction in a particular context, other than that they do not understand its use.

I have presented the child's acquisition of *I* and *you*, and particularly of *I*, as an enormous achievement against daunting odds. It could be, however, that the child has already built up a framework for identifying persons and that the pronouns map on to it in a fairly straightforward manner. As I noted earlier, children generally use proper names to refer to themselves and to others before they use the appropriate pronouns. Furthermore, parents also use proper names frequently when speaking with very young children, and may also use gesture, particularly pointing. Durkin, Rutter and Tucker (1982) and Durkin, Rutter, Room and Grounds (1982) have suggested that proper names may be used to facilitate communication in the context of an instruction to act or an attention-orienting utterance. Now it could also be that these devices in some way make the child's induction into the appropriate use of personal pronouns easier. But, although a number of authors have noted the developmental shift from a frequent use of proper names to a greater use of pronouns, I have not seen an account of precisely how such a process might work.

Place deixis

Here and there
In Chapter 1, I discussed ways in which the child may focus on the object of another's attention by tracking the direction of gaze, body orientation and pointing. Deictic terms such as *here* and *there* are just two of a number of linguistic terms used to specify location. Of course, it is a big leap from being able to follow a line of gaze to being able to interpret and to use the conventions of language.

Whereas *I* and *you* refer to the speaker and the addressee respectively, *here* and *there* are not necessarily related to a place near the speaker and a place near the addressee; rather, they refer to a place near and a place farther from the *speaker*. *I* and *you*, then, are mutually exclusive (except in cases where *you* is used in the sense of *one*). In contrast, although *here* refers to a place near the speaker it may also include the addressee's position; similarly, *there* may be a place far from both of them. It would seem to depend on the positioning of the two participants in relation to the places being contrasted; thus, participants at opposite ends of a particular distance will be distinguished as being *here* and *there*, whereas those in relative proximity will be described as being *here* and the place farther away from both of them will be described as *there*. Another problem with *here* and *there* is that, unlike *I* and *you*, there is no clear boundary between them; it is difficult to say when *here* becomes *there*! Furthermore, whereas *I* and *you* are primarily deictic terms and do not have other uses (except, as given above, when *you* means *one*), *here* and *there* may be used in deictic and nondeictic ways. *There*, in particular, may be used in utterances like 'There are three books on the desk.'

Bearing in mind these problems, it would not be at all surprising if young children did not grasp the deictic meaning of *here* and *there* until much later than they grasp *I* and *you*. Two main principles in fact have to be grasped: the speaker is the point of reference, and the terms contrast a place near to and a place far from that point.

If we look at the frequency with which children hear the terms *here* and *there* (see Wales, 1979, p. 243, for summary of data from Cross), *there* is used by adults almost three times as frequently as *here* in their speech to children. If frequency alone were an important predictor, obviously *there* should have special status. But, as we saw with *I* and *you*, frequency was not a useful predictor at all. In fact, with *here* and *there* Clark and Sengul (1978) make the opposite prediction. They point out that *here* refers to the speaker's place, and may or may not include the addressee's place, but *there* can refer to many places distant from the speaker. Thus, *there* shifts reference more than *here*. It is likely, then, that when children start to use these terms they will use *here* correctly rather than *there*. In fact both terms appear very early in children's speech but they are used in rather different ways. It is indeed *here* which is used to draw attention to a location; *there* may be used to indicate that an action has been completed (Griffiths, 1974; Carter, 1975). Nevertheless, children do contrast locations, but they do so by using gesture, usually a point, along with the linguistic term *here*; thus, they say *here* and point to a near location, and they also say *here* and point to a location farther away. Adults also very often use gesture as an accompaniment to their deictic term (see Wales,

Speaker 2

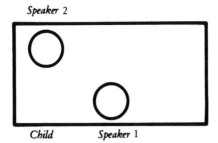

Child   Speaker 1

Figure 7.2: The experimental layout used by Clark and Sengul (1978, Figure 1, p. 465). The speaker sat either at the same side of the table as the child (Speaker 1) or on the opposite side (Speaker 2). (Reprinted with the permission of the publisher.)

1979, p. 254, for data tabulated from Cross). Whereas *I* and *you* are used correctly by age 2 or 2½ years, this is not the case with *here* and *there*; in Clark and Sengul's study (to be discussed later) the correct contrastive use was still not achieved at age 4.

Because of the difficulties of assessing the *contrast* of *here* and *there* in production data, Clark and Sengul (1978) argue that we must look at comprehension studies to find out when and how children work out the contrast. In their task the child sat at a table on which were placed two discs – one opposite her and one to the side. The speaker sat near one or another of the discs (see Figure 7.2).

Matching pairs of toy animals were placed on the discs and the child was given instructions like, 'Make the dog over here/there turn around.' When the speaker sat beside the child the *here* instructions were responded to correctly more than were the *there* instructions; the converse was true when the speaker sat opposite the child. The youngest children (average age 3 years 3 months) did not contrast the terms: most of them picked up the animal on their own side of the table regardless of instruction and speaker position; a small group choose the animal near the speaker. Clark and Sengul referred to these groups as 'child-centred' and 'speaker-centred' respectively. Slightly older children (average age 3 years 10 months) showed a partial contrast: some were correct on both terms when the speaker was beside them but were wholly or partially incorrect when the speaker was opposite them; others were correct with the speaker opposite but wrong with her beside them. Again these two groups could be

Speaker 1

Child

Speaker 2

Figure 7.3: The child is equidistant from each speaker.

described as child- or speaker-centred respectively. Eight months later some of the children were retested and it was found that those who had been child-centred at the no contrast stage were also child-centred at the partial contrast stage; similarly, speaker-centred no contrast children had become speaker-centred partial contrast children. The oldest children, between 4 and 5 years, and a group of adults used the terms in the correct contrastive way and used the speaker as the point of reference.

Other studies which add support to Clark and Sengul's findings are de Villiers and de Villiers (1974), Wales (1979), Tanz (1980) and Tfouni and Klatzky (1983). The de Villiers study and that of Tfouni and Klatzky found that, in a comprehension task in which the experimenter sat opposite the child, *there* was understood correctly more often than *here*. The study by Wales was very extensive and included a number of further conditions. Generally, the three main stages found by Clark and Sengul were supported, although the partial contrast stage was less clear-cut. Wales, Tanz, and Tfouni and Klatzky included a 'neutral' condition in which two speakers were contrasted and the child sat to the side (see Figure 7.3).

Thus, the speakers were equidistant from the child, the advantage

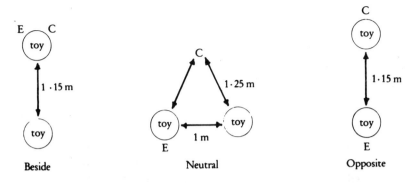

Figure 7.4: The three conditions used by Charney (1979, Figure 1, p. 72) in her study of *here* and *there*. (Reprinted with the permission of the publisher.)

being that the child could not simply select the location near herself. Both Wales and Tanz again found more correct responses to *here* than *there*, but Tfouni and Klatzky found the opposite.

One study with completely contradictory findings is that of Charney (1979): she found more correct responses of *there* in the beside condition, *here* in the opposite condition, and *there* in the neutral condition (see Figure 7.4).

Charney argues that the instructions given to the child in previous studies have been too complex (e.g. 'Make the horse over here/there jump up and down') in that the child must work out not only which object should be selected but also what action should be performed. If the child has a limited processing capacity, she may use most of it on deciding which action to perform and may then fall back on a near-self location. Charney claims that her instructions ('Which one is over here/there?') circumvent this problem and allow the child to concentrate on location. Clearly, it is most important that this issue be sorted out. In the meantime, we can only sum up the predominant pattern which has emerged so far.

As with the terms *I* and *you*, children are most likely to select the most stable referent to work on first. The most stable referent is the child herself, so in comprehension tasks most very young children select a place near themselves. A smaller but substantial group of children however select a place near the speaker in comprehension tasks. The first, child-centred, group must learn not only to contrast the terms along a distance dimension but also that the terms are related to the *speaker's* point of view. Perhaps the speaker-centred children can be regarded as more advanced since they already have the 'speaker principle'; they need only to acquire the 'distance principle'. One might predict that the speaker-centred children would achieve full contrast before the child-centred children.

I have already pointed out that *I* and *you* are mutually exclusive in referring respectively to speaker and addressee; they are also discrete in that a clear boundary exists between who is speaker and who is not. *Here* and *there* are used with reference to the speaker's position, but the boundary between *here* and *there* is not so definite as that between *I* and *you*. Furthermore, both terms may be used non-deictically as well as deictically. It is not surprising to find that correct use of *here* and *there* is achieved later than *I* and *you*. But there is a problem with this conclusion. When *I* and *you* are normally used, they are not backed up to any great extent by gesture; in contrast, gesture is extremely important in the use of *here* and *there*. Studies, such as that of Clark and Sengul, which have omitted gesture (for the very sound reason that they wish to study the child's understanding of the *linguistic* terms) may grossly underestimate the child's abilities in normal interaction. Naturalistic studies may well reveal that children do not normally find *here* and *there* as confusing as the experimental studies suggest. In fact Tfouni and Klatzky (1983) found that their 3½-year-olds achieved near-perfect performance when the experimenter used a pointing gesture along with the deictic term.

In front of and behind

In front of and *behind* are mutually exclusive in that what is in front of a reference point cannot also be behind it. However, when the terms are used deictically the point of view to which they relate is not so clear. Whereas *here* and *there* are related to the speaker's viewpoint, *in front* and *behind* may be related to the speaker's viewpoint, to the addressee's viewpoint, or to some other perspective. Indeed when these terms are used deictically, the speaker may need to indicate whose viewpoint is being adopted in order to avoid ambiguity, e.g. 'It's behind *you*' or 'It's behind the tree from where *you* are looking'. Despite the potential problems, the recipient of instructions containing these terms generally adopts her own perspective. Lynn Taylor and I compared a condition in which the experimenter sat beside the subject and shared her perspective, with one in which the experimenter sat opposite the subject. A fence stretched across the table. The subject was given a small brick and was told, 'Put the brick in front of (behind) the fence'. Overwhelmingly, most subjects, aged 4 to 9 years and a group of adults, related the terms to their own viewpoint: *in front of* meant 'near themselves' and *behind* meant 'away from themselves'. De Villiers and de Villiers (1974), in a *production* task, also compared conditions in which the experimenter (recipient of message) sat beside or opposite the child. This time, the child told the *experimenter* where to place the object. The children used the terms in relation to the experimenter's viewpoint. Thus, it is the recipient's perspective, not the speaker's, to which these terms relate.

We might expect that *in front of* and *behind* would be used first in a nondeictic way, since the terms can be *tied* to a particular feature of an object and do not shift when different speakers take the floor. Thus, 'in front of' or 'behind the doll' refers to a particular location near the doll's face or back, respectively. Indeed, Tanz (1980), in her study of 3- to 5-year-olds' comprehension, found that the nondeictic system precedes the deictic one.

When featured objects are used, since both deictic and nondeictic interpretations of the terms are possible, there is potential ambiguity. These coincide when, for instance, a doll faces the observer, but conflict when it faces away (see Figure 7.5). When there is no gesture to clarify the terms, most people normally assume the nondeictic rather than the deictic sense. This is particularly true of children (Tanz, 1980; Cox, 1981a), but a minority of adults do take the deictic option (Cox, 1981a).

Since children, at least by the age of 7 years, can respond deictically in tasks involving non-featured objects (Kuczaj and Maratsos, 1975; Cox, 1979, 1981b; Tanz, 1980), I wondered if I could also get them to respond deictically in a featured-object task. I tried to find out if they are actually aware of the possible deictic interpretation of terms like *in front of* and *behind* even when the nondeictic interpretation may be very dominant.

Two experiments involved a treasure hunt game (Cox, 1985b). In the first one, a rectangular clock tower stood in the middle and on top of a closed, shallow box; there were four trapdoors in the box, one near each side of the clock tower (see Figure 7.6). The clock tower could face towards, away from, to the right or to the left of the child. The child was told that some treasure was hidden beneath one of the trapdoors and that a clue had been left as to its whereabouts. For each

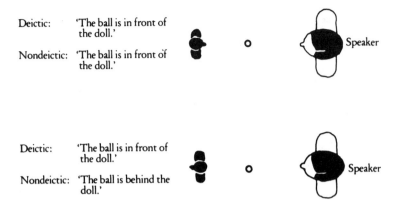

Deictic: 'The ball is in front of the doll.'

Nondeictic: 'The ball is in front of the doll.'

Deictic: 'The ball is in front of the doll.'

Nondeictic: 'The ball is behind the doll.'

Speaker

Speaker

Figure 7.5: Deictic and nondeictic interpretations coincide when a doll faces the speaker, but conflict when it faces away.

orientation of the clock, the clue was 'The treasure is *in front of/ behind* the clock'. As had been found previously, most subjects interpreted the terms in a nondeictic way: *in front of* meant 'near the clock face' and *behind* meant 'near the back of the clock', regardless of its orientation. Subjects were asked to make a second guess as to where the treasure might be hidden. Whereas 4- to 8-year-olds responded randomly on their second guess, the 10-year-olds and adults tended to repeat their first response. So there was no evidence of an understanding of the deictic interpretation of the terms, even among adults. In fact, many subjects stated verbally that no other location was possible.

In the second experiment a similar procedure was followed and the subjects were rewarded by consistently finding the treasure in the location compatible with the nondeictic interpretation of the terms. But then the location of the treasure was changed so that only a deictic search strategy would be successful. The speed with which the subjects switched strategy (measured by the number of trials to criterion) increased with age: most adults were successful but many of the 4-year-olds continued to use a nondeictic strategy and did not find the treasure even after twenty trials.

It seems very difficult, then, for young children to appreciate that the terms *in front of* and *behind*, when referring to featured objects, *could* have a deictic meaning, and indeed most adults do not normally interpret the terms in this way either. But this may be true only in

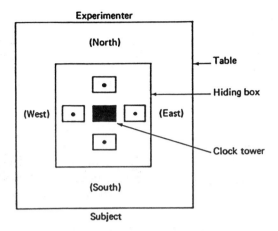

Figure 7.6: The arrangement of materials in the treasure hunt game (Cox, 1985b). (Reprinted with the permission of the publisher.)

certain kinds of tasks. Although both the deictic and nondeictic options were available in the treasure hunt game, the choice may not have been equal. The featured clock tower may have given an overwhelming cue that a nondeictic interpretation was appropriate; the mere presence of observers (the experimenter and the subject) may not have been sufficient to make a deictic interpretation of the terms equally likely.

Sarah Isard and I decided to design some tasks in which the options could be made equal or even biased towards the deictic rather than the nondeictic interpretation (Cox and Isard, 1990). Five- to 6-year-olds and 9- to 10-year-olds were invited to position a little man *in front of* or *behind* a toy car which pointed either away from them or to the right. When the observer's viewpoint was not emphasized and the children were simply asked to 'Put the man *in front of/behind* the car', both age groups responded in the predicted nondeictic way, placing the man near the front or back of the car regardless of its orientation. So far, these findings supported those of previous studies.

The next step was to emphasize the observer's viewpoint by saying, 'Let me see the man standing *in front of* the car' and 'Hide the man *behind* the car'. Although we had expected that this emphasis on viewpoint would prompt a change of response, the children still responded in a nondeictic way. We then tried a more richly contextualized task, recasting the instructions into a game format: the children pretended to take a photograph of the man *in front of* the car and also hid him *behind* the car in a game of hide and seek. This time their responses were split: half the children in both age groups opted for the deictic and half for the nondeictic interpretation. So, even in a task in which the observer's viewpoint is made highly salient, the nondeictic response has not been overridden.

Finally, we tried the game format again but this time took out the spatial terms themselves, so that the children were asked where the man should stand in order to have his photograph taken and where he should go in order to hide. It was only under these conditions that most of the children responded in a deictic way. So, although children can respond deictically, when nonfeatured objects are used or when the spatial terms are omitted from a featured-objects task, the terms *in front of* and *behind* in conjunction with featured objects seem to have a very powerful effect – namely, that children respond in a nondeictic manner.

What must the child learn about the deictic meaning of the terms *in front of* and *behind*? That they are mutually exclusive and refer to the opposite sides of a referent object, that they lie along the horizontal-frontal axis emanating from the observer, and that *in front of* refers to the observer's side whereas *behind* refers to the far side of the object. (It should be pointed out that although this is true for most cultures, Hill (1978) has found that the Hausa-speakers of Nigeria operate rather differently: *in front of* refers to the far side of the object and *behind* refers to the near side from the observer's viewpoint.) As with the other terms discussed above, we may predict that young children will not fully contrast the two terms and use them as mutually exclusive and opposite to one another; they may not alight on the correct axis, nor indeed on the intended observer.

When asked to place a ball *in front of* or *behind* another 'referent' ball, children below about age 4 years do not restrict themselves to the horizontal-frontal axis: they may also place their ball to the left or right sides, or above or below the referent. But by about age 4 or 5, they do restrict their placements to this axis (Cox, 1979, 1981a and b).

Do children contrast the two terms correctly? If we refer to the discussions of *I* and *you* and *here* and *there* above, we might again suppose that the child would use herself as the main reference: she should have a bias towards locations near herself (in front) rather than farther away (behind). Thus, errors should occur more with *behind* and this term may be interpreted by the child as if it meant *in front*. This is the prediction of various researchers (e.g. H. Clark, E. Clark, and Osgood) whose positions are detailed and reviewed by Tanz (1980). Interestingly, the evidence does not support the prediction: *behind* (or *in back of*) is generally used and interpreted correctly before *in front of* (Museyibova, 1961; Kuczaj and Maratsos, 1975; Piérart, 1977; Washington and Naremore, 1978; Cox, 1979; Harris and Strommen, 1979; Tanz, 1980).

How do we explain this very surprising result? It was argued above that children first deal with terms which have more stable referents. Thus, the child first understands *you* (rather than *I/me*) when used by others and uses *I/me* correctly (rather than *you*) because the referent, i.e. the child herself, does not shift. Now when we come to the deictic terms *in front of* and *behind*, in a comprehension task these refer to the child's own perspective and they each have fixed referents; one does not shift more than the other. So the acquisition of *behind* before *in front of* can have nothing to do with the extent of shifting reference. What it may have to do with is the way it is highlighted in communication. Both adults and children use the terms *behind* or *back* more frequently than *in front of* (Rinsland, 1945; Lorge, 1949; Jones and Wepman, 1966; Bloom, 1973; Wells, 1975) and this may be because, as a number of writers (e.g. Johnston and Slobin, 1979; Leehey and Carey, 1978; Harris and Strommen, 1979; Tanz, 1980; Abkarian, 1983) have suggested, there is more need to tell someone that an object is behind and perhaps hidden by another than there is to say that an object is in front of another and in full view. If an object is in front of something else and one person asks 'Where is it?', the other person may reasonably look and point and say 'There'. It is not necessary to relate the object to another in the environment. On the other hand, if the object is behind another and cannot efficiently be indicated by gesture, it will be more informative if it is related to another landmark by linguistic means – 'It's behind *x*'. Thus, the child learns that *behind* generally relates one object to another, but she may not realize that *in front of* can also serve a similar function. It is not until the age of about 6 years, according to my data (Cox, 1979, 1981a and b), that the locative meanings of both *in front of* or *behind* are mastered.

Most of the experimental work on *in front of* and *behind* has concentrated on the child's comprehension of these terms when used by the adult experimenter. Jane Ryder Richardson and I (Cox and

Ryder Richardson, 1985) were interested in how children themselves, aged between 3 and 10 years, would describe the spatial relationship between two objects. We placed two differently-coloured balls, one in front of other, before the child and asked her to describe this arrangement so that a friend, sitting beside her but separated by a screen, could arrange her two identical balls in the same way. We found that the 3-year-olds and, to a large extent, the 4-year-olds gave insufficient information, simply saying, 'It's here' or 'That one's there'. The 5-year-olds, however, had begun to use spatial terms such as *at the front/back* or environmental landmarks, e.g. 'The red ball is towards the window'. By the age of 6, spatial terms predominated although a substantial minority of children up to the age of 10 used environmental terms or a combination of spatial and environmental terms. We found that an adult group used exclusively spatial terms and that the term *behind*, as opposed to *at the back*, was particularly an adult term.

In this study the subject's orientation to her task materials was the same as that of her friend; thus, a correct description of her own view would also be sufficient to allow her friend to reproduce the same spatial arrangement of objects. As far as I am aware, the only study which has asked children to produce a spatial description when the child's view and the other observer's view conflict is that of de Villiers and de Villiers (1974). Unfortunately, it is difficult to make sense of their findings as the tabulated data for the same *vs.* different perspective conditions conflict with the graphs drawn from the same data. One would predict, however, that giving a description about another's perspective when that perspective differs from one's own would be more difficult than simply describing one's own view. As yet, we do not have systematic comparisons between comprehension and description tasks involving featured- and non-featured objects and when the child either does or does not share the same view as the other observer.

Summary

The importance of studying the child's acquisition of deictic terms is that these provide an opportunity to tap the child's understanding of the changing roles of conversational participants and the shifting referents to which the terms relate. It is clear that children do not learn these terms by a simple association between a word and an object, nor are they influenced directly by the frequency with which they hear the terms in the adult speech around them. But, by the age of about 2 or 2½ years they have mastered the use of *I/me* and *you* to refer to the speaker and addressee, respectively, and have done so with minimal error; other terms, such as the locative contrasts *here* and *there* and *in front of* and *behind* are worked out later.

The evidence in this chapter, although far from complete, shows that the child first relates deictic terms to her own position. Some researchers have assumed that this 'self-centred' beginning necessarily implies that the child is egocentric. However, as I argued in Chapter 1 with regard to the young child's use of her own position in space, taking herself as a reference point does not necessarily imply that she is egocentric, in the sense that she is 'locked in' and unaware of others; it is simply a useful and stable reference point to adopt. After all, the child has to start *somewhere*, and self, being stable, seems a sensible choice. The point is that in order to use the terms correctly to refer to *herself*, the child must have first understood how they are used by other people; she *then* has to reverse the roles and apply them to herself. As Tanz (1980, p. 162) puts it, the child 'cannot have grasped this egocentric formula without having understood at some level that other speakers organize the system with themselves at centre. Thus, any child who has mastered the shifter properties of *I* and *you* or *me* and *you* in ordinary conversation has achieved some degree of decentering'.

Note

1. I have also noticed, and Maratsos (1979, p. 233) makes the point too, that children often use the accusative form *me* instead of the nominative *I*.

Conclusion to Part III

We already know from Chapter 1 that very young babies and their parents engage in 'dialogues'. Their turn-taking games may simply entail looking at the other person and then looking away. Babies can also follow a parent's line of gaze and discover what she is attending to; of course the parent may use a 'package' of cues such as gaze, pointing, shaking the object, as well as a verbalization to attract the baby's attention. Two very important features of a conversation, then – turn-taking and co-attending to the same subject-matter – are well-established long before the child actually begins to talk. And, indeed, as Bruner (1983, p. 122) points out, 'it is highly doubtful that children could learn language . . . were they either irreversibly or implacably egocentric'.

I wanted to see how the child might learn to be a participant in a conversation and examined the notion that adults' baby-talk might be an important factor in facilitating children's language development. It is interesting that adults generally do not correct children's errors in an overt and explicit way. Nevertheless, it seems that adults do give corrective feedback, but in a more subtle and implicit way, by modelling the correct form in their replies to the sense of the child's utterance. Whether or not the child makes use of this feedback remains to be demonstrated. Adults' use of baby-talk seems better explained as a way of *communicating* with their cognitively and linguistically immature children, rather than a means of teaching them grammar. But, in communicating messages to the children, baby-talk may also facilitate the child's role as a conversational participant. Thus, the adults' recasts and expansions of the children's own utterances may continue and develop a topic, and parents' frequent 'tag' questions may be designed to cue the child that it is her turn to contribute. So baby-talk, as well as being a response to a cognitively and linguistically immature listener, may also teach the child how to be an effective communicator herself.

I then considered how children themselves might speak to listeners of different ages. The evidence suggests that children are engaged in different activities with listeners of different ages. Whereas their interaction with parents is more participative, with babies they are concerned to show them things, tell them things, and to prohibit and restrict them. In doing so, different features of language are used: longer and more complex utterances are addressed to parents; shorter, and simpler utterances are addressed to babies. In addition, more proper names are used with babies than with adults, and the talk is delivered at a higher pitch. These activity differences in themselves show that children treat the two age groups differently. There is some further evidence that children can adjust their speech to different age groups even when engaged in the *same* kind of activity. Although the younger children are limited to the adoption of different pitches when addressing listeners of varying ages, those from about 5 years of age can make syntactic changes also.

In their verbal interactions with those around them children develop procedures for making inferences concerning the points of view of others. The 2-year-olds studied by Keenan and Klein distinguished whether or not their listeners were attending to them, and if they were not they did not elaborate their topic and often used repetition to persist with their original proposal. Only when this received some form of acknowledgement by the listener, such as repetition of what was first said, would they continue. Such interpretative skills, however, are not just confined to the beginning of interaction sequences. They are integral to children's mastery of the deictic terms, and they become especially apparent in cases where the child is involved in some form of communication difficulty. By the age of 4, children have a variety of techniques available to them when a question is not answered by a parent, some of which treat the parent as not having heard the original question, others treating the parent as having heard but choosing not to respond. Wootton has noted how children's positioning of address terms in their follow-up turn parallels these two possibilities, the address term at the beginning of the turn functioning as an attention-getter, at the end of the turn as a solicit device.

Cases where the child's respondent resorts to clarification requests constitute another form of communication difficulty. Here, children are frequently confronted with questions like, 'What?' or 'Pardon?', which locate either part or all of what the child has said as problematic. Children not only recognize this, but through their replies can indicate their analysis of the problem that their recipient is having. In some cases they may simply repeat their original utterance, and in other cases correct it or elaborate it in some way; in certain types of sequence they may simply say 'Please', indicating that they have interpreted the adult's utterance as a politeness request. In spite of the fact that in a small set of cases there is evidence of misinterpretation of the clarification request by the child, in many cases there is every indication that children accurately identify the type of problem the parent is having.

The different points of view of speaker and listener are marked in all languages by deictic terms, *I* and *you*, *here* and *there*, and so on. The referents of these terms change as different people take on the roles of speaker and listener. A competent use and understanding of the terms, then, indicates an understanding of the shifting roles of conversational participants.

A general finding which emerges from the studies of deictic terms, discussed in Chapter 7, is that children seem to work out the meaning of the terms with reference to themselves first. Thus they respond to sentences referring to themselves (*you*) earlier than those referring to the adult speaker (*I/me*). It seems as if the child uses herself as a starting point, and this notion also emerged in Part I in the discussion of children's understanding of others' visual percepts. I suggested there that the child's use of self as a reference point should not necessarily be interpreted in an egocentric way, but as a useful strategy for working out what other people are referring to, either verbally or visually.

When the child begins to *use* pronouns rather than proper names in her own speech, she uses those terms which refer to herself (*I/me*) earlier than those which refer to her addressee (*you*); meanwhile, she continues to address listeners with proper names. Nevertheless, in using *I* and *me* appropriately, she must already have understood how others use the terms with reference to themselves; when she herself became a speaker, she must then have applied the pronouns to her own point of view. So, again, the child seems to use self as a starting point, but this does not necessarily imply a lack of understanding of others.

Not only are the roles of speaker and listener marked in conversation, so also are the locations which they occupy or want to refer to. Thus, a speaker may refer to the place that she occupies as *here* and contrast it with a place farther away, *there*. A speaker can also relate one object to another from another's point of view: for example, she may describe one object as being *in front of* or *behind* another from the observer's viewpoint. Generally, the research studies show that children comprehend the meaning of *there*, when used by other people, before the meaning of *here*. This pattern also fits in with the development of personal pronouns: the term which refers to the *child's* position is understood first. The acquisition of *in front of* and *behind*, however, do not seem to fit in with this self-reference pattern. *Behind* is used and understood earlier than *in front of*. The reason is probably because *behind*, rather than *in front of*, conveys more information about the location of hidden objects.

Whereas personal pronouns generally have only deictic meanings, locative terms can also have nondeictic as well as deictic meanings. This potential ambiguity of meaning may lead to some difficulty in young children's understanding of their use. However, in practice, children and adults may use non-verbal gestures, such as gaze and pointing, to help clarify their meaning. Nevertheless, it seems that the nondeictic use may be understood before the deictic use. This is not surprising since the introduction of a shifting point of view must surely make the deictic use more complex. The nondeictic use is related to a feature in the environment which remains the same for all observers. Thus, 'in front of the house' means near the 'front' door regardless of which direction the observer approaches the house. The nondeictic use rests on a stable referent and, in this respect, is less complex than the deictic.

PART IV What's on your Mind?

In this last section of the book I shall consider what children understand about the more covert and mentalistic aspects of other people – that is, what is going on in their minds. To a greater or lesser extent we all appreciate that, like ourselves, other people have thoughts, desires and intentions and are also capable of feeling a range of different emotions. Often we can see the outward signs of what others are experiencing but we also make inferences and assumptions even when no such signs are present and can predict reasonably accurately what others will think and feel should certain circumstances arise. We have what many writers have termed a *theory of mind*. How does such knowledge come about? And do young children also have a theory of mind?

Piaget believed that the very young baby cannot distinguish between the 'self' and the 'other' and that the notion of the independent existence of oneself and one's own actions in a world of other independent objects (including people) takes a considerable time to develop. Later, when the young child becomes aware of the world of thoughts, intentions and desires, she cannot distinguish between those belonging to herself and those belonging to others. For Piaget such behaviour is indicative of the child's basic egocentrism.

As we have seen in earlier chapters, although young children are not as competent as older children and adults, they are in fact more capable than Piaget supposed. Yet, we still need to find out whether they can distinguish between things which are real and those which are only imagined, whether they understand that other people have thoughts and feelings, whether or not their understanding is basically the same if less sophisticated than older children's and adults', and how their understanding comes about and develops. The research effort in this area has flourished since the early 1980s, but there is as yet no clear consensus on these issues and this is one of the reasons why this topic is both exciting but often difficult to grasp.

Although there are of course many different mental states, the research to date has investigated very few of them. For this reason my review will be very selective. In Chapter 8 I shall concentrate almost exclusively on the child's understanding of the *belief* state of herself or of other people – that is, what she thinks people believe about a given situation – and on her assumption that people will act on those beliefs rather than on the objective facts. In Chapter 9 I shall go on to discuss the child's understanding of *emotional* states, her understanding of how people with different beliefs and desires will feel in particular circumstances and how the child comes to realize that, potentially, one's feelings are private but that one can attempt to mislead others by effecting a particular public display.

It turns out that even very young children behave as if they have considerable understanding of what goes on in people's minds. But, as we have seen in earlier chapters, these children still have a long way to go before they achieve an adult 'theory of mind'.

8 I know what you're thinking

In the first year of life the infant's knowledge of the world depends to a very great extent on her direct perception of it. We can think of the input from direct perception as forming a mental model of the real situation – Perner (1988) calls this a *knowledge base* but Leslie (1988) calls it a *primary representation*. The infant, according to Perner (1990), is capable of updating this *single model* as new information about a changing situation is perceived; but since she is capable of generating only one model, she cannot compare her present situation with how it was in the past nor how it might be in the future. If the infant is to progress beyond this immediate reality she must develop some mechanism whereby elements from her knowledge base can be put into different models and can be rearranged in different ways. Only when she can generate and compare these *multiple models* can she consider what is the case now compared with what used to be the case or what is the case now and what might be the case in the future. In fact, beginning in their second year, young children *can* represent alternative states – when they pretend, for example, that an object or an action is something other than it appears.

Pretense

The research studies reviewed by Fein (1981) support a claim made by Piaget (1962) that the incidence of pretend play rises and then falls again between the ages of 1 to 6 years. The child's earliest pretend gestures, appearing at about 12 or 13 months, are directed towards herself rather than to others. So, for example, she may pretend to feed herself. Over the next year or 18 months these self-referenced behaviours decline and other-referenced behaviours increase. At first, the child is the active agent in the pretense and treats the other (often

Figure 8.1: A 22-month-old girl pretends to feed her teddy bear. (Photograph by Ida Neal.)

a doll) as a passive partner (see Figure 8.1). Increasingly, however, the child is able to treat the doll as if it were acting on its own behalf. This ability to use dolls to represent more complex roles continues to develop from age 2 to 6 or 7 years.

Between the ages of about 19 to 24 months the child increasingly uses one object to substitute for another. A banana may usefully serve as a pretend telephone; while holding one end to her ear, the child speaks into the other end. She knows that the object *is* a banana and yet at the same time can behave towards it as if it were a telephone. This dependence on the actual presence of a substitute object eventually declines and by the age of 4 years half of the child's pretend episodes do not depend on the immediate presence of a physical object.

At the age of about 3 years, children engage much more in *social* pretend play involving pretend scenarios with peers or adults, although it is not clear whether this increase is accompanied by a decrease in solitary pretense. Also at this age children begin to *communicate* about their pretense. Thus, Garvey and Berndt (1977) reported that all their 3- to 5-year-old dyads commented on their pretend roles. Although the children's comments on their own pretend roles were the most prevalent, the most striking shift with age was the increase in comments about joint- or partner-activities, e.g. 'Are you going to be the bride?' and 'Pretend you hate fish'.

Children's pretense, then, is one example of their ability to generate and compare multiple models. Another example is their ability to distinguish between their apprehension of a real object *vs.* their thought about the object, to be discussed in the next section.

The real and the imagined

Most of us have no problems at all in distinguishing between those objects which are real, in the sense that we can see them or touch them, and those which are figments of our imagination, thoughts or dreams. In considering whether a chair, for example, is a real object or an imagined one we may refer to at least three criteria (Wellman, 1988). First of all, we have direct behavioural-sensory evidence of the real object – we can see it, touch it, sit on it, etc. – but not of the imagined chair. Secondly, the real chair is public in the sense that other people can also see it, touch it and sit on it whereas the imagined chair is not. Thirdly, under normal circumstances the real chair will continue to exist over time whereas the idea of a chair will not be so consistent.

In order to assess children's ability to distinguish between the real and the imagined, Wellman and Estes (1986) presented young children with two contrasting characters, a boy who had a cookie *vs.* a boy who *thought* about a cookie. Other mental–real contrasts included the mental activities of *dreaming, remembering* and *pretending*. Three-, 4- and 5-year-olds were asked whether or not the cookie or the thought could be seen, touched or manipulated, whether either could be seen by someone else and whether either could be manipulated in the future. The children were very good at ascribing behavioural-sensory, public and consistent status to the real but not to the mental items, and even 75 per cent of the 3-year-olds responded in this way.

So, Wellman and Estes have shown that young children as well as adults can distinguish real from imagined items and can use the same criteria in this process. Interestingly, when children do make errors they mistake real items for mental ones just as often as they mistake mental items for real ones. Wellman and Estes carried out further studies in order to tidy up some possible objections to their research design, but again confirmed their finding that even 3-year-olds can distinguish between real items and those which are imagined.

In a further set of studies, Estes, Wellman and Woolley (1989) wanted to see if 3- to 5-year-olds could still distinguish between real objects and thoughts even in situations seemingly ripe for realistic confusions. The children were asked questions about (1) a real object, for example, a deflated balloon, (2) a real deflated balloon hidden in a box, and (3) a mental image of a deflated balloon. The mental image of the balloon, in particular, was referred to as 'a picture in your head'; this terminology was chosen deliberately in order to invite the possible confusion of an image with a real picture. The experimenter's questions reflected the three criteria used in the previous set of studies. For example, with respect to the image of a balloon the questions were: 'That balloon in your head, can you see it with your eyes?', 'Can I see it with my eyes?', 'Just by thinking about it, can you make it stretch out long and skinny?'. Even the 3-year-olds could distinguish between the real object and the mental entity. They said that they couldn't touch the imagined object because 'it's only pretend' or 'it's not real'. They also said that they couldn't touch a real hidden object, but in this case they didn't use the language of mental states in their explanation; instead, they said they couldn't touch the hidden object because it had 'gone away'.

A decoupling mechanism

A mechanism by which multiple models can be generated has been suggested by Leslie (1988). Unfortunately he calls these further models *meta-representations* which leads to some confusion since other researchers, such as Perner, do not use *meta-representational* in this way. Basically, a meta-representation (for Leslie) is an internal representation consisting of three parts: *agent–informational relation–'expression'*. The agent represents a person such as *I* or *Mummy*. The expression is a piece of information that has been *decoupled* from its normal use as in 'this object (banana) is a telephone'. The informational relation does the job of linking the agent, the decoupled expression and the primary representation (the normal meaning of the term *banana*). Examples of informational relations are *pretend* or *think*. So, the child might generate the meta-representation *I pretend 'this banana is a telephone'*.

Because any agent, the self or another, can be nominated, the child does not need different mechanisms to represent another's pretense or belief as distinct from her own. Thus, the theory can explain why the appearance of pretense in self and its understanding in others appear at approximately the same time. Furthermore, any primary expression can replace *expression* so that the theory can cope with children's representations of what literally is the case as well as what is false. In other words, the same representational code can be used for perceiving a situation and for pretending about a situation, and this makes the theory particularly parsimonious. The appearance of this decoupling mechanism at the age of approximately 18 months may simply be due to a process of maturation (Leslie, 1987); on the other hand, Perner (1990) has argued that in fact it may have been there from the beginning but its use may have had to wait for the firm establishment of the earlier, primary (single model) system.

False beliefs

Young children clearly have an impressive understanding of which phenomena are real and which are pretend or imaginary and, indeed, even by the age of 2½ to 3 years, they engage in conversations about the mental states of thinking, remembering, pretending, and so on (e.g. Shatz, Wellman and Silber, 1983). Nevertheless, below the age of 4 or 5 years they appear to have difficulty in predicting the behaviour of someone who holds a mistaken or false belief. In order to investigate children's capabilities regarding this problem, researchers have used a variety of *false belief* tasks. I shall describe one, the Sally–Anne task, used by Baron-Cohen, Leslie and Frith (1985). The child is shown two dolls, Sally and Anne (see Figure 8.2). Sally hides a marble in a basket and then goes out for a walk. While she is away, Anne takes the marble from the basket and hides it in a box. Sally returns and wants her marble. The child is asked some control questions to make sure she has followed these events; she is then asked the key question, 'Where will Sally look for her marble?'.

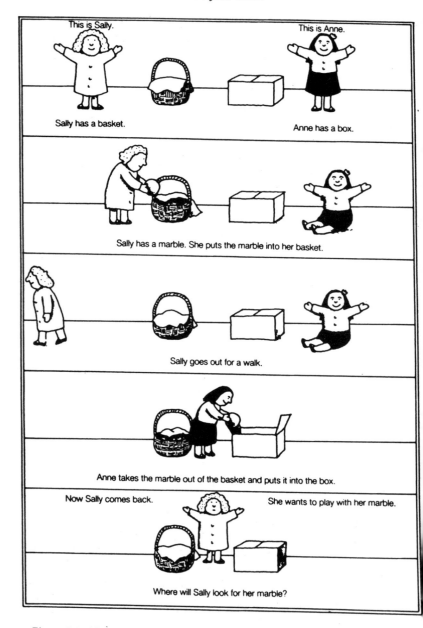

Figure 8.2: The Sally–Anne task (Frith, 1989, Figure 10.1, p. 160). (Reprinted with the permission of the author and the artist, Axel Scheffler.)

Children aged 4 years and above answer the question correctly. They understand that Sally will look for the marble in the basket because that is where she believes the marble to be, even though this belief is mistaken. In contrast, most normal 3-year-olds (Perner, Leekam and Wimmer, 1987) and autistic children (Baron-Cohen, Leslie and Frith, 1985), even with a mental age of 7 years and above, fail the task by saying that Sally will look for the marble where it actually is, in the box.

Other false belief tasks are based on Flavell's appearance–reality distinction (Flavell, Flavell and Green, 1983). An example is the Smarties task (Perner, Leekam and Wimmer, 1987) (see Figure 8.3) which gives similar results to the Sally–Anne task. Twenty-nine 3-year-olds were asked what they thought was in a Smarties tube. Not surprisingly, they all answered 'Smarties'. The experimenter then opened the tube and showed the children that in fact there was only a pencil inside. The tube was closed again and the children were asked some questions, including 'What will [name of friend] think is in here?'. Thirteen of the 29 children correctly answered that their friend would believe there to be Smarties in the tube – these successful children tended to be the slightly older ones, 3½- to 4-year-olds – but 16 children failed and claimed that their friend would think there would be a pencil inside. Subsequent studies by Gopnik and Astington (1988), Wimmer and Hartl (1991) and Gopnik and Slaughter (in press) have shown that the younger children not only fail to predict their friend's false belief but also fail to remember their own initial false belief, namely that the tube contains Smarties.

The child's theory of mind

What the results of the false belief tasks may show is that only at the age of about 4 years do children begin to develop a *theory of mind*, the notion that people's behaviour can be explained in terms of the beliefs they hold about a situation. Thus, the 4-year-old predicts that Sally will search for her marble in the basket because that is where Sally believes her marble to be, even though that belief is false. Although the 3-year-old can conceive of (or represent) both a true or a false location of the marble, she cannot conceive of (or represent) Sally's misrepresentation of its location. Since she cannot do this, she will not

Figure 8.3: The Smarties task (Frith, 1989, Figure 10.2, p. 162). (Reprinted with the permission of the author and the artist, Axel Scheffler.)

use Sally's false belief as a guide in predicting where Sally will search. Consequently, she will predict that Sally will search for the marble in the place where it actually is; there would be no reason for her to search in a place where the marble is not located.

So, the possession of a theory of mind refers not simply to the fact that the child knows, believes or feels something or that she recognizes these mental states in others; rather, it means that the child is able to *reflect on* her own and on other people's knowledge, beliefs and feelings or, to put it another way, the child can form *meta-representations*.

Now, there is some confusion in the literature regarding the exact nature of such a theory and a problem which clouds the issue, as Johnson (1988) points out, is that researchers have sometimes used the same terminology to refer to different things or different terminology to refer to the same things. Whereas Piaget, for example, used the term *presentation* or *knowledge* to refer to the child's possession of some information, feeling or belief, more recent researchers have used such terms as *primary representation* (Leslie) or *knowledge base* (Perner). Similarly, in considering the child's ability to reflect on her own thoughts, feelings and beliefs or on those of others, Piaget used the term *representation* but more recent researchers prefer the term *meta-representation*, except that Leslie uses it in a different way.

As well as this lack of consensus regarding the terminology, there are also researchers who doubt whether the child's theory of mind can really be called a theory in the sense that an adult might have a theory of, say, planetary motion (Harris, 1989). In order to explain planetary motion we invoke a nonobservable, theoretical entity – namely, gravity. Similarly, children are supposed to invoke nonobservable states – beliefs and desires – in order to explain a person's behaviour. But, argues Harris, beliefs and desires are not in fact *un*observable. They are states which the child herself has and, furthermore, can report on; there is nothing hidden about them. So, complex though the young child's understanding of her own and others' mental states may be, we may be claiming too much in using the term 'theory' in the same sense that adults use it to explain phenomena in the physical world.

Meta-representation

We might consider that a main criterion for the child's possession of a theory of mind, as I suggested in the previous section, is her ability to form *meta-representations*. This raises the problem of what meta-representations actually are, at what age children become capable of constructing them and, in turn, at what age they can be said to have acquired a theory of mind.

Although Leslie (1988) acknowledges that 4-year-olds can respond correctly in false belief tasks but that 3-year-olds cannot, the abilities he claims for 3-year-olds suggest that they have already made considerable progress towards the acquisition of a theory of mind. His justification for this claim is that the further or secondary mental models which these young children can construct via the process of decoupling are in fact *meta-representations*. Perner (1988 and 1990), in contrast, although he agrees that the young child can form both primary mental models and further models and also accepts Leslie's account of the decoupling mechanism which enables the child to generate these further models, nevertheless disagrees about the nature of the 3-year-olds' abilities. Specifically, he does not accept that the further multiple models which the child is capable of constructing are meta-representational. For Perner, *meta-representation* should be used in a recursive way to denote not simply a further representation but rather a representation of a representation *as* a representation (Perner, 1990). Since, for Perner, 3-year-olds do not have the capacity for such meta-representational thinking they cannot therefore be said to have a theory of mind.

Perner (1988) explains the difference between the representational systems of the 3- and 4-year-old by using an example concerning Mary's belief about the location of an ice-cream van. Mary has been misinformed about the location of the ice-cream van: she believes it to be in the park whereas in fact it is at the church. Both the 3- and the 4-year-old understand that Mary is under a misapprehension, but according to Perner they conceptualize Mary's false belief in different ways. From her knowledge base, the 3-year-old generates two models, one describing the real situation and one describing the false situation (see Figure 8.4). The child conceives of Mary's false belief simply by associating her with the mental model of the false situation. Perner calls this young child a *situation theorist*. But, although she can construct alternative mental models and can compare them with the real situation this does not, according to Perner, constitute a meta-representation. And, if the child must be able to use a meta-representation in order to be deemed to have a theory of mind, then the 3-year-old does not possess one. Perner (1990) prefers to think of the 3-year-old as having *a mentalistic theory of behaviour* but not *a representational theory of mind*.

The 4-year-old, in contrast to the younger child, can conceive of Mary's false belief by constructing a model such as, 'Mary's belief that the ice-cream van is in the park misrepresents the real situation that the van is actually at the church' (see Figure 8.4). So, this child can construct a mental model of a situation which itself represents or misrepresents a situation.

This ability to generate meta-representations is, for Perner, a more stringent criterion of the existence of a theory of mind. Chandler (1988) would also agree; however, as we shall see later, he does not accept that many of the false belief tasks currently employed in the literature yield positive proof that the children who pass do so by means of the meta-representational thought I have just outlined.

To summarize, the 3-year-olds' problems in the Sally–Anne and Smarties tasks are not to do with their inability to represent alternative views of a situation. Rather, according to Perner, they centre around the young child's inability to construct a model which represents a misrepresentation of the true situation. In order to succeed in the Sally–Anne task, for instance, children need to construct a mental model that Sally's belief that the marble is in the basket misrepresents the actual situation that the marble is in fact in the box. Because 3-year-olds have no means of modelling a misrepresentation in this meta-representational way, they cannot predict accurately what Sally will do; neither are they able to work out their friend's mistaken belief or indeed their own initial false belief in the Smarties task.

How are beliefs formed?

In considering the 3-year-olds' problems with false belief tasks, Leslie (1988) has focused on the possibility that they may not yet appreciate that mental states can be *caused* by real events. The child has to realize that Sally's exposure to the marble in the basket will *cause* her to believe that that is where it is. Subsequently, Sally's nonexposure to the marble's change of location does not alter her belief; when she returns her unchanged belief will determine where she searches for the marble. Similarly, in the Smarties task the friend's exposure to the Smarties tube will *cause* her to believe that it contains Smarties and her nonexposure to the pencil will leave her belief unchanged. The

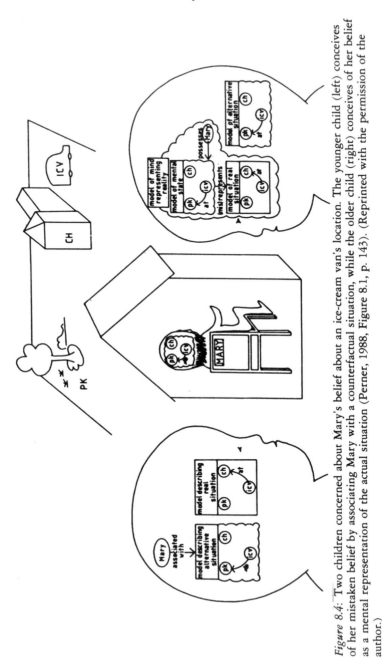

Figure 8.4: Two children concerned about Mary's belief about an ice-cream van's location. The younger child (left) conceives of her mistaken belief by associating Mary with a counterfactual situation, while the older child (right) conceives of her belief as a mental representation of the actual situation (Perner, 1988, Figure 8.1, p. 143). (Reprinted with the permission of the author.)

friend's unchanged belief will determine what she says is in the tube. Unless the child has realized that events can cause mental states, and vice versa, she is unlikely to monitor very closely these details of the situations that people are exposed to with a view to working out their resulting mental states. It is interesting that 9 of those 16 children who failed the Smarties test (Perner *et al.*, 1987) nevertheless were able to say that they themselves had held the false belief that the tube contained Smarties; yet, they failed to say that their friend would hold the same false belief. This suggests that these children did not know where their false belief had come from and that they did not know how to go about predicting what their friend's belief would be.

Leslie is arguing, then, that although 3-year-olds know that concrete objects and events can cause people to behave in certain ways and that they can represent the mental states of themselves and others, these two abilities run essentially in parallel (see Figure 8.5). It is not until around the age of 4 years that the child forges links between these two systems and extends the possible causes of behaviour to include mental states (see Figure 8.6).

Whereas Leslie sees the 4-year-old's success in a false belief task as depending on a greater understanding of the causal role of mental states, Perner takes the contrasting view: the 4-year-old's understanding of the causal role develops as a *consequence* of her emerging concept of mental representation. The difference in their views depends crucially on these researchers' contrasting positions regarding the 3-year-old's ability (Leslie) or inability (Perner) to meta-represent mental states, as I outlined in an earlier section.

Other researchers, such as Wellman (1988), also recognize that an explanation is needed to account for the 3-year-olds' failure and the 4-year-olds' success in the false belief tasks. Unlike Perner in particular, however, Wellman is less well disposed to the notion that the younger children *lack* a theory of mind and that its acquisition is what heralds the 4-year-olds' success in the task. Wellman argues that by the age of 2½ to 3 years children engage in conversations about mentalistic states which indicates that they do in fact possess a theory of mind. They may not be so proficient as older children but they are, nonetheless, engaged in essentially the same kind of activity, namely trying to understand the internal states – beliefs, desires, intentions, etc. – of themselves and others. While not denying these impressive endeavours of such young children, Perner in contrast would not wish to ascribe a theory of mind to them.

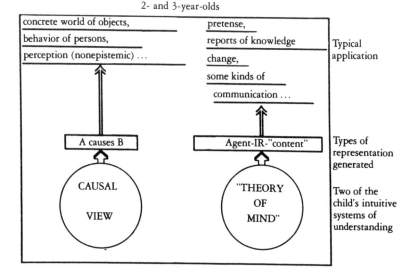

Figure 8.5: According to Leslie (1988, Figure 2.4, p. 37) the causal view and the 'theory of mind' of 2- to 3-year-olds are independent. (Reprinted with the permission of the author.)

Along with other researchers, Wellman argues that the 3-year-old's theory of mind changes over time because her notion of the mind itself changes. At an early stage, the child sees the mind as a repository of its owner's thoughts and beliefs. Later, not only does the mind hold thoughts and beliefs, it also reasons, hypothesizes and plans using this information. In support of this view, Johnson and Wellman (1982) found that although preschool children realize there is a distinction between real things and actions *vs.* thoughts and ideas, they say that the mind and the brain are involved only in mental activities such as thinking, dreaming and remembering but not in walking, kicking, seeing and hearing.

The child's idea of the mind, then, changes from its being a container of information to its being an information processor and interpreter. The younger children understand that people encounter things in the real world and therefore know about them or, conversely, fail to encounter them and therefore remain ignorant of

4-year-olds

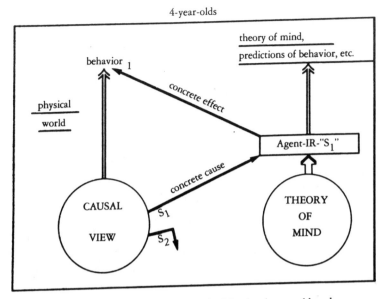

Figure 8.6: The two systems become linked in the 4-year-old and constitute a theory of mind (Leslie, 1988, Figure 2.5, p. 38). (Reprinted with the permission of the author.)

them; they also appreciate that they can imagine or dream of real things. What they fail to understand, however, is *how* their knowledge of things and events has come about. They may know *that* they know, but not *how* they know it. Despite some apparent differences, this position of Wellman's does not seem to me to be very different from that put forward by Leslie.

The child's developing theories of mind

Many researchers have concentrated on children of preschool or early school age, on whether or not they possess a theory of mind and on the different characteristics of those who do and those who do not. From this body of work, the reader could be forgiven for assuming that when children do acquire such a theory – somewhere between the ages of 4 to 6 years – that they have acquired something the same as or very similar to an adult's concept. But, intuitively we recognize that such an early acquisition of a full-blown understanding of others' minds is unlikely.

Someone who has expressed similar doubts is Chandler (1988), an established researcher actively involved in work on role-taking skills in children long before the recent surge in interest in the child's theory of mind (e.g. Chandler, 1973). Not only does he believe that the child's understanding of her own and other people's beliefs develops further after the age of about 4 to 6 years, but he also suspects that the acquisition of a theory of mind which seems to occur somewhat abruptly at this age is, in fact, in place in some form at an even earlier age. If he is right, Chandler's position argues for a less dramatic watershed in development at age 4 to 6 years than other researchers would advocate and a more protracted later development, perhaps through a series of different theories of mind. In charting these developments, Chandler also argues that the mere addition of more and more recursive steps – e.g. 'I know that you know what I know' – fails to capture some of the important differences which actually differentiate the childish theories of mind from those of the more mature person.

Some of the evidence that very young children possess some sort of theory of mind is available from many of the studies I have already outlined in this book. Even 2-year-olds are quite competent at, for example, pointing out and showing things to another person and, conversely, at hiding something from them. The desire and ability to do this suggests that these children hold certain beliefs about the state of the other person and how that state can be changed. Chandler also agrees with Wellman that the very young child's use of mental state verbs and her ability to engage in pretend play give added weight to the argument that she has acquired the rudiments of some sort of theory of mind. The case could be made even stronger, according to Chandler (Chandler, Fritz and Hala, 1989), if it could be shown that the young child can engage in deceitful behaviour in order to engender a false belief in another person. And Chandler *et al.* have provided such evidence: children as young as 2½ years practised a variety of deception strategies in order to prevent a seeker finding some hidden treasure; these practices included destroying clues and producing false trails. In the face of such compelling evidence it is certainly difficult to deny that the young child possesses at least a fledgling theory of mind. Perner (1990), however, is sceptical. He maintains that the children's responses in the Chandler *et al.* study were the result of massive prompting by the experimenter and were not indicative of true deception.

Just as it is possible that very young children may have been underestimated, so according to Chandler the child who passes the false belief task may in fact have been overestimated. This is because researchers such as Wimmer and Perner (1983) claim too much for the false belief task, namely that the successful child understands that both Sally and Anne, for example, apprehend the same stimulus material in different ways. This is what Flavell calls a Level 2 accomplishment – a notion I discussed in Chapter 2 in relation to the child's visual perspective-taking abilities – and means that the child understands that two people can interpret the same stimulus in different ways. But Chandler argues that the two protagonists in the false belief task do *not* have equal access to the same material; Anne (and the child) has access to all of the information but Sally to only part of it. In fact, Chandler argues, to achieve success in this task the child requires merely Level 1 ability, the appreciation that two different people may have different interpretations resulting from their exposure to different events. Thus, although a 4-year-old may be able to solve the false belief task she may not solve it in the same way that many researchers have been assuming and therefore may not possess such a sophisticated theory of mind as they have advocated.

The shift from Flavell's Level 1 to Level 2 can be demonstrated using some of the role-taking tasks devised by Flavell in the 1960s (e.g. Flavell, 1968). In one example the child is asked to describe the significance of a dog sitting beneath an apple tree, a scene witnessed by both the child herself and a protagonist in the story. The child but not the protagonist has previously observed the dog chasing a boy into the tree. Another task involves the child's interpretation of her own view of a cartoon drawing and that of another person who has only a keyhole view of a small portion of the picture. The important point is that in these two tasks, in contrast to the false belief task, the child is asked how the same *shared views* of two people might be different, even though one has been more fully informed than the other. This Level 2 task is not passed until children are about 6 or 7 years old (Chandler and Helm, 1984; Taylor, 1988).

Even when the child of school age comes to understand that the same material or event can be interpreted in different ways, she nevertheless assumes that one interpretation is in fact correct (Chandler, 1987). It is not until the adolescent period that young people begin to appreciate that there may be no one objective and truthful interpretation but many different subjective views. In Chandler's terms, adolescents begin 'to shift primary responsibility for the knowing process from the objects to the subjects of thought' (Chandler, 1988, p. 409).

Summary

I have outlined some of the issues involved in the recent research on the child's developing theory of mind. Researchers such as Wellman and Chandler seem to be particularly in favour of the very young child – say, at age 2 years – having considerable intuition regarding other people's minds. Leslie is also impressed by the 3-year-olds' ability to represent mental states in themselves and others. Perner, while not denying that 3-year-olds can engage in pretend play and may be able to assess whether or not a statement about a situation is true or false, believes nevertheless that these children cannot be said to have a theory of mind. This does not emerge until about the age of 4 years, when children begin to be able to form meta-representations of a model of a true (or false) situation.

Whereas many of these researchers argue that a fairly sophisticated theory of mind is in place somewhere between the ages of 4 to 6 years, Chandler believes that the child's abilities at this age have been greatly overestimated partly because the tasks used for assessment can be solved in a less complicated way than many researchers have supposed. It may be, then, that the child's ability to reflect on her own and others' mental states does not emerge until the age of about 6 or 7 years and that she will have to proceed through a number of intervening stages before she acquires a truly adult understanding. As Chandler points out, '. . . one must in all likelihood be mature in order to have a mature theory of mind' (Chandler, Fritz and Hala, 1989, p. 1275).

9   I know how you feel

A body of literature has been built up, particularly during the 1970s, on children's role-taking ability, their ability to put themselves into another person's shoes and to appreciate their feelings in different situations. This literature, it seems to me, focused more on the *correlates* of this ability rather than on how children actually come to *understand* their own and other people's emotions. In my opinion a more recent book – Paul Harris's *Children and Emotion* (1989) – provides a more interesting and useful account of children's developing understanding of emotions. I make no apologies for drawing quite heavily upon it in this chapter and recommend it to the reader for a fuller discussion of some of the issues I shall outline here.

Facial expressions

The claim that the different facial expressions of emotion – happiness, anger, sadness, and so on – are both *universal* and *innate* goes back at least as far as Darwin (1872). The cross-cultural data collected by Ekman (Ekman and Friesen, 1971; Ekman, 1973) lend considerable support to the first part of this claim and the findings of a number of studies on the young infant's ability to produce several different facial expressions support the second part, namely that the production of facial expressions is an innate ability and does not depend on imitation or learning. In one study, for example, newborns were given liquids which were slightly sweet or very sweet and slightly bitter or very bitter (Ganchrow, Steiner and Daher, 1983). The neonates' expressions were recorded and judges, though they themselves did not know which liquids the subjects had tasted, were asked to say whether the expressions indicated the babies' enjoyment or dislike of the liquids. It turned out that the sweet liquids elicited a more enjoyable facial expression whereas the bitter liquids elicited an expression of dislike. Furthermore, the judges could tell from the intensity of the expression whether a baby had tasted the mild or the stronger version.

This kind of evidence strongly suggests that the expression of at least some basic emotions is innate and that we do not have to learn how to express them by copying other people. This suggestion may sit uneasily, however, with another piece of evidence of the neonate's ability, that she may be able to imitate the tongue protrusions of an adult model (see Chapter 1). But, even if neonates do have this ability (and this is by no means generally accepted) it does not necessarily imply that their normal production of facial expressions is learned through imitation. Indeed, as Harris (1989) argues, even if they can imitate different expressions when a model is present, it is difficult to see how such young babies could know the different contexts in which to produce them. All in all, then, it is highly likely that the production of facial expressions such as happiness, anger and distress is innate.

In fact, Darwin's claim about the facial expression of emotion went further than his statements about its innateness and universality. He actually said that we have an innate ability to *recognize* the facial expressions of emotion. The baby is supposed to be able to discriminate the different facial expressions of the people she sees around her. Again, Harris cites evidence in support of Darwin's claim. In one study (Caron, Caron and Myers, 1982), babies between the ages of 4 and 7 months were shown pictures of four different women who expressed either happiness or surprise. The older babies tended to look less and less as each picture of the same emotion was presented. But, if a picture of a new emotion was presented – surprise or happiness, depending on the emotion already seen – these older babies renewed their interest.

The second study cited by Harris shows that not only can 7-month-old infants recognize the same facial expression in different people, but that they also expect a particular expression to be linked with a certain tone of voice (Walker-Andrews, 1986). These infants were shown two films side-by-side, one of a face displaying a happy expression and another of one displaying an angry expression. As well as seeing the faces the infants could also hear a soundtrack of either a happy or an angry voice. The question was, given a particular voice-tone, which face would the infants attend to? They tended to look at the face which matched the voice, the happy face for the happy voice and the angry face for the angry voice.

Further evidence with even younger infants comes from Haviland and Lelwica (1987) who asked mothers to engage in dialogues with their 10-week-old babies and to adopt the facial expressions and voice-tone of three emotions – happiness, sadness or anger. The babies could discriminate the three different emotions and responded to them in different ways: they looked happy when the mother expressed happiness, they looked angry or became still when the mother expressed anger, and engaged in mouthing, chewing and sucking when the mother expressed sadness. Despite these impressive discriminatory abilities, however, we do not know what the facial expressions actually *mean* to the infant, as Harris points out. Even though she may be able to tell a happy face from an angry one and may be able to match a facial expression to a particular voice-tone, it does not follow that she will understand what the facial expression actually implies – that someone is happy, angry, and so on. In order to pursue this issue, we need to look at the babies' reactions to the facial expressions they see. And, indeed, Haviland and Lelwica have pointed out that their babies were not simply imitating the mothers' expressions; their stilling or 'freezing' posture, for instance, when the mother became angry was not in imitation of the mother's expression and was also similar to the freezing behaviour seen in older children when parents are angry.

Further evidence of the infant's meaningful interpretation of the adult's expression comes from a study of 12- to 18-month-olds carried out by Klinnert (1984). The infant was introduced on three separate trials to three new toys. In each trial the toy was at some distance away from the infant. When she had looked towards her mother, the mother adopted a particular facial expression: a smile, a fearful expression or a neutral expression. In fact, the expression for the first toy had no effect. But, for the second and third toys, the infants tended to respond to their mothers' fearful expression by approaching her more quickly, remaining with her and touching her. These results suggest that the infant is looking 'for guidance' from her mother's reactions to objects; in particular, she is inhibited about investigating an object when the mother has exhibited a fearful expression.

At the end of her first year, then, the young child can express a number of different emotions, can discriminate them in other people's facial expressions and has some understanding regarding the meaning of these different expressions.

Understanding through pretense

Although we know that, even during their first year, infants often react to the distress of other people by becoming upset themselves (Zahn-Waxler and Radke-Yarrow, 1982), it has been argued (e.g. Hoffman, 1981) that this reaction is no more than 'emotional contagion' and does not imply a concern for other people at all; supposedly, this emotional contagion is later converted in some way into a sympathetic concern. Now, although he does not deny the occurrence of such emotional contagion, Harris maintains that this is *not* how young children come to understand how other people feel. Rather, Harris's view is that since the young child is already aware of the various emotions she herself has experienced on different occasions she can imagine what another person must feel *without simultaneously having to experience that same emotion herself.*

This developing ability to understand other people's states of mind may be enhanced or even brought about by the child's capacity for pretense, which itself begins about the age of 12 to 13 months and continues to develop until at least the age of 4 years and beyond (Fein, 1981). Indeed, Harris claims that pretense 'is a key that unlocks the minds of other people and allows the child temporarily to enter into their plans, hopes and fears' (Harris, 1989, p. 52); it enables the child to imagine how others feel even though she does not share those same feelings.

In predicting what another person will feel, the child is not simply associating and remembering particular situations and particular emotions – an objection levelled by Chandler and Greenspan (1972) – but, according to Harris, can take into account the specific desires of individual people which may result in their experiencing different emotions even though they are in the same situation.

In order to demonstrate this understanding that the same situation can provoke different emotions in different people depending on each person's particular desires Harris has used stories involving animal characters (Harris, Johnson, Hutton, Andrews and Cooke, 1989). The children are told, for example, that Ellie the elephant wants a drink. Half are told that she doesn't like milk and only likes coke; the other half are told she doesn't like coke and only likes milk. A neutral, opaque bottle is produced which, the children are told, contains a drink. They are asked how Ellie will feel – happy or sad – if she should find milk or coke in the bottle. The children then open up the bottle to reveal the contents; half the children find the preferred drink and half find the nonpreferred one. Finally, the experimenter asks whether Ellie is happy or sad. The researchers found that 5-year-olds and, to a large extent, even 3-year-olds predicted that Ellie would be happy if the bottle turned out to contain the drink she prefers but sad if it should contain the drink she does not like. Further, although the 3-year-olds were less accurate than the 5-year-olds, both age groups were able to adjust their prediction if needs be when they saw the actual contents of the bottle. These results show that preschool children understand that people with different likes and dislikes can have different feelings about a given situation.

Being provocative

By the age of about 20 months young children are more active in their response to other people's emotions and can even take steps to bring about emotional change in others. So, for example, they understand not only that someone is distressed, but also recognize what that person is distressed about and may be able to exhibit appropriate 'comforting' behaviour. As well as displaying this concern for others, children at this stage can also antagonize others, especially their siblings, and bring about distress (Dunn, 1988). In fact, the radical swings in behaviour, from being so caring one minute to being so beastly the next, often leave parents totally perplexed. But all this may be evidence that their offspring have begun to identify the conditions or actions which will curtail or promote a particular emotional state in another person. Indeed, it has been suggested that these exasperating children are actually more socially engaged and/or better able to work out what will soothe or upset another person than are others who seem to engage much less in both kinds of behaviour. It is not clear, however, how these caring and hurting behaviours are actually related and there may be individual differences which, as yet, remain uncharted.

One cause of individual differences may be the differences in parenting, specifically in the way that parents interpret another's emotional state (Zahn-Waxler, Radke-Yarrow and King, 1979; Miller and Sperry, 1987). For example, those parents who provide statements of principle when their children have upset others (e.g. 'People are not for hitting' or 'You must never poke anyone's eyes') tend to produce children who are more caring and comforting when confronted with another child's distress. There is evidence that abusing parents, in contrast, seem to produce children in the preschool who do not comfort other children in distress; instead, they may simply look on or become upset themselves or actually become hostile and aggressive to the distressed child (Main and George, 1985).

Despite their different ways of responding to distress in others, children from different backgrounds have very similar views regarding the fundamental transgressions of other people's rights (Smetana, Kelly and Twentyman, 1984). Even though they may indulge in causing distress to others they nevertheless recognize, by the age of 3 to 5 years, that being aggressive towards another child, for example, is a very serious transgression, whereas putting their toys away in the wrong place is a relatively minor infringement of the rules. Although parents and teachers will often treat an infringement of a minor rule as seriously as they do a major one, children of course have direct feedback from the victims of their aggression and in this way may learn the significance of moral *vs.* conventional rules.

So, normal children as well as those who have been abused may indulge, to differing degrees, in behaviour which is hurtful and distressing to others. Yet these children will also agree that such behaviour is wrong. Harris suggests that we can resolve this paradox by realizing that it must be difficult for young children to use their knowledge to guide their own actions. It is one thing to make moral judgements when one is detached from a situation, but quite another to respond in a rational way when one is caught up in the situation itself – a problem not confined to the young child but also experienced by the adult too.

Hidden emotions

Although there may be individual differences, it is usually not difficult for an adult to know what a very young child is feeling because she usually displays her feelings overtly through her facial expressions, bodily posture and vocalizations. An older child or an adult may have cause to hide her true feelings and to display some other emotional state instead.

In order to find out how well children can hide their feelings, Saarni

(1984) presented 6- to 10-year-olds with a parcel containing an attractive gift after they had completed an experimental task. The gift was greeted very enthusiastically by all the children. On a second occasion the expectant children were presented with a rather drab gift. This time it was greeted with suppressed disappointment – a slight smile and mumbled thanks – but the children were not able to put on a completely convincing face.

Even younger children, 3- to 4-year-olds, were studied by Cole (1986). After the children had rank ordered a set of toys, they received the least-preferred item. They opened the parcel either with the experimenter present or alone. Video-recordings revealed that when they were alone the children expressed spontaneous and open disappointment but when the experimenter was there they tried to conceal their disappointment with a half-smile. These findings show that from the age of about 3 years children can at least *attempt* to adapt their facial expressions in order to express an emotion they do not actually feel even if they are not very successful.

However, a problem with the interpretation of these findings in both Saarni's and Cole's studies, as Harris points out, is that we do not know whether the children were really trying to conceal their true feelings or whether they were merely being polite even in the face of disappointment. In saying 'thank you' and effecting a smile they may simply have gone through a well-practised and automatic politeness routine and may not have realized that they had displayed an emotion that they did not feel. In other words, they may not have *deliberately* tried to conceal their disappointment at all.

This issue is addressed by Harris, Donnelly, Guz and Pitt-Watson (1986) in their comprehension studies in which children from 3 to 10 years were told stories. A happy or sad event befell the main character and, for good reason, this character needed to hide her feelings. An example is: 'Diana is playing a game with her friend. At the end of the game Diana wins and her friend loses. Diana tries to hide how she feels because otherwise her friend won't play any more.' The child was then asked how Diana really feels and also what emotion appears on her face. Other stories concerned characters who felt upset but have to look cheerful. In all cases, the actual emotions were not named, so the child had to work these out for herself; she could not simply repeat what she had heard.

The older children, from 6 to 10 years, had no difficulty with the task. They understood that a character might feel happy but try to look sad, or vice versa. In other words they appreciated that a person's real feelings might be different from the emotion they actually displayed. The younger children, 3- to 4-year-olds, were also good at judging what the characters' real feelings were. In addition, the 4-year-olds, but not the 3-year-olds, understood the reasons for the main characters' wanting to hide their feelings. Both of these younger age groups, however, had great difficulty in predicting what expression the main characters would have on their faces. What they did not seem to appreciate was that an expressed emotion can be different from what the person actually does feel. These findings, then, suggest that the children aged from 6 to 10 years in Saarni's study really were trying to suppress their disappointment but that the 3- to 4-year-olds in Cole's study were probably not making a deliberate effort to do this.

Harris has looked carefully at the way that 6-year-olds articulate the differences between real and apparent emotions (Harris and Gross, 1988). It turns out that many of them can embed three or even four clauses in their explanations of why a story character would wish to hide her true feelings and display a different emotion. So, for example, the child might say, 'She didn't want her sister to know that she hided her toy' or 'She didn't want her friend to know that she really feels happy that she won'. These kinds of explanations suggest that 6-year-olds appreciate that the adoption of the apparent emotion by the character is intended to create a false impression and deliberately to mislead other people. Gross and Harris (1988) checked this by asking the children a further question in the story task, e.g. 'How does Diana's friend think that Diana feels?'. These 6-year-olds had no difficulty in understanding that by putting on a particular facial expression a character can mislead others into thinking that that is how she really feels.

As Harris says, this ability requires considerable conceptual sophistication. First of all, the child must understand how the situation looks from two different points of view: the real feelings of the character *vs.* her apparent feelings taken by her friend to be genuine. But, further, the child must appreciate the *intended relationship* between these two points of view, namely that the main character has deliberately arranged the conditions which have brought about these two different perspectives and has done so in order to mislead her friend.

In the kinds of task used by Harris and other researchers, the child knows what the story character really feels and also knows that this character wants to hide her real feelings and substitutes some other emotion. But, in real life when the child is not privy to this information, how successful is she at diagnosing the truthfulness of other people's emotional displays? And how does she come to realize that *she* can mislead others by adopting a facial expression which belies her real feelings? How is it that she realizes that one's feelings can be private and not automatically on public display?

Harris dismisses the notion that children, somewhere between the ages of 4 and 6 years of age, make this change simply through a progressive refinement of their observational skills. The shift, he argues, is in fact a *cognitive discovery*. And the child makes this discovery by realizing that her facial expressions are sometimes interpreted by others as signalling an emotion different from the one she actually has. The child observes the onlooker's reaction and reflects on the cause, namely her own facial expression. The realization that it is this displayed emotion and not her real emotion which the onlooker takes to be the true state of affairs suggests to the child the potential privacy of that real emotion and the possibility of concealing it from others. The child must have a co-ordinated understanding of both perspectives – her own real feelings and the way that she imagines the onlooker sees her feelings – and must keep in mind both of these very different points of view.

Although I do not doubt Harris's claim that the child does in fact make a cognitive discovery and that this *could* come about in the way he suggests, it seems to me that there is another more plausible possibility. And this is the idea put forward by DePaulo and Jordan (1982) that there is an excellent training ground available for children which enables them to develop and practise skills for concealing their true feelings and beliefs and for presenting a different 'face' to others. The training ground referred to is the very varied and rich world of children's games. In numerous party games (such as the button game analyzed by Sacks, 1980, and discussed in Chapter 1 of this volume), board games, card games and sports the participants need both to produce and to detect verbal and nonverbal cues designed to deceive and outwit other players. In the button game, the child must adopt a neutral or innocent face if she really does have the button or a guilty face if she does not have it. In chess or checkers she must suppress her excitement when she sees the possibility of a winning move so as not to give the game away.

This training ground provides a context in which deceit and lying are both sanctioned and expected and in which the child's deception abilities are developed in fairly rigid and predictable situations. It may be that children are able to generalize these skills to real-life contexts – in some cases for socially acceptable ends such as suppressing the truth in order not to upset or embarrass others or, alternatively, for more dubious reasons of personal gain at the expense of other people. The implication of all this is that the realization that one can present a face to the world that is at odds with one's true feelings may not be a *lone* discovery on the child's part but may in fact come about through the expectation of others in a *social context*.

Summary

It is highly likely that the facial expressions of basic emotions such as happiness, anger and sadness are both universal and innate. Certainly, very young babies produce these different expressions and can also discriminate them in other people. By the end of their first year, infants also have some understanding of the meaning of these expressions, that is, in their implications for what other people are feeling.

During their second year young children become more active and make attempts to alter the emotional states of others: they show caring behaviour when someone is upset and, in contrast, will deliberately provoke hurt and anger in others. Their understanding of how other people feel may be related to their capacity for pretense, enabling them to imagine how someone feels without, at the same time, having to experience that emotion themselves. And, by the age of 3 years, they can work out that different people may feel different things even when confronted by the same situation.

Even though preschool children know a good deal about other people's emotional states, they have some difficulty in understanding that a person can have a private feeling and yet at the same time display a completely different one. It is not until the age of about 6 years that children really get to grips with this distinction and begin to be able deliberately to mislead others as to their true feelings.

Conclusion to Part IV

In this section I have discussed some of the work on the young child's understanding of people's different beliefs about a given situation and her understanding of people's emotional states. Since we presume that the same basic processes underlie the child's understanding of all mental states, my separation of these topics seems somewhat arbitrary. It does in fact reflect the pattern of the research effort in the area at present.

Beginning in their second year, young children have some intuitive understanding of people's beliefs and feelings and, particularly through their capacity for pretense, they can imagine that things might be different from how they actually are – they can pretend that an object is a different object and that they feel an emotion that in fact they do not have. Later, children recognize that they and others can hold a false belief – a belief that something is the case when in fact it is not. They also understand that a person's feelings depend not only on the situation they find themselves in but also on their own particular desires – their likes and dislikes, and so on.

Despite these impressive abilities, however, it is likely that these young children do not represent their knowledge in the same way as do older children, a distinction I have already discussed in relation to children's visual perspective-taking skills (Chapter 2). Their relatively immature way of representing mental states prevents them from solving some of the more complicated false belief and role-taking tasks presented by researchers. By the age of about 6 or 7 years, however, they appreciate that different people can interpret the same information in different ways and that a person can feel one emotion while at the same time publicly displaying an entirely different one. Development does not end here, though, even though much of the research covers only a fairly limited age span. No doubt in the near future research studies will cover a wider age range and will also integrate the different topics within this general area.

Bibliography

Abkarian, G. G. (1983) More negative findings for positive prepositions. *Journal of Child Language, 10,* 415–29.

Acredolo, L. P. (1978) Development of spatial orientation in infancy. *Developmental Psychology, 14,* 224–34.

Acredolo, L. P. (1979) Laboratory versus home: the effect of environment on the 9-month-old infant's choice of spatial reference system. *Developmental Psychology, 15,* 666–7.

Andersen, E. S. (1984) The acquisition of sociolinguistic knowledge: some evidence from children's verbal role-play. *The Western Journal of Speech Communication, 48,* 125–44.

Anderson, J. W. (1972) Attachment behaviour out of doors. In Blurton-Jones, N. (Ed.) *Ethological Studies of Child Behaviour.* Cambridge: Cambridge University Press.

Baillargeon, R. (1987) Young infants' reasoning about the physical and spatial properties of a hidden object. *Cognitive Development, 2,* 179–200.

Bakeman, R. and Adamson, L. B. (1984) Coordinating attention to people and objects in mother–infant and peer–infant interaction. *Child Development, 55,* 1278–89.

Bakker-Renes, H. and Hoefnagel-Hoehle, M. (1974) Situatie verschillen in taalgebruik (Situation differences in language use). Master's thesis, University of Amsterdam.

Baron-Cohen, S., Leslie, A. M. and Frith, U. (1985) Does the autistic child have a 'theory of mind'? *Cognition, 21,* 37–46.

Barrett, M. D., Beaumont, A. V. and Jennett, M. S. (1985) Some children do sometimes do what they have been told to do: task demands and verbal instructions in children's drawing. In Freeman, N. H. and Cox, M. V. (Eds.) *Visual Order: The Nature and Development of Pictorial Representation.* Cambridge: Cambridge University Press.

Barrett, M. D. and Bridson, A. (1983) The effect of instructions upon children's drawings. *British Journal of Developmental Psychology, 1,* 175–8.

Bates, E. (1979) *The Emergence of Symbols: Cognition and Communication in Infancy.* New York: Academic Press.

Bates, E., Benigni, L., Bretherton, I., Camaioni, L. and Volterra, V. (1979) Cognition and communication from nine to thirteen months: correlational findings. In Bates, E. *The Emergence of Symbols.* New York: Academic Press.

Bayraktar, R. (1985) Cross-cultural analysis of drawing errors. In Freeman, N. H. and Cox, M. V. (Eds.) *Visual Order: The Nature and Development of Pictorial Representation*. Cambridge: Cambridge University Press.

Bee, H. (1975) *The Developing Child*. New York: Harper and Row.

Berman, P. W. (1976) Young children's use of the frame of reference in construction of the horizontal, vertical, and the oblique. *Child Development*, 47, 259–63.

Berman, P. W., Cunningham, J. G. and Harkulich, J. (1974) Construction of the horizontal, vertical and oblique by young children: failure to find the oblique effect. *Child Development*, 45, 474–8.

Bjorklund, D. F. (1987) A note on neonatal imitation. *Developmental Review*, 7, 86–92.

Bloom, L. (1973) *One Word at a Time*. The Hague: Mouton.

Bower, T. G. R. (1974) *Development in Infancy*. San Francisco: Freeman.

Bower, T. G. R. (1979) *Human Development*. San Francisco: Freeman.

Bower, T. G. R., Broughton, J. M. and Moore, M. K. (1970) Infant responses to approaching objects: an indicator of response to distal variables. *Perception and Psychophysics*, 9, 193–6.

Bower, T. G. R. and Wishart, J. G. (1972) The effects of motor skill on object permanence. *Cognition*, 1, 165–72.

Braine, M. D. S. (1962) Piaget on reasoning: a methodological critique and alternative proposals. In Kessen, W. and Kuhlman, C. (Eds.) *Thought in the Young Child, Monographs of the Society for Research in Child Development*, 27, 41–61.

Brazelton, T., Koslowski, B. and Main, M. (1974) The origins of reciprocity: the early mother–infant interaction. In Lewis, M. and Rosenblum, L. (Eds.) *The Effect of the Infant on its Caregiver*. New York: Wiley.

Bremner, J. G. (1978) Egocentric versus allocentric spatial coding in nine-month-old infants: factors influencing the choice of code. *Developmental Psychology*, 14, 346–55.

Bremner, J. G. (1980) The infant's understanding of space. In Cox, M. V. (Ed.) *Are Young Children Egocentric?* London: Batsford Academic.

Bremner, J. G. (1984) Errors towards the perpendicular in children's copies of angular figures: a test of the bisection interpretation. *Perception*, 13, 117–28.

Bremner, J. G. (1988) *Infancy*. Oxford: Blackwell.

Bremner, J. G. and Bryant, P. E. (1977) Place versus response as the basis of spatial errors made by young infants. *Journal of Experimental Child Psychology*, 23, 162–71.

Bremner, J. G. and Moore, S. (1984) Prior visual inspection and object naming: two factors that enhance hidden feature inclusion in young children's drawings. *British Journal of Developmental Psychology*, 2, 371–6.

Bremner, J. G. and Taylor, A. J. (1982) Children's errors in copying angles: perpendicular error or bisection error? *Perception*, 11, 163–71.

Brener, R. (1983) Learning the deictic meaning of third person pronouns. *Journal of Psycholinguistic Research*, 12, 235–62.

Bridges, A. and Rowles, J. (1985) Young children's projective abilities: what can a monster see? *Educational Psychology*, 5, 251–66.

Brittain, W. L. (1976) The effect of background shapes on the ability of children to copy geometric forms. *Child Development*, 47, 1179–81.

Brodzinsky, D. M., Jackson, J. P. and Overton, W. F. (1972) Effects of perceptual shielding in the development of spatial perspectives. *Child Development*, 43, 1041–6.

Brown, R. (1977) Introduction. In Snow, C. and Ferguson, C. (Eds.) *Talking to Children: Language Input and Acquisition*. Cambridge: Cambridge University Press.

Brown, R. and Fraser, C. (1964) The acquisition of syntax. In Bellugi, U. and Brown, R. (Eds.) *Monographs of the Society for Research in Child Development*, 29, No. 1, 43–79.

Brown, R. and Hanlon, C. (1970) Derivational complexity and order of acquisition in child speech. In Hayes, J. R. (Ed.) *Cognition and the Development of Language*. New York: Wiley.

Brown, R. and Herrnstein, R. J. (1975) *Psychology*. London: Methuen.

Bruner, J. S. (1974/5) The ontogenesis of speech acts. *Journal of Child Language*, 2, 1–19.

Bruner, J. S. (1975) From communication to language – a psychological perspective. *Cognition*, 3, 255–87.

Bruner, J. S. (1982) The organization of action and the nature of the adult-infant transaction. In Tronick, E. (Ed.) *Social Interchange in Infancy: Affect, Cognition and Communication*. Baltimore: University Park Press.

Bruner, J. (1983) *Child's Talk. Learning to Use Language*. Oxford: Oxford University Press.

Bruner, J., Caudill, E. and Ninio, A. (1977) Language and experience. In Peters, R. S. (Ed.) *John Dewey Reconsidered*. London: Routledge and Kegan Paul.

Bushnell, I. W. R., Sai, F. and Mullin, J. T. (1989) Neonatal recognition of the mother's face. *British Journal of Developmental Psychology*, 7, 3–15.

Butterworth, G. E. (1977) Object disappearance and error in Piaget's Stage 4 task. *Journal of Experimental Child Psychology*, 23, 391–401.

Butterworth, G. E. (1981) Structure of the mind in human infancy. Paper presented to the International Society for the Study of Behavioral Development, Toronto, Canada.

Butterworth, G. E. (1987) Some benefits of egocentrism. In Bruner, J. S. and Haste, H. (Eds.) *Making Sense: The Child's Construction of the World*. London: Methuen.

Butterworth, G. E. and Cochran, E. (1980) Towards a mechanism of joint visual attention in human infancy. *International Journal of Behavioral Development*, 3, 253–72.

Butterworth, G. E. and Grover, L. (1988) The origins of referential communication in human infancy. In Weiskrantz, L. (Ed.) *Thought Without Language*. Oxford: Clarendon Press.

Butterworth, G. E. and Jarrett, N. (1980) The geometry of pre-verbal communication. Paper presented at the British Psychological Society Developmental Psychology Section Conference, Edinburgh.

Caron, R. F., Caron, A. J. and Myers, R. S. (1982) Abstraction of invariant face expressions in infancy. *Child Development, 53*, 1008–15.

Carter, A. L. (1975) The transformation of sensori-motor morphemes into words: a case study of the development of 'here' and 'there'. *Papers and Reports on Child Language Development, 10*, 31–48. Stanford University, California, U.S.A.

Carter, A. L. (1978) From sensori-motor vocalizations to words. In Lock, A. (Ed.) *Action, Gesture and Symbol: The Emergence of Language*. London: Academic Press.

Cazden, C. (1965) Environmental assistance to the child's acquisition of grammar. Doctoral Dissertation, Harvard University.

Cazden, C. (1970) The situation: a neglected course of social class differences in language use. *Journal of Social Issues, 26*, 35–60.

Chandler, M. J. (1973) Egocentrism and antisocial behavior: an assessment and training of social perspective-taking skills. *Developmental Psychology, 9*, 326–32.

Chandler, M. J. (1987). The Othello effect: essay on the emergence and eclipse of skeptical doubt. *Human Development, 30*, 137–59.

Chandler, M. J. (1988) Doubt and developing theories of mind. In Astington, J. W., Harris, P. L. and Olson, D. R. (Eds.) *Developing Theories of Mind*. New York: Cambridge University Press.

Chandler, M. J., Fritz, A. S. and Hala, S. (1989) Small-scale deceit: deception as a marker of two-, three-, and four-year-olds' early theories of mind. *Child Development, 60*, 1263–77.

Chandler, M. J. and Greenspan, S. (1972) Ersatz egocentrism: a reply to H. Borke. *Developmental Psychology, 7*, 104–6.

Chandler, M. J. and Helm, D. (1984) Developmental changes in the contributions of shared experience to social role-taking competence. *International Journal of Behavioral Development, 7*, 145–56.

Charney, R. (1979) The comprehension of 'here' and 'there'. *Journal of Child Language, 6*, 69–80.

Charney, R. (1980) Speech roles and the development of personal pronouns. *Journal of Child Language, 7*, 509–29.

Chiat, S. (1981) Context-specificity and generalisation in the acquisition of pronominal distinction. *Journal of Child Language, 8*, 75–91.

Chiat, S. (1982) If I were you and you were me: the analysis of pronouns in a pronoun-reversing child. *Journal of Child Language, 9*, 359–79.

Clark, E. V. and Sengul, C. J. (1978) Strategies in the acquisition of deixis. *Journal of Child Language, 5*, 457–75.

Coie, J. D., Costanzo, P. R. and Farnill, D. (1973) Specific transitions in the development of spatial perspective-taking ability. *Developmental Psychology, 9*, 167–77.

Cole, P. M. (1986) Children's spontaneous control of facial expression. *Child Development, 57*, 1309–21.

Collis, G. M. (1977) Visual co-orientation and maternal speech. In Schaffer, H. R. (Ed.) *Studies in Mother–Infant Interaction*. London: Academic Press.

Collis, G. M. and Schaffer, H. R. (1975) Synchronization of visual attention in mother–infant pairs. *Journal of Child Psychology and Psychiatry, 16,* 315–20.

Condon, W. S. and Sander, L. (1974) Neonate movement is synchronized with adult speech: interactional participation and language acquisition. *Science, 183,* 99–101.

Cooley, C. H. (1908) A study of the early use of self-words by a child. *Psychological Review, 15,* 339–57.

Corsaro, W. A. (1976) The clarification request as a feature of adult interactive styles with young children. *Language and Society, 6,* 183–207.

Cox, M. V. (1978a) Order of acquisition of perspective-taking skills. *Developmental Psychology, 14,* 421–2.

Cox, M. V. (1978b) The development of perspective ability in children. *International Journal of Behavioral Development, 1,* 247–54.

Cox, M. V. (1978c) Spatial depth relationships in young children's drawings. *Journal of Experimental Child Psychology, 26,* 551–4.

Cox, M. V. (1979) Young children's understanding of 'in front of' and 'behind' in the placement of objects. *Journal of Child Language, 6,* 371–4.

Cox, M. V. (1980) Visual perspective-taking in children. In Cox, M. V. (Ed.) *Are Young Children Egocentric?* London: Batsford Academic.

Cox, M. V. (1981a) Interpretation of the spatial prepositions 'in front of' and 'behind'. *International Journal of Behavioral Development, 4,* 359–68.

Cox, M. V. (1981b) The development of children's use and interpretation of spatial terms. Social Science Research Council Report HR 6069/1 and 2.

Cox, M. V. (1981c) One thing behind another: problems of representation in children's drawings. *Educational Psychology, 1,* 275–87.

Cox, M. V. (1985a) One object behind another: young children's use of array-specific or view-specific representations. In Freeman, N. H. and Cox, M. V. (Eds.) *Visual Order: The Nature and Development of Pictorial Representation.* Cambridge: Cambridge University Press.

Cox, M. V. (1985b) Deictic and nondeictic interpretations of *in front of* and *behind* in fronted object tasks. *International Journal of Behavioral Development, 8,* 183–94.

Cox, M. V. (1986) Cubes are difficult things to draw. *British Journal of Developmental Psychology, 4,* 341–5.

Cox, M. V. (1989) Knowledge and appearance in children's pictorial representation. *Educational Psychology, 9,* 15–25.

Cox, M. V. and Isard, S. (1990) Children's deictic and nondeictic interpretations of the spatial locatives *in front of* and *behind*. *Journal of Child Language, 17,* 481–8.

Cox, M. V. and Martin, A. (1988) Young children's viewer-centred representations: drawings of a cube placed inside or behind a transparent or opaque beaker. *International Journal of Behavioral Development, 11,* 233–45.

Cox, M. V. and Ryder Richardson, J. (1985) How do children describe spatial relationships? *Journal of Child Language, 12,* 611–20.

Cox, M. V. and Willetts, E. (1982) Childhood egocentrism: the order of acquisition of before-behind and left-right relationships. *British Journal of Educational Psychology, 52,* 366–9.

Crook, C. K. (1983) The perpendicular error and the vertical effect. Paper presented at the Conference on Graphic Representation, University of York.

Crook, C. K. (1985) Knowledge and appearance. In Freeman, N. H. and Cox, M. V. (Eds.) *Visual Order: The Nature and Development of Pictorial Representation.* Cambridge: Cambridge University Press.

Cross, T. G. (1977) Mothers' speech adjustments: the contribution of selected child listener variables. In Snow, C. and Ferguson, C. (Eds.) *Talking to Children: Language Input and Acquisition.* Cambridge: Cambridge University Press.

Cross, T. G. (1978) Mothers' speech and its association with linguistic development in young children. In Waterson, N. and Snow, C. (Eds.) *The Development of Communication.* Chichester: Wiley.

Darwin, C. (1872) *The Expression of the Emotions in Man and Animals.* London: Murray.

Davis, A. M. (1983) Contextual sensitivity in young children's drawings. *Journal of Experimental Child Psychology, 35*, 478–86.

Davis, A. M. (1984) Noncanonical orientation without occlusion: children's drawings of transparent objects. *Journal of Experimental Child Psychology, 37*, 451–62.

Dayton, G. O., Jones, M. H., Giu, P., Rawson, R. H., Steele, B. and Rose, M. (1964) Developmental study of coordinated eye movements in the human infant: 1 – visual activity in the newborn: a study based on induced autokinetic nystagmus recorded by electrooculography. *Archives of Ophthalmology, 71*, 865–70.

DePaulo, B. M. and Jordan, A. (1982) Age changes in deceiving and detecting deceit. In Feldman, R. S. (Ed.) *Development of Non-Verbal Behavior in Children.* New York: Springer.

De Villiers, P. and de Villiers, J. (1974) On this, that, and the other: nonegocentrism in very young children. *Journal of Experimental Child Psychology, 18*, 438–47.

Donaldson, M. (1978) *Children's Minds.* Glasgow: Fontana/Collins.

Dubery, F. and Willats, J. (1972) *Drawing Systems.* London: Studio Vista.

Dunkeld, J. and Bower, T. G. R. (1979) Infant smiling in different situations. Unpublished manuscript, University of Edinburgh.

Dunn, J. (1988) *The Beginnings of Social Understanding.* Oxford: Blackwell.

Dunn, J. and Kendrick, C. (1982) The speech of two- and three-year-olds to infant siblings: 'baby talk' and the context of communication. *Journal of Child Language, 9*, 579–95.

Durkin, K., Rutter, D. R., Room, S. and Grounds, P. (1982) Proper name usage in maternal speech: a longitudinal study. In Johnson, C. E. and Thew, C. L. (Eds.) *Proceedings of the Second International Congress for the Study of Child Language,* Washington, D. C.: University Press of America.

Durkin, K., Rutter, D. R. and Tucker, H. (1982) Social interaction and language acquisition: motherese help you? *First Language, 3*, 107–20.

Ekman, P. (1973) Cross-cultural studies of facial expression. In Ekman, P. (Ed.) *Darwin and Facial Expression.* New York: Academic Press.

Ekman, P. and Friesen, W. (1971) Constants across culture in the face and emotion. *Journal of Personality and Social Psychology,* 17, 124–9.

Elliot, A. J. (1981) *Child Language.* Cambridge: Cambridge University Press.

Estes, D., Wellman, H. M. and Woolley, J. D. (1989) Children's understanding of mental phenomena. In Reese, H. W. (Ed.) *Advances in Child Development and Behavior.* Orlando, Florida: Academic Press.

Fantz, R. L. (1963) Pattern vision in newborn infants. *Science,* 140, 296–7.

Fehr, L. A. (1978) Methodological inconsistencies in the measurement of spatial perspective taking ability: a cause for concern. *Human Development,* 21, 302–15.

Fein, G. G. (1981) Pretend play in childhood: an integrative review. *Child Development,* 52, 1095–118.

Ferguson, C. A. (1977) Baby talk as a simplified register. In Snow, C. E. and Ferguson, C. A. (Eds.) *Talking to Children: Language Input and Acquisition.* Cambridge: Cambridge University Press.

Fishbein, H. D., Lewis, S. and Keiffer, K. (1972) Children's understanding of spatial relationships: coordination of perspectives. *Developmental Psychology,* 7, 21–33.

Flavell, J. (1968) in collaboration with Botkin, P., Fry, C., Wright, J. and Jarvis, P. *The Development of Role-Taking and Communication Skills in Children.* New York: Wiley.

Flavell, J. H. (1974) The development of inferences about others. In Mischel, T. (Ed.) *Understanding Other Persons.* Oxford: Blackwell.

Flavell, J. H. (1978) The development of knowledge about visual perception. In Keasey, C. B. (Ed.) *Nebraska Symposium on Motivation.* Lincoln: University of Nebraska Press.

Flavell, J. H., Everett, B. A., Croft, K. and Flavell, E. R. (1981) Young children's knowledge about visual perception: further evidence for the Level 1–Level 2 distinction. *Developmental Psychology,* 17, 99–103.

Flavell, J. H., Flavell, E. R. and Green, F. L. (1983) Development of the appearance–reality distinction. *Cognitive Psychology,* 15, 95–120.

Flavell, J. H., Shipstead, S. G. and Croft, K. (1978) Young children's knowledge about visual perception: hiding objects from others. *Child Development,* 49, 1208–11.

Fogel, A. and Hannan, T. E. (1985) Manual actions of nine- to fifteen-week-old human infants during face-to-face interaction with their mothers. *Child Development,* 56, 1271–9.

Fontaine, R. (1984) Imitative skill between birth and six months. *Infant Behavior and Development,* 7, 323–33.

Franco, F. and Butterworth, G. E. (1988) Manual pointing, visual checking and vocalization in infancy. Paper presented at the Annual Conference of the British Psychological Society Developmental Section, Coleg Harlech, Wales.

Freeman, N. H. (1980) *Strategies of Representation in Young Children.* London: Academic Press.

Freeman, N. H., Eiser, C. and Sayers, J. (1977) Children's strategies in producing 3-D relationships on a 2-D surface. *Journal of Experimental Child Psychology,* 23, 305–14.

Freeman, N. H. and Janikoun, R. (1972) Intellectual realism in children's drawings of a familiar object with distinctive features. *Child Development,* 43, 1116–21.

Frith, U. (1989) *Autism.* Oxford: Basil Blackwell.

Furrow, D., Nelson, K. and Benedict, H. (1979) Mothers' speech to children and syntactic development: some simple relationships. *Journal of Child Language,* 6, 423–42.

Ganchrow, J. R., Steiner, J. E. and Daher, M. (1983) Neonatal facial expressions in response to different qualities and intensities of gustatory stimuli. *Infant Behavior and Development,* 6, 473–84.

Gardner, H. (1972) The development of sensitivity to figural and stylistic aspects of paintings. *British Journal of Psychology,* 63, 605–15.

Garnica, O. K. (1977) Some prosodic and paralinguistic features of speech to young children. In Snow, C. and Ferguson, C. (Eds.) *Talking to Children: Language Input and Acquisition.* Cambridge: Cambridge University Press.

Garnica, O. K. (1978) Non-verbal concomitants of language input to children. In Waterson, N. and Snow, C. (Eds.) *The Development of Communication.* Chichester: Wiley.

Garvey, C. (1977) The contingent query: a dependent act in conversation. In Lewis, M. and Rosenblum, L. (Eds.) *Interaction, Conversation and the Development of Language: The Origins of Behavior. Vol. V.* New York: Wiley.

Garvey, C. and BenDebba, M. (1978) An experimental investigation of contingent query sequences. *Discourse Processes,* 1, 36–50.

Garvey, C. and Berndt, R. (1977) Organization of pretend play. *Catalogue of Selected Documents in Psychology,* 7, 1589.

Garvey, C. and Hogan, R. (1973) Social speech and social interaction: egocentrism revisited. *Child Development,* 44, 562–8.

Gelman, R. and Shatz, M. (1977) Appropriate speech adjustments: the operation of conversational constraints on talk to two-year-olds. In Lewis, M. and Rosenblum, L. (Eds.) *Interaction, Conversation and the Development of Language.* New York: Wiley.

Gesell, A., Thompson, H. and Amatruda, C. S. (1934) *Infant Behavior: Its Genesis and Growth.* New York: McGraw Hill.

Gibson, J. J. (1950) *The Perception of the Visual World.* Cambridge, Mass.: Riverside Press.

Gibson, J. J. (1966) *The Senses Considered as Perceptual Systems.* Boston: Houghton Mifflin.

Gibson, J. J. (1979) *The Ecological Approach to Visual Perception.* Boston: Houghton Mifflin.

Gleason, J. Berko (1973) Code switching in children's language. In Moore, T. E. (Ed.) *Cognitive Development and the Acquisition of Language.* New York: Academic Press.

Gleitman, L. R., Newport, E. L. and Gleitman, H. (1984) The current status of the motherese hypothesis. *Journal of Child Language,* 11, 43–79.

Glucksberg, S., Krauss, R. M. and Weisberg, R. (1966) Referential communication in nursery school children: method and some preliminary findings. *Journal of Experimental Child Psychology,* 3, 333–42.

Golinkoff, R. M. and Ames, G. J. (1979) A comparison of fathers' and mothers' speech with their young children. *Child Development, 50*, 28–32.

Goodenough, F. (1926) *The Measurement of Intelligence by Drawings.* New York: World Books.

Gopnik, A. and Astington, J. W. (1988) Children's understanding of representational change and its relation to the understanding of false belief and the appearance–reality distinction. *Child Development, 59*, 26–37.

Gopnik, A. and Slaughter, V. (in press) Young children's understanding of changes in their mental states. *Child Development.*

Goren, C. C., Sarty, M. and Wu, P. Y. K. (1975) Visual following and pattern discrimination of face-like stimuli of newborn infants. *Pediatrics, 56*, 544–9.

Granrud, C. E. and Yonas, A. (1984) Infants' perception of pictorially specified interposition. *Journal of Experimental Child Psychology, 37*, 500–11.

Greenman, G. W. (1963) Visual behaviour of newborn infants. In Solnit, A. J. and Provence, S. A. (Eds.) *Modern Perspectives in Child Development,* New York: Hallmark.

Griffiths, P. (1974) *That there* deixis 1: *that.* Unpublished paper, University of York.

Gross, D. and Harris, P. L. (1988) Understanding false beliefs about emotion. *International Journal of Behavioral Development, 11*, 475–88.

Grover, L. (1988) Comprehension of manual pointing gesture in human infants. Doctoral thesis, University of Southampton.

Hagen, M. A. (1976) Development of ability to perceive and produce pictorial depth cue of overlapping. *Perceptual and Motor Skills, 42*, 1007–14.

Hagen, M. A. (1985) There is no development in Art. In Freeman, N. H. and Cox, M. V. (Eds.) *Visual Order: The Nature and Development of Pictorial Representation.* Cambridge: Cambridge University Press.

Hagen, M. A. and Elliott, H. B. (1976) An investigation of the relationship between viewing condition and preference for true and modified linear perspective with adults. *Journal of Experimental Psychology: Human Perception and Performance, 2*, 479–90.

Haith, M. M. (1966) The response of the human newborn to visual movement. *Journal of Experimental Child Psychology, 3*, 235–43.

Hall, E. (1970) A conversation with Jean Piaget and Bärbel Inhelder. *Psychology Today, 3*, 25–32 and 54–6.

Hannan, T. E. (1987) A cross-sequential assessment of the occurrences of pointing in 3- to 12-month-old human infants. *Infant Behavior and Development, 10*, 11–22.

Harkness, S. (1977) Aspects of social environment and first language acquisition in rural Africa. In Snow, C. E. and Ferguson, C. A. (Eds.) *Talking to Children: Language Input and Acquisition.* Cambridge: Cambridge University Press.

Harris, D. B. (1963) *Children's Drawings as Measures of Intellectual Maturity.* New York: Harcourt, Brace and World.

Harris, L. J. and Strommen, E. A. (1979) The development of understanding of the spatial terms *front* and *back. Advances in Child Development and Behavior, 14*, 149–207.

Harris, P. L. (1989) *Children and Emotion: The Development of Psychological Understanding.* Oxford: Blackwell.

Harris, P. L., Donnelly, K., Guz, G. R. and Pitt-Watson, R. (1986) Children's understanding of the distinction between real and apparent emotion. *Child Development, 57,* 895–909.

Harris, P. L. and Gross, D. (1988) Children's understanding of real and apparent emotion. In Astington, J. W., Harris, P. L. and Olson, D. R. (Eds.) *Developing Theories of Mind.* New York: Cambridge University Press.

Harris, P. L., Johnson, C. N., Hutton, D. Andrews, G. and Cooke, T. (1989) Young children's theory of mind and emotion. *Cognition and Emotion, 3,* 379–400.

Haviland, J. M. and Lelwica, M. (1987) The induced affect response: 10-week-old infants' responses to three emotional expressions. *Developmental Psychology, 23,* 97–104.

Hayes, L. A. and Watson, J. S. (1981) Neonatal imitation: fact or artifact? *Developmental Psychology, 17,* 655–60.

Hill, C. (1978) Linguistic representation of spatial and temporal orientation. *Proceedings of the Berkeley Linguistic Society, 4,* 524–39.

Hirsh-Pasek, K., Treiman, R. and Schneiderman, M. (1984) Brown and Hanlon revisited: mothers' sensitivity to ungrammatical forms. *Journal of Child Language, 11,* 81–8.

Hoffman, M. L. (1981) Perspectives on the difference between understanding people and understanding things: the role of affect. In Flavell, J. and Ross, L. (Eds.) *Social Cognitive Development.* Cambridge: Cambridge University Press.

Hood, B. and Willatts, P. (1986) Reaching in the dark to an object's remembered position: evidence for object permanence in 5-month-old infants. *British Journal of Developmental Psychology, 4,* 57–65.

Hoy, E. (1974) Predicting another's visual perspective: a unitary skill? *Developmental Psychology, 10,* 462.

Hughes, M. and Donaldson, M. (1979) The use of hiding games for studying the coordination of viewpoints. *Educational Review, 31,* 133–40.

Hustler, D. (1981) Some comments on clarification requests: a response to Langford. In French, P. and Maclure, M. (Eds.) *Adult-Child Conversation.* London: Croom Helm.

Huxley, R. (1970) The development of the correct use of subject personal pronouns in two children. In Flores D'Arcais, G. B. and Levitt, W. J. M. (Eds.) *Advances in Psycholinguistics.* Amsterdam: North Holland.

Ibbotson, A. and Bryant, P. E. (1976) The perpendicular error and the vertical effect in children's drawing. *Perception, 5,* 319–26.

Ives, W. (1980) Preschool children's ability to coordinate spatial perspectives through language and pictures. *Child Development, 51,* 1303–06.

Ives, W. (1983) The development of strategies for coordinating spatial perspectives of an array. In Olson, D. R. and Bialystock, E. (Eds.) *Explorations in Inner Space: Aspects of the Development of Spatial Cognition.* Hillsdale, New Jersey: Erlbaum.

Jacobson, J. L., Boersma, D. C., Fields, R. B. and Olson, K. L. (1983)

Paralinguistic features of adult speech to infants and small children. *Child Development, 54,* 436–42.

Jacobson, S. W. (1979) Matching behavior in the young infant. *Child Development, 50,* 425–30.

Jahoda, G. (1981) Drawing styles of schooled and unschooled adults: a study in Ghana, *Quarterly Journal of Experimental Psychology, 33A,* 133–43.

Jakobson, R. (1960) Why 'mama' and 'papa'? In Kaplan, B. and Wapner, S. (Eds.) *Perspectives in Psychological Theory.* New York: Wiley.

Jakobson, R. (1968) *Child Language, Aphasia, and Phonological Universals.* The Hague: Mouton.

James, W. (1890) *The Principles of Psychology.* New York: Holt.

Johnson, C. N. (1988) Theory of mind and the structure of conscious experience. In Astington, J. W., Harris, P. L. and Olson, D. R. (Eds.) *Developing Theories of Mind.* New York: Cambridge University Press.

Johnson, C. N. and Wellman, H. M. (1982) Children's developing conceptions of the mind and brain. *Child Development, 53,* 222–34.

Johnston, J. R. and Slobin, D. I. (1979) The development of locative expressions in English, Italian, Serbo-Croatian and Turkish. *Journal of Child Language, 6,* 529–45.

Jones, L. V. and Wepman, J. M. (1966) *A Spoken Word Count: Adults.* Chicago: Language Research Association.

Kanner, L. (1949) Problems of nosology and psychodynamics of early infantile autism. *American Journal of Orthopsychiatry, 19,* 416–26.

Kavanaugh, R. D. and Jirkovsky, A. M. (1982) Parental speech to young children: a longitudinal analysis. *Merrill-Palmer Quarterly, 28,* 297–311.

Kaye, K. (1982) *The Mental and Social Life of Babies.* Chicago: University of Chicago Press.

Keenan, E. O. and Klein, E. (1975) Coherency in children's discourse. *Journal of Psycholinguistic Research, 4,* 365–80.

Kellman, P. J. (1984) Perception of three-dimensional form by human infants. *Perception and Psychophysics, 36,* 353–8.

Kermoian, R. and Campos, J. J. (1988) Locomotor experience: a facilitator of spatial cognitive development. *Child Development, 59,* 908–17.

Kessen, W., Haith, M. M. and Salapatek, P. (1970) Human infancy: a bibliography and guide. In Mussen, P. (Ed.) *Carmichael's Manual of Child Psychology.* New York: Wiley.

Kielgast, K. (1971) Piaget's concept of spatial egocentrism: a reevaluation. *Scandinavian Journal of Psychology, 12,* 179–91.

Klinnert, M. (1984) The regulation of infant behavior by maternal facial expression. *Infant Behavior and Development, 7,* 447–65.

Kuczaj, S. A. (1982) On the nature of syntactic development. In Kuczaj, S. A. (Ed.) *Language Development. Vol. 1. Syntax and Semantics.* Hillsdale, New Jersey: Erlbaum.

Kuczaj, S. A. and Maratsos, M. P. (1975) On the acquisition of *front, back* and *side. Child Development, 46,* 202–10.

Langford, D. (1981) The clarification request in conversation between mothers and their children. In French, P. and Maclure, M. (Eds.) *Adult–Child Conversation.* London: Croom Helm.

Lee, M. (1989) When is an object not an object? The effect of 'meaning' upon the copying of line drawings. *British Journal of Psychology, 80,* 15–37.

Leehey, S. C. and Carey, S. (1978) Up front: the acquisition of a concept and a word. Paper presented at the 10th Child Language Research Forum, Stanford, California.

Lempers, J. D. (1979) Young children's production and comprehension of nonverbal deictic behaviours. *The Journal of Genetic Psychology, 135,* 93–102.

Lempers, J. D., Flavell, E. R. and Flavell, J. H. (1977) The development in very young children of tacit knowledge concerning visual perception. *Genetic Psychology Monographs, 95,* 3–53.

Leslie, A. M. (1987) Pretense and representation: the origins of 'Theory of Mind'. *Psychological Review, 94,* 412–26.

Leslie, A. (1988) Some implications of pretense for the development of theories of minds. In Astington, J. W., Harris, P. L. and Olson, D. R. (Eds.) *Developing Theories of Mind.* New York: Cambridge University Press.

Leung, E. H. L. and Rheingold, H. L. (1981) Development of pointing as a social gesture. *Developmental Psychology, 17,* 215–20.

Levinson, S. C. (1983) *Pragmatics.* Cambridge: Cambridge University Press.

Liben, L. (1978) Perspective-taking skills in young children: seeing the world through rose-coloured glasses. *Developmental Psychology, 14,* 87–92.

Liben, L. and Belknap, B. (1981) Intellectual realism: implications for investigation of perceptual perspective-taking in young children. *Child Development, 52,* 921–4.

Light, P. H. and Humphreys, J. (1981) Internal spatial relationships in young children's drawings. *Journal of Experimental Child Psychology, 31,* 521–30.

Light, P. H. and MacIntosh, E. (1980) Depth relationships in young children's drawings. *Journal of Experimental Child Psychology, 30,* 79–87.

Light, P. and Nix, C. (1983) 'Own view' versus 'good view' in a perspective-taking task. *Child Development, 54,* 480–3.

Lorge, I. (1949) *The Semantic Count of the 570 Commonest English Words.* New York: Teachers College, Columbia University.

Luquet, G. H. (1913) *Les Dessins d'un Enfant.* Paris: Alcan.

Luquet, G. H. (1927) *Le Dessin Enfantin.* Paris: Alcan.

Machover, K. (1953) Human figure drawings of children. *Journal of Projective Techniques, 17,* 85–91.

Macnamara, J. T. (1982) *Names for Things.* Cambridge, Mass.: MIT Press.

Main, M. and George, C. (1985) Responses of abused and disadvantaged toddlers to distress in agemates: a study in the day care setting. *Developmental Psychology, 21,* 407–12.

Maratos, O. (1973) The origin and development of imitation in the first six months of life. Doctoral thesis, University of Geneva.

Maratsos, M. P. (1979) Learning how to and when to use pronouns and determiners. In Fletcher, P. and Garman, M. (Eds.) *Language Acquisition,* Cambridge: Cambridge University Press.

Masangkay, Z. S., McCluskey, K. A., McIntyre, C. W., Sims-Knight, J., Vaughn, B. E. and Flavell, J. H. (1974) The early development of inferences about the visual percepts of others. *Child Development, 45,* 357–66.

Masur, E. F. (1982) Mothers' responses to infants' object-related gestures: influences on lexical development. *Journal of Child Language, 9,* 23–30.

McDonald, L. and Pien, D. (1982) Mother conversational behaviour as a function of interactional intent. *Journal of Child Language, 9,* 337–58.

McGarrigle, J. and Donaldson, M. (1974) Conservation accidents. *Cognition, 3,* 341–50.

McNeill, D. (1963) The psychology of *I* and *you*: a case history of a small language system. Paper presented at the American Psychological Association Symposium on Child Language.

Meltzoff, A. N. and Moore, M. K. (1977) Imitation of facial and manual gestures by human neonates. *Science, 198,* 75–80.

Meltzoff, A. N. and Moore, M. K. (1983) Newborn infants imitate adult facial gestures. *Child Development, 54,* 702–9.

Meltzoff, A. N. and Moore, M. K. (1985) Cognitive foundations and social functions of imitation and intermodal representation in infancy. In Mehler, J. and Fox, R. (Eds.) *Neonate Cognition: Beyond the Blooming Buzzing Confusion.* Hillsdale, New Jersey: Erlbaum.

Messer, D. J. (1983) The redundancy between adult speech and nonverbal interaction: a contribution to acquisition? In Golinkoff, R. M. (Ed.) *The Transition from Prelinguistic to Linguistic Communication.* Hillsdale, New Jersey: Erlbaum.

Meyer, E. (1935) *La Répresentation des Relations Spatiales chez l'Enfant.* Universitaire de Genève: Institut des Sciences de l'Education.

Miller, P. and Sperry, L. L. (1987) The socialization of anger and aggression. *Merrill Palmer Quarterly, 33,* 1–32.

Minnigerode, F. A. and Carey, R. N. (1974) Development of mechanisms underlying spatial perspectives. *Child Development, 45,* 496–8.

Mitchelmore, M. C. (1978) Developmental stages in children's representations of regular solid figures. *Journal of Genetic Psychology, 133,* 229–39.

Moore, V. (1986) The use of a colouring task to elucidate children's drawings of a solid cube. *British Journal of Developmental Psychology, 4,* 335–40.

Morss, J. R. (1987) The construction of perspectives: Piaget's alternative to spatial egocentrism. *International Journal of Behavioral Development, 10,* 263–79.

Murchison, C. and Langer, S. (1927) Tiedemann's observations on the development of the mental faculties of children. *Pedagogical Seminary and Journal of Genetic Psychology, 34,* 205–30.

Murphy, C. M. (1978) Pointing in the context of a shared activity. *Child Development, 49,* 371–80.

Murphy, C. M. and Messer, D. J. (1977) Mothers, infants and pointing: a study of a gesture. In Schaffer, H. R. (Ed.) *Studies in Mother-Infant Interaction.* London: Academic Press.

Museyibova, T. A. (1961) The development of an understanding of spatial relations and their reflection in the language of children of preschool age. In Anan'yev, B. G. and Lovov, B. F. (Eds.) *Problemy Vospriyatiya Prostranstva i Prostranstvennykh Predstavleniy.* Moscow (*Problems of Spatial Perception and Spatial Concepts.* N.A. S.A., June 1964.)

Naeli, H. and Harris, P. (1976) Orientation of the diamond and the square. *Perception*, 5, 73–8.

Nelson, K. E. (1976) Facilitating children's syntax acquisition. *Developmental Psychology*, 13, 101–7.

Nelson, K. E., Carskaddon, G. and Bonvillian, J. D. (1973) Syntax acquisition: impact of experimental variation in adult verbal interaction with the child. *Child Development*, 44, 497–504.

Newport, E. L. (1976) Motherese: the speech of mothers to young children. In Castellan, N. J., Pisoni, D. B. and Potts, G. R. (Eds.) *Cognitive Theory 2.* Hillsdale, New Jersey: Erlbaum.

Newport, E. L., Gleitman, H. and Gleitman, L. R. (1977) Mother, I'd rather do it myself: some effects and noneffects of maternal speech style. In Snow, C. and Ferguson, C. (Eds.) *Talking to Children: Language Input and Acquisition.* Cambridge: Cambridge University Press.

Newson, J. and Newson, E. (1975). Intersubjectivity and the transmission of culture. *Bulletin of the British Psychological Society*, 28, 437–45.

Nigl, A. J. and Fishbein, H. D. (1973) Children's ability to coordinate perspectives: Cognitive factors (1). In Preiser, W. F. E. (Ed.) *Environmental Design Research, Vol. 2.* Stroudsberg, Pennsylvania: Dowden, Hutchinson and Ross.

Ninio, A. and Bruner, J. (1978) The achievement and antecedents of labelling. *Journal of Child Language*, 5, 1–15.

O'Hare, D. and Westwood, H. (1984) Features of style of classification: a multivariate experimental analysis of children's responses to drawings. *Developmental Psychology*, 20, 150–8.

Pechmann, T. and Deutsch, W. (1982) The development of verbal and nonverbal devices for reference. *Journal of Experimental Child Psychology*, 34, 330–41.

Perner, J. (1988) Developing semantics for theories of mind: from propositional attitudes to mental representation. In Astington, J. W., Harris, P. L. and Olson, D. R. (Eds.) *Developing Theories of Mind.* New York: Cambridge University Press.

Perner, J. (1990) *Understanding the Representational Mind.* Cambridge, Mass.: MIT Press.

Perner, J., Kohlmann, R. and Wimmer, H. (1984) Young children's recognition and use of the vertical and horizontal in drawings. *Child Development*, 55, 1637–45.

Perner, J., Leekam, S. and Wimmer, H. (1987) Three-year-olds' difficulty in understanding false belief: cognitive limitation, lack of knowledge, or pragmatic misunderstanding? *British Journal of Developmental Psychology*, 5, 125–37.

Phillips, W. A., Hobbs, S. B. and Pratt, F. R. (1978) Intellectual realism in children's drawings of cubes. *Cognition*, 6, 15–33.

Phillips, W. A., Inall, M. and Lauder, E. (1985) On the discovery, storage and use of graphic descriptions. In Freeman, N. H. and Cox, M. (Eds.) *Visual Order: The Nature and Development of Pictorial Representation.* Cambridge: Cambridge University Press.

Piaget, J. (1926) *The Language and Thought of the Child.* London: Routledge and Kegan Paul.

Piaget, J. (1951) *Play, Dreams and Imitation in Childhood,* London: Heinemann.

Piaget, J. (1954) *The Construction of Reality in the Child.* New York: Basic Books.

Piaget, J. (1962) *Play, Dreams and Imitation in Childhood.* New York: Norton.

Piaget, J. and Inhelder, B. (1956) *The Child's Conception of Space.* London: Routledge and Kegan Paul.

Piaget, J. and Inhelder, B. (1969) *The Psychology of the Child.* London: Routledge and Kegan Paul.

Piérart, B. (1977) L'acquisition du sens des marquers de relation spatial 'devant' et 'derrière'. *Année Psychologique,* 77, 95-116.

Pillow, B. H. and Flavell, J. H. (1986) Young children's knowledge about visual perception: projective size and shape. *Child Development,* 57, 125-35.

Pratt, F. (1985) A perspective on traditional artistic practices. In Freeman, N. H. and Cox, M. V. (Eds.) *Visual Order: The Nature and Development of Pictorial Representation.* Cambridge: Cambridge University Press.

Pratt, K. C. (1954) The neonate. In Carmichael, L. (Ed.) *Manual of Child Psychology.* New York: Wiley.

Presson, C. C. and Somerville, S. C. (1985) Beyond egocentrism: a new look at the beginnings of spatial representation. In Wellman, H. (Ed.) *Children's Searching: The Development of Search Skill and Spatial Representation.* Hillsdale, New Jersey: Erlbaum.

Preyer, W. (1896) *The Senses and the Will.* New York: Appleton-Century-Crofts.

Reissland, N. (1988) Neonatal imitation in the first hour of life: observations in rural Nepal. *Developmental Psychology,* 24, 464-9.

Ricci, C. (1887) *L'Arte dei Bambini.* Bologna: N. Zanichelli.

Ricks, D. M. and Wing, L. (1975) Language, communication and the use of symbols in normal and autistic children. *Journal of Autism and Childhood Schizophrenia,* 5, 191-221.

Rinsland, H. D. (1945) *A Basic Vocabulary of Elementary School Children.* New York: Macmillan.

Rutter, M., Greenfield, D. and Lockyer, L. (1968) A five to fifteen year follow-up study of infantile psychosis. In Chess, S. and Thomas, A. (Eds.) *Annual Progress in Child Psychiatry and Child Development.* New York: Brunner/Mazel.

Saarni, C. (1984) Observing children's use of display rules: age and sex differences. *Child Development,* 55, 1504-13.

Sachs, J. and Devin, J. (1976) Young children's use of age-appropriate speech styles in social interaction and role-playing. *Journal of Child Language,* 3, 81-98.

Sacks, H. (1980) Button, button, who's got the button? *Sociological Inquiry,* 50, 318-27.

Sacks, H. and Schegloff, E. (1974) Two preferences in the organisation of reference to persons in conversation and their interaction. In Avison, N. H. and Wilson, R. J. (Eds.) *Ethnomethodology: Labelling Theory and Deviant Behavior.* London: Routledge and Kegan Paul.

Salatas, H. and Flavell, J. H. (1976) Perspective-taking: the development of two components of knowledge. *Child Development, 47,* 103–9.

Scaife, M. and Bruner, J. S. (1975) The capacity for joint visual attention in the infant. *Nature, 253,* 265–6.

Schaffer, H. R., Hepburn, A. and Collis, G. M. (1983) Verbal and nonverbal aspects of mothers' directives. *Journal of Child Language, 10,* 337–55.

Shatz, M. (1982) On mechanisms of language acquisition: can features of the communicative environment account for development? In Gleitman, L. and Wanner, E. (Eds.) *Language Acquisition: the State of the Art.* Cambridge: Cambridge University Press.

Shatz, M. and Gelman, R. (1973) The development of communication skills: modifications in the speech of young children as a function of listener. *Monographs of the Society for Research in Child Development, 38,* No. 5.

Shatz, M., Wellman, H. M. and Silber, S. (1983) The acquisition of mental verbs: a systematic investigation of the first reference to mental state. *Cognition, 14,* 301–21.

Shirley, M. M. (1931–33) *The First Two Years: A Study of Twenty-Five Babies* (3 Vols.). Minneapolis: University of Minnesota Press.

Smetana, J. G., Kelly, M. and Twentyman, C. T. (1984) Abused, neglected and maltreated children's conceptions of moral and socio-conventional transgressions. *Child Development, 55,* 277–87.

Snow, C. E. (1972) Mothers' speech to children learning language. *Child Development, 43,* 549–65.

Snow, C. E. (1977a) The development of conversation between mothers and babies. *Journal of Child Language, 4,* 1–22.

Snow, C. E. (1977b) Mothers' speech research: from input to interaction. In Snow, C. and Ferguson, C. (Eds.) *Talking to Children: Language Input and Acquisition.* Cambridge: Cambridge University Press.

Snow, C. E. (1986) Conversations with children. In Fletcher, P. and Garman, M. (Eds.) *Language Acquisition.* Cambridge: Cambridge University Press. 2nd edition.

Strayer, J. (1977) The development of personal reference in the language of two-year-olds. Doctoral Thesis, Simon Fraser University, British Columbia, Canada.

Sugarman-Bell, S. (1978) Some organizational aspects of preverbal communication. In Markova, I. (Ed.) *The Social Context of Language.* Chichester: Wiley.

Sylvester-Bradley, B. and Trevarthen, C. (1978) Baby talk as an adaptation to the infants' communication. In Waterson, N. and Snow, C. (Eds.) *The Development of Communication.* Chichester: Wiley.

Tanaka, Y. (1968) Children's representation of spatial transformation. *Japanese Journal of Educational Psychology, 16,* 124.

Tanz, C. (1980) *Studies in the Acquisition of Deictic Terms.* Cambridge: Cambridge University Press.

Taylor, M. (1988) Conceptual perspective taking: children's ability to distinguish what they know from what they see. *Child Development, 59*, 703–18.

Taylor, M. and Bacharach, V. R. (1982) Constraints on the visual accuracy of drawings produced by young children. *Journal of Experimental Child Psychology, 34*, 311–29.

Tfouni, L. V. and Klatzky, R. L. (1983) A discourse analysis of deixis: pragmatic, cognitive and semantic factors in the comprehension of 'this', 'that', 'here' and 'there'. *Journal of Child Language, 10*, 123–33.

Trevarthen, C. (1977) Descriptive analyses of infant communicative behaviour. In Schaffer, H. R. (Ed.) *Studies in Mother-Infant Interaction.* London: Academic Press.

Trevarthen, C. (1979) Communication and cooperation in early infancy: a description of primary intersubjectivity. In Bullowa, M. (Ed.) *Before Speech: The Beginnings of Interpersonal Communication.* Cambridge: Cambridge University Press.

Vinter, A. (1986) How do imitative skills evolve during the first months of life? Paper presented at the 2nd European Conference on Developmental Psychology, Rome.

Vygotsky, L. S. (1962) *Thought and Language.* Cambridge, Mass.: MIT Press.

Wales, R. (1979) Deixis. In Fletcher, P. and Garman, M. (Eds.) *Language Acquisition.* Cambridge: Cambridge University Press.

Walker-Andrews, A. S. (1986) Intermodal perception of expressive behaviors: relation of eye and voice? *Developmental Psychology, 22*, 373–7.

Washington, D. and Naremore, R. (1978) Children's use of spatial prepositions in two and three dimensional tasks. *Journal of Speech and Hearing Research, 21*, 151–65.

Wellman, H. M. (1988) First steps in the child's theorizing about the mind. In Astington, J., Harris, P. L. and Olson, D. R. (Eds.) *Developing Theories of Mind.* New York: Cambridge University Press.

Wellman, H. M. and Estes, D. (1986) Early understanding of mental entities: a reexamination of childhood realism. *Child Development, 57*, 910–23.

Wells, G. (1975) Language development in pre-school children. Transcripts, University of Bristol.

Werner, H. and Kaplan, B. (1963) *Symbol Formation.* New York: Wiley.

Willats, J. (1977) How children learn to represent three-dimensional space in drawings. In Butterworth, G. (Ed.) *The Child's Representation of the World.* New York: Plenum Press.

Willats, J. (1985) Drawing systems revisited: the role of denotation systems in children's figure drawings. In Freeman, N. H. and Cox, M. V. (Eds.) *Visual Order: The Nature and Development of Pictorial Representation.* Cambridge: Cambridge University Press.

Wimmer, H. and Hartl, M. (1991) The Cartesian View and theory of mind: developmental evidence from understanding false belief in self and other. *British Journal of Developmental Psychology, 9*, 125–38.

Wimmer, H. and Perner, J. (1983) Beliefs about beliefs: representation and constraining function of wrong beliefs in young children's understanding of deception. *Cognition, 13*, 103–28.

Wolff, P. H. (1963) Observations on the early development of smiling. In

Foss, B. M. (Ed.) *Determinants of Infant Behaviour. Vol 2.* New York: Wiley.

Wootton, A. J. (1981) Children's use of address terms. In French, P. and Maclure, M. (Eds.) *Adult-Child Conversation.* London: Croom Helm.

Wykes, T. (1981) Inference and children's comprehension of pronouns. *Journal of Experimental Child Psychology, 32,* 264–78.

Wykes, T. (1983) The role of inferences in children's comprehension of pronouns. *Journal of Experimental Child Psychology, 35,* 180–93.

Zahn-Waxler, C. and Radke-Yarrow, M. (1982) The development of altruism: alternative research strategies. In Eisenberg-Berg, N. (Ed.) *The Development of Prosocial Behavior.* New York: Academic Press.

Zahn-Waxler, C., Radke-Yarrow, M. and King, R. A. (1979) Child rearing and children's prosocial dispositions towards victims of distress. *Child Development, 50,* 319–30.

Zinober, B. and Martlew, M. (1985) Developmental changes in four types of gesture in relation to acts and vocalizations from 10–21 months. *British Journal of Developmental Psychology, 3,* 293–306.

Name Index

Subject Index